D1155667

TRUE STORIES

TRUE STORIES

SELECTED, TRANSLATED, AND ARRANGED

FROM THE BEST SOURCES

BY

Mother Francis Raphael, OSD

AKA Augusta Theodosia Drane

Caritas Publishing

Originally published in 1855 as *Catholic Legends* by Augusta Theodosia Drane, (whose name as a Religious was Mother Francis Raphael, OSD). Edited and republished by Caritas Publishing in 2021. Note that the word "legend," while formerly meaning an historical account involving marvelous subject matter, has since devolved to indicate a narrative that is *not* true. Since the accounts of the present volume are culled from authentic and credible sources, and are thus trustworthy of belief, the word "legend" has been changed to "story." The Publisher has also added true stories from *Legends of the Seven Capital Sins* and *Legends of the Commandments of God*, by J. Collin de Plancy.

Republished on the Feast of St. Anselm, April 21, 2021.

Cover design by George Ramsis: georgeramsis45@yahoo.com

Special thanks to Mary Ellen.

Paperback ISBN: 978-1-945275-63-0

Hardback ISBN: 978-1-945275-62-3

CATHOLIC
Stories

CONTENTS

PREFACE

The design with which these stories and anecdotes have been collected has been to furnish a few examples of that singular beauty which is so intimately associated with the Catholic Church and everything that proceeds from her. Undoubtedly these stories are substantially true, being founded on distinct and actual facts, and being a representation of what does appear continually in the history of the mysterious intercourse between the visible and the invisible. They are to the eye of the mind what a painting of any long past actual event is to the eye of the body, conveying a vivid idea of what in substance occurred, but accompanied with various accessories, as colouring, and light and shade, which spring from the painter's imagination, and serve to impress the living reality on the spectator's mind. As such, they are not only interesting and beautiful, but positively instructive.

Mother Francis Raphael, OSD
1855

THE STORY OF THE
HERMIT NICHOLAS

A t the close of the year 1481, on the eve of St. Thomas, the deputies of the free Confederation of High Germany met in full assembly at Stantz, in the canton of Unterwald. They were, for the most part, men who, by their bravery and skill in battle, no less than by their wisdom and prudence in time of peace, had acquired great consideration among their countrymen; and they had assembled on this occasion to deliberate upon matters of the gravest import to the common welfare.

At this period the cities and states of the Swiss Confederation were at the height of their prosperity; the fruit of three memorable victories over the forces of the Duke of Burgundy.

Six years had not elapsed since the first of these— that of Granson. In this famous engagement, the Confederates had humbled the haughty arrogance of Charles the Bold: his fine army, three times stronger than their own, had been cut in pieces; and this hitherto unconquered hero, the master of the richest provinces on this side the Alps— the two Burgundies, Gueldres, and almost all Belgium,— this warrior, before whom France trembled, and whom Lorraine had been unable to resist, fled from the field of battle with only six companions. Four hundred pieces of artillery, six hundred banners, his ducal hat, his sword of state, the three large diamonds, celebrated through Europe, which were destined at a subsequent period to adorn the crowns of mighty potentates;—in a word, a camp which was unequalled in riches and magnificence throughout Christendom, and could only be compared to the camps of the Turks, fell into the hands or poor mountaineers, who, with the help of God, had defended their liberty against the cupidity and pride of a foreign foe. The second battle took place on the plains of Morat. Charles of Burgundy was supported by Savoy, Milan, and Italy. The Swiss had for auxiliaries, Austria, the cities of Alsace, and Réné, Duke of Lorraine. The Confederates fought with unabated heroism, and all the might of Burgundy failed to overpower them. His army was again routed with enormous loss, and Charles fled a second time, having with him only thirty men. The Confederates, after the battle, fell on their knees in thanksgiving for the success of their arms; the trumpets poured forth a joyous blast; messengers, decorated with green branches, ran in all haste through the towns and villages, and the bells rang out exulting peals; sounds of triumph echoed from the depths of the valley to the solitary chalêt at the foot of those eternal glaciers, where dwell the chamois and the vulture.

The third of these great battles was fought by the Swiss near Nancy. The Burgundian, in his despair, had collected all that remained of his forces, and having on this occasion to contend with troops superior to his own, he displayed a valour worthy of his name and ancestors. But all his efforts were in vain; and Charles, the last of his house on the throne of Burgundy, was once more totally defeated.

The reputation of the Swiss became so great in consequence of these successes, that the most powerful princes of Europe sent ambassadors to their assemblies, and sought their alliance. At the negotiations held at Zurich, in 1478, for concluding peace with Burgundy, were to be seen envoys from the Emperor of Germany, the King of France, the Archduke of Austria, and counts and lords from far and near. The Swiss had no longer a single enemy to fear.

But notwithstanding these brilliant victories, these distinguished marks of respect, and their increasing internal prosperity, the deputies of the Confederates assembled at Stante in 1481 did not wear so serene an aspect as might have been expected. They cast at one another dark and distrustful glances; and none would have conjectured that these were the same men who, a little before, had fought so loyally one for the other, and who had owed the success of their arms to their unbroken unity. But the Swiss of that age were men; and the men of that day were little different from those of the present; the very prosperity which God had granted them became their misfortune. Their coffers were full of gold; but the old manner of life, in which their fathers found strength and contentment, had become distasteful to them. The immense booty taken from the Burgundians, and the payments made on various accounts by France, had occasioned large sums of money to circulate among the people; and the Swiss, overcome by the seductions of gold, had lost something of their pure and disinterested love for their country. The heart of more than one old Confederate must have bled to see the ancient sentiments of loyalty and the fear of God so visibly declining among the people; and their former simplicity and purity of manners giving place insensibly to corruption and disorder. The authorities sought zealously to arrest the progress of evil. But laws could not long preserve their vigour, when vice poisoned the soul of the community. The arrogance of youth no longer yielded the respect due to age; and this deterioration of manners threatened to bring about the ruin of the country.

The minds of the Confederates had been already so warped by jealousy and selfishness, that the members of the assembly of Stantz could come to no mutual understanding, and were unceasingly embittered against each other. There were two parties in the assembly at variance with each other; that of the towns, and that of the country. The peasants of Uri, of Schwytz, and Unterwalden, cantons which gave birth to the Swiss League, who pastured their flocks in safety in high valleys, inaccessible to the enemy, desired peace beyond everything; and distrusted the ambition and cupidity of the citizens, who would draw them needlessly into interminable wars. They sought to maintain the Swiss Confederation within its ancient limits, and were not disposed to strengthen the opposite party by the admission of new towns. On the contrary, the towns of Lucerne, of Berne, and of Zurich exerted themselves to obtain admittance into the Confederation for Soleure and Fribourg; because they themselves lay exposed to the attacks of the enemy, Switzerland not having as yet any natural frontier; and these towns had fought faithfully for Switzerland in the wars against Charles, and the Confederates in the hour of danger had promised to admit them into the league.

To this source of discord was added the envy excited by the division of the Burgundian booty and the foreign subsidies. It was in vain that the cantons of Glarus and Zug sought to interpose their mediation, and that meetings were held in various places to reconcile differences. And now the Confederates were assembled for consultation for the last time at Stantz. The animosity of party, however, was so great, that after three sessions of angry debates, the members rose with agitated countenances, and separated without taking leave of one another, to meet again, perhaps, only in the conflict of civil war. That which neither the power of Austria, nor the audacious might of Charles of Burgundy, had ever been able to accomplish, the Swiss were themselves in danger of bringing about by their internal dissensions; and the liberty and happiness of their country stood in the most imminent peril.

These considerations filled all good citizens with sorrow

and alarm; and, amongst others, a curé of Stantz, named Henri Im Grand, a Lucernois, and a man full of piety and zeal for the good of his country. As he reflected on the danger which threatened her, his thoughts turned to the holy hermit, Brother Nicholas, of Kauft. "This man," said he to himself, "lives in the presence of God; a divine blessing is certainly with him; all honour him as a saint; he is, perhaps, the only man whose voice will command attention from these adverse parties." The man of God rose up, took his staff, and ascending the valley of Enstmosn, crossed the Kernwald to the peaceful solitude where dwelt the hermit-saint.

Let us leave the good curé to accomplish his journey with the help of God; he has almost four leagues to travel, and the Swiss leagues are a good measure; and while we meantime inquire who is this Brother Nicholas, and in what manner a poor hermit in his solitude has acquired such influence and authority.

The man who at this epoch, not only in the mountains of Switzerland, but even through Christendom, was known and venerated under the name of Nicholas de Flue, was born in the higher valley of Unterwald sixty-four years previously (in 1417), at the time the bishops of the Catholic Church sat in the Council of Constance. The cottage of his parents was situated in a peaceful and woody country, near the high mountains of Sachslen. Not far distant is the beautiful lake of the four cantons, surrounded by smiling meadows, and enamelled with odoriferous flowers, its waters are clear as a mirror; all manner of fish may be seen sporting in its depths, and every variety of aquatic plants floating on its surface. From the crystal basin which laves their foot, the mountains rise high into the azure regions of the air, and upon their declivity are the pretty huts of the shepherds sheltered by dark forests; while grazing flocks give life to the landscape, the lofty summits of these mountains are covered with eternal snows, and penetrate the clouds, towering far above all surrounding objects. Upon the shores of the lake, in the valleys, and on the hills, are charming villages, beautiful churches, and modest chapels. Crosses in many parts mark the spots where a good action has been performed, or a crime committed; or where the wild and frightful aspect of nature makes the heart shudder from the consciousness of guilt, and cast itself helplessly on God. Four cantons, Uri, Schwytz, Lucerne, and Unterwalden, the native country of Brother Nicholas, surround this beautiful lake; the whole forming a magnificent panorama of mountains, elevating the soul by its grandeur and variety. It was here that Nicholas de Flue was born; in one of these solitary valleys, where the silence is broken only by the bell of the herd, the wild song of the birds of the forest, and the murmur of Alpine torrents. He was descended from a race of good and pious shepherds, in whom were transmitted from father to son the ancient virtues of the Swiss, and who enjoyed during successive centuries the esteem of their fellow-countrymen. His parents had an honest competence; and, after the example of their fathers, they adhered steadfastly to the true and ancient faith, respected the laws of their country, and brought up their children in piety and virtue. They tended their flocks with unwearied care; and, after a life of tranquillity, fell asleep in God, full of confidence; for they had walked before Him, like the patriarchs, to the borders of Jordan. The young Nicholas grew up beneath their salutary tutelage, and manifested always an obedient spirit and a love of virtue; gentle and pious even from the days of his childhood. It was often remarked by those around him, that after the hard labour of a whole day in the fields, when he returned home in the evening, he would disappear by stealth to pray in some secret place. His spirit began thus early to mortify the body, in order to give itself without distraction to elevated contemplation. When some one, out of kindness, warned him not to ruin his health in his youth by such severe fasts as he was accustomed to observe, he replied, with sweetness, that such was the will of God concerning him. Notwithstanding his fervent and austere devotion, his demeanour was cheerful and affable; and he discharged with fidelity all the duties which his condition of life imposed upon him. He entered upon manhood endowed with a noble firmness of soul, a penetrating intelligence, and great purity of heart. In his twenty-third year he took arms, at the call of the magistrates, in the campaign against Zurich; and again, fourteen years later, at the time of the occupation of Thurgovia, when he commanded, as captain, a company of 100 men, and manifested such bravery, that his country decreed him a gold medal as a recompense. A yet more honourable circumstance in the same expedition was the saving of the monastery of the valley of St. Catherine, near Diessenhofen, which to this day reveres him as its deliverer. It was owing to his exhortations that the Swiss relinquished their design of setting fire to the abbey, in order to expel the enemy, who abandoned it soon after of their own accord. In battle he carried his sword in one hand, his chaplet in the other: he showed himself at once a fearless soldier and a merciful Christian, protecting the widow and the orphan, and not permitting the conquerors to perpetrate acts of violence against the vanquished.

Arrived at manhood, Nicholas married, in obedience to the wishes of his parents; choosing from among the maidens of the canton a virtuous young girl, named Dorothy Wysyling. They had ten children, five sons and five daughters, from whom sprang a numerous and honourable posterity, which never lost the remembrance of its ancestors.

Nicholas was himself unanimously elected governor and judge of Obwalden. His conduct in this important post may be gathered from what the curé, Henri Im Grand, his director and friend, revealed after his death. Nicholas had one day said to him on this subject, "I have received from God the gift of an upright spirit. I have been often consulted in the affairs of my country; I have also pronounced many judgments; but, through Divine grace, I do not remember to have acted against my conscience in any thing: I have never regarded persons, nor have I ever departed from the ways of justice." The high dignity of Landamman was decreed him by the General Assembly several times; but he feared the great responsibility; and, without doubt, he felt also that God had reserved him for some other and greater thing.

Nicholas had thus lived fifty years for the good of his country and family, and esteemed by all, when, in the year 1467, he felt himself moved by an ardent desire of being more intimately united with God, in a life of entire separation from the world. His eldest son, Jean de Flue, thus speaks of him: "My father always retired to rest at the same time as his children and servants; but every night I saw him rise again, and heard him praying in his chamber until morning. Many times, also, he would repair in the silence of the night to the old church of St. Nicholas, or to other holy places. These hours of solitude were to him the happiest moments of his life; and the interior impulse became even more powerful to consecrate the remainder of his life to the devout contemplation of eternal truths. God also favoured him frequently with miraculous intimations of His divine will. On one occasion, when he went to visit his flock at a place called Bergnatt, according to his wont, he knelt upon the grass, and began to pray, when God vouchsafed him a consoling vision. He beheld a fragrant lily, white as snow, come out of his mouth, and rise towards heaven. Whilst he regaled himself with the perfume and beauty of the flower, his flock came gambolling towards him, and amongst them a noble horse. As he turned to look, the lily inclined itself towards the horse, which advanced and drew it from his mouth; by which Nicholas was made to understand that the treasure to which he should aspire was in heaven; and if his heart was not wholly detached from the things of earth, he would forfeit the possession of the celestial joys reserved for him."

Another time, while engaged in the ordinary business of his house, he saw three men approach him, of venerable aspect, one of whom addressed him thus:

"Tell us, Nicholas, will you put body and soul into our power?"

"I give myself to none," replied he, "but the Almighty God, whom I have long desired to serve with my soul and body."

At these words the strangers turned with a smile one towards the other, and the first answered: "Because thou hast given thyself wholly to God, and art bound to Him for ever, I promise that in the 70th year of thine age thou shalt be delivered from all the troubles of this world. Remain, then, constant in thy resolution, and thou shalt carry in heaven a victorious banner in the midst of the armies of God, if thou hast borne with patience the cross that we leave thee."

Upon this the three men disappeared. These and similar apparitions confirmed him in his resolution of separating from the world. At length he disclosed to his wife the desire of his soul, and entreated her, for the love of God, to give him permission to fulfil the vocation which God had indicated to him. She consented with calm resignation, and Nicholas began at once to arrange the affairs of his house, assigning to each of his children his part of the inheritance. He then assembled all his household,—his old father, 70 years of age, his wife, his children, and his friends: he appeared before them barefoot and bareheaded, clothed in the long robe of a pilgrim, with a staff and chaplet in his hand; he thanked them for all the kindness they had shown him, exhorted them for the last time to fear God before all things; then he gave them his blessing and departed. That this separation was a trial to him, was evidenced by his frequent expressions of thankfulness to God that He had strengthened him to overcome for His service the love he bore to his wife and children.

Nicholas set out for the place whither God should see good to lead him with a tranquil heart: he would not remain in his own neighbourhood, lest he should become a subject of scandal, and be regarded as an impostor assuming an appearance of sanctity; at the same time he dreaded ostentation, and endeavoured to conceal his great piety as much as possible from the eyes of men. Crossing the fertile valleys and the verdant mountains of his country, he arrived at the limits of the Confederation. When not far from Aaran, upon the Hanenstein, which then separated Burgundy from Switzerland, at a spot whence he could see beyond the frontiers the little town of Liechtstall, he had a remarkable vision. The town, with its houses and towers, appeared to him enveloped in flames. Terrified with this spectacle, he entered into conversation with a peasant whom he found in a neighbouring farm-house; and after some preliminary discourse, he made known to him his purpose, begging him to point out a solitary spot where he might be able to carry it into effect. This man counselled him to remain in his own country; because, as the Confederates were not always well received in other parts, he might be unfavourably regarded, and his retreat be disturbed, besides, there were deserts enough in Switzerland where he might serve God in peace. Brother Nicholas thanked his host for this good counsel, and retook the same evening the road to his native place. He passed the night in a field in the open air, reflecting on the end of his pilgrimage, and praying God to enlighten him. Soon he fell asleep, but suddenly beheld himself surrounded with a bright light, and it seemed to him as though a cord drew him towards his own country. This supernatural light penetrated his whole interior, and caused him, as he afterwards declared, a suffering as from the sharp incisions of a knife. The following morning he rose, and went the same day without stopping as far as Melchthal, his native place: he repaired to one of his pastures called the Kluster; there he made a little hut of branches and leaves under a strong larch, in the midst of thorny bushes, and remained without discovery till the eighth day, neither eating nor drinking, but absorbed in prayer and meditation on divine things. Some hunters in pursuit of game in the forest first became aware of his retreat, and spoke of him to his brother Pierre de Flue, who came to entreat him not to suffer himself to die with hunger in so wild a solitude. Brother Nicholas begged him to be without uneasiness on his account, since he had experienced no evil result up to that time. Nevertheless, that he might not seem to tempt God, he sent secretly for the curé of Kerns, a venerable priest, named Oswald Isner, and acquainted him with the whole case. This good man gave the following testimony after the hermit's death, as may be read in the parish record of the year 1488:

"When Br. Nicholas had passed eleven days without food, he sent for me, and asked me whether he should take some nourishment or continue his trial, as he had always desired to be able to live without eating, in order to be more effectually separated from created things. When I saw and comprehended that this could come only from the source of divine love, I counselled Br. Nicholas to persevere as long as he found himself able; and from this time to the day of his death, a period of more than twenty years, he continued to dispense with bodily food. As the pious brother was more familiar with me than with any other person, I sought earnestly to learn from him how his strength was sustained; and one day he told me in great secrecy, that when he assisted at Mass, and the priest communicated, he received a strength which enabled him to refrain from all other nourishment."

When the fame of this miraculous life spread abroad, people flocked from all parts to see a man whom God had so distinguished, and to convince themselves of its reality by personal observation. It may well be imagined that no woodsman in the canton went to fell a tree, no shepherd to visit his pastures, without seeking an interview with this wonderful inhabitant of the solitude. His quiet life was in consequence so much disturbed, that he determined to seek a more isolated spot. After traversing several of the wildest valleys with this intention, he beheld above a gloomy gorge, down which the Melch precipitates itself with deafening roar, a brilliant light descending from heaven. Obedient to this indication of the will of God, he built there a little hut, surrounded with thick underwood, situated only a quarter of a league from his former house. But the same year, his neighbours, the inhabitants of Obwalden, edified by his holy life, and knowing him to be neither an impostor nor a vain enthusiast, built him a chapel with a small cell attached, and presented it to him as a mark of their affection. Brother Nicholas entered this new dwelling, and continued there to serve God in the same supernatural life. Meanwhile the renown of his extraordinary mode of existence extended far and wide: many were unwilling to believe that a man could thus live miraculously by the sole grace of the Almighty, whilst others glorified God on his behalf.

It was only on Sundays and festival days that he left his cell, and assisted with the rest of the parishioners at divine service in the church of Sachslen. Once a year he repaired to Lucerne for the great procession, and to visit the celebrated places of pilgrimage, as well as those to which the Church had granted indulgences. When the journey became too fatiguing on account of his advanced age, and the gifts of pious persons enabled him to procure the services of a priest, he heard Mass daily in his own chapel, and confessed and received the Holy Communion frequently. He consecrated to the service of God all the hours from midnight to midday, at which time he prayed and meditated, especially on the passion of Jesus Christ our Saviour, who, as he said, communicated to him in the exercise a miraculous strength, a supernatural food.

During the remainder of the day, from midday to the evening, he received those who visited him; or, when the weather was fine, he would traverse the mountains praying, or visit his friend Brother Ulrich, and converse with him on divine things. Ulrich was a German gentleman originally from Bavaria, who, after many remarkable adventures, had quitted the world to establish himself near Nicholas in this solitude. Lodged in the hollow of a rock, he led a life similar to his, save only that he could not dispense with food, which the pious country-people provided for him. In the evening Brother Nicholas resumed his prayers; then he went to take a short repose upon his couch, which consisted only of two planks, with a piece of wood or a stone for a pillow.

The holy and miraculous life of a man so entirely separated from the world, inspired all Christians, without distinction of rank, with such confidence in the power of his prayers, and in the wisdom of his counsels, that in the Swiss cantons and elsewhere, whoever was in trouble or anxiety, or desired sound advice in public or private affairs, went to seek Brother Nicholas in his asylum, to receive from him direction and consolation, and to recommend himself to his prayers. Generals and statesmen, bishops and scholars, did not think it beneath their dignity to visit, in these wild defiles, this poor hermit, who could neither read nor write; and they went away astonished at the simple wisdom, the clear and profound insight into things divine and human which he manifested. Those who from far and near repaired in pilgrimage to Einsiedeln, to invoke the holy Mother of God, did not think they could return in peace to their firesides, if they had not visited and conversed with Brother Nicholas.

It need not, then, excite astonishment that the curé Henri Im Grand should have placed his hope in Brother Nicholas. Let us now see how the zealous priest succeeded in his undertaking.

Night was already far advanced when the curé Henri arrived before the hermitage. The cell where the pious brother had lived for so many years was so low that he touched the ceiling with his head: it was not three feet in length, and only half that width; to the right and left were little windows the size of a man's hand, and a door and window opened to the chapel. No other furniture was to be seen but the bed, with its old gray coverlet, on which the hermit reposed.

The good curé explained to the brother the great danger in which the country was involved: he informed him how deplorable had been the issue of the assembly, and implored him in the name of God to come and succour his poor country in the present emergency. Brother Nicholas replied with his usual calm gravity: "Return," said he, "to Stantz; tell the envoys of the Confederation that Brother Nicholas has something to propose to them, and that he will repair to them speedily."

The curé, full of hope, resumed his journey with all possible speed; he hastened to the inns where the deputies were preparing for departure, and conjured them, with tears in his eyes, in the name of God and of Brother Nicholas, to be again reconciled, and to listen for the last time to the counsels and proposition of the pious hermit. They consented; and some hours after, the brother appeared in the midst of the assembly.

Notwithstanding his great age, Nicholas had performed this long and difficult journey without resting; his fine majestic figure, which time had scarcely bent, was to be seen advancing across the market-place of Stantz to the town-hall. He wore, according to custom, his simple dark-coloured dress, which descended to his feet; he carried his chaplet in one hand, and grasped his staff with the other; he was, as usual, barefoot and bareheaded; and his long hair, a little touched by the snows of age, fell upon his shoulders. When the holy man entered the hall before all the Confederates, and they beheld the peace which irradiated his countenance, and the heavenly light which shone from his eyes, a profound veneration for the humble servant of God penetrated the whole assembly, and they responded to his friendly salutation by rising spontaneously and bowing low before him. After a few moments, silence was broken by the fine and sonorous voice of the hermit, who addressed them thus:

"Dear lords, faithful Confederates, I salute you in the name of God, our good Father and Master, who has sent me here, that I may exhort you touching your dissensions, which are likely to bring about the ruin of our beloved country. I am a poor unlearned man; but I will give you counsel in all the sincerity of my heart, and will speak to you as God inspires me. Would that my words may bring you to unity and peace! O dear Confederates! discuss your affairs in a spirit of friendship and kindness; for one good leads to another. Believe me that it is to a steadfast union that you and your fathers owe your prosperity. And since, in recompense of this concord, God has vouchsafed you such noble victories, would you, through jealousy and avarice, separate to your mutual destruction? Keep yourselves carefully from all dissension, from all distrust; in God we ought always to find peace: God, who is peace itself, is not subject to any change; but discord is the parent of change, and leads to destruction. For this cause I conjure you, dear Confederates of the country, receive into your alliance the two good towns of Fribourg and Soleure; they have given you faithful succour in danger, they have suffered with you good and bad fortune, and they have lost much in your cause. I will not only exhort and counsel you, I will also entreat you earnestly, because I know that it is the will of God. A time will come when you will have great need of His assistance and support. And you, Confederates of the cities! renounce these rights of security which you have established with these two cities; for they are a source of discord. Do not extend too far the circle of the Confederation, that you may the better maintain peace and unity, and enjoy in repose the liberty so dearly purchased. Do not meddle with too many external affairs, nor ally yourselves with foreign powers. O dear Confederates! accept neither presents nor subsidies of money, that you may not appear to have sold your country for gold, that jealousy and selfishness may not germinate amongst you and poison your hearts. Preserve in all your relations your natural justice; divide the booty according to the service rendered, the conquered lands according to the localities. Do not be drawn into unjust wars by the hope of pillage; live in peace and in good understanding with your neighbours; if they attack you, defend your country valiantly, and fight like staunch men. Practise justice amongst yourselves, and love one another as Christian allies. May God protect you, and be with you for all eternity!"

Thus spoke Nicholas de Flue; and God gave His grace to the words of the holy anchorite, says the worthy chronicler Ischudi; so that in one hour all difficulties were smoothed away, and base passions were silent through shame before the severe counsel of a man who appeared before this assembly with his hands raised towards heaven, even as a prophet sent from God.

The Confederates, in accordance with Nicholas's advice, received into their league the towns of Fribourg and Soleure; the ancient treaties of alliance were confirmed, and further consolidated by being established on the basis of new laws unanimously enacted. The pacification of all the Swiss cantons, the maintenance of public order, and of the authority of the magistrates against the disturbers of the peace, the division of booty according to the rule given by Nicholas,— such were the points upon which the Confederates, who had so long contended with so much animosity, came this same day to an entire agreement.

The brother returned the same evening to his peaceful hermitage. At Stantz the bells were rung, and sounds of rejoicing floated across the lakes and through the valleys to all the villages and towns of Switzerland, from the snowy heights of St. Gothard to the smiling plains of Thurgovia. There was as much joy and gladness everywhere as after the victories of Granson and Morat, and with as just cause: for there the Confederates had delivered their country from foreign enemies; here they saved it from their own passions. Their true deliverer, who had obtained for them this victory over themselves, was the poor Brother Nicholas, and as such he was everywhere recognised and extolled.

The towns and countries of the Confederation, and above all Soleure and Fribourg, satisfied with the happy termination of their dissensions, testified their gratitude to the brother by sending him letters of thanks and precious gifts. He accepted the latter only when they were destined to adorn the chapel, for he wished that they should honour God alone as the author of all good. In accordance with this desire, the inhabitants of Soleure sent him twenty gold florins to found a perpetual Mass. Fribourg did the same. Berne sent a courier with a letter of thanksgiving and a handsome present. The answer which the brother returned, through the medium of his son John, exists to this day in the archives of Soleure, to which city it was presented by Berne. Soleure also testified her gratitude to the curé Henri Im Grand, who had brought the brother to Stantz. From this time the general veneration for, and confidence in, Brother Nicholas increased continually.

Nicholas lived six years longer in his peaceful retreat, rich in benedictions. At length the time arrived when God would call His faithful servant from the miseries of the world to eternal joys in His unchangeable presence.

The whole life of the saint had been an unceasing combat with his earthly nature,—a combat which was to continue to his latest hour, in order that he might be adorned in heaven with crowns of patience and meekness, virtues which had enabled him to support every trial on earth. Before his death God sent him a sharp sickness, in which indescribable pains penetrated to the very marrow of his bones.

In this condition of suffering he turned from side to side, writhing upon his couch like a worm trodden under foot. These frightful pains lasted eight days, during which his body was as it were annihilated: he bore them with perfect resignation, and continued to exhort those who surrounded his bed of death so to conduct themselves in this life that they might leave it with a peaceful conscience. "Death," said he, "is terrible; but it is still more terrible to fall into the hands of the living God." When his pains were a little relieved, and the moment of death drew near, Nicholas desired with all the ardour of devotion to receive the sacred Body of the Saviour, and to be strengthened by the Sacrament of Extreme Unction. Near the dying man stood his faithful companion Brother Ulrich, his old friend Henri Im Grand, and the pious anchorite Cecil, who after his death led for seventy years the same solitary life in a neighbouring cell; his faithful wife and children also gathered round him. In their presence he received the holy Sacraments with tokens of deep humility; then he thanked God anew for all the benefits He had dispensed to him, prostrated himself, and died the death of the just.

This event took place on the first day of the spring of the year 1487, the feast of St. Benedict, the same on which seventy years previous he was born.

The lily had been the favourite symbol of this pure calm soul; the lily in flower, resplendent with a divine glory, was Brother Nicholas himself, the humble servant of God, whose name it is said even St. Charles Borromeo never pronounced but with uncovered head.

Note

The magistrates of the canton, desiring to verify the fact of the monastic life of Blessed Nicholas, sent officers, who, for the space of a month, occupied day and night all the avenues of his retreat, in order that no person might bring provisions. Thomas, Suffragan Bishop of Constance, subjected the brother to a similar test when he consecrated the chapel; and after him, Bishop Otho visited the hermit. The Archduke Sigismond of Austria sent, for the same purpose, his physician, the learned and skilful Binkard de Horneck, in order that he might attentively observe Nicholas during several days and nights. Frederic III., Emperor of Germany, also appointed delegates to examine him; but all these expedients served only to confirm the truth. Those who visited him were so struck with the piety and humility of the servant of God, that all their doubts vanished, and they left him penetrated with the most profound respect. When asked how he could exist without food, his simple reply was, "God knows."

THE CHURCH OF
SAINT SABINA

The Catholic traveller, whose devotion leads him to some of those many churches of modern Rome which are in one way or another like volumes of the stories of saints, can hardly fail to visit, among others, the Convent of Santa Sabina on the Aventine Hill, once the residence of St. Dominic, and which from his time to our own has ever continued to be occupied by his children. It is full of him and of his order. There, as you stand outside, you may see green lanes winding down among the almond-trees to the long road of the Via Appia which lies below, where, by the way-side, stands the Convent of San Sisto, which he gave up to the nuns whom he planted there, whilst he himself came with his brethren to reside at Santa Sabina. One may fancy it the very path worn by the holy patriarch's feet on those daily visits which we are told he paid to his spiritual daughters; for it seems to have no other purpose than, as it were, to be a green cloister between the two Churches of Santa Sabina and San Sisto. If you look above the door, as you pull the convent-bell, you will see a half-defaced fresco, depicting one in the white habit and black mantle of the Friars-Preachers; whilst on either side are angels with torches in their hands, who seem lighting him on his way.

It is St. Dominic, who was himself so escorted one night on his return to his convent; and whom the angels "left courteously" (as one of his biographers says) at this very door at which you stand. You step into the cloister; and before entering the church, you may see, in the little quadrangular enclosure, the orange-tree planted by his own hand. Lift the heavy curtain, and you stand within the church itself; scarcely altered in its general features, though six hundred years have passed since he kept his nightly vigils and disciplined himself to blood within its walls, or took his scanty rest leaning against one of those pillars on a stone you may see on the right hand engraved with his name, and preserved there for the veneration of the faithful. It is not a rich or highly-ornamented church. No long line of chapels on either side dazzle the eye with their pictures; the nave is bare and unbroken in its severe and majestic solemnity. On the arch above the choir there is a mystic painting of sheep clustered on a grassy lawn round a fountain of running water: it preserves something of the character of those traditionary representations of Christ and His Apostles you may see in the old golden mosaics of the more ancient basilicas. And there are other paintings, which repeat to you again and again whole chapters of the early romantic chronicles of the Friars-Preachers. In one the young Napoleon is raised to life by the prayer of St. Dominic; in another, Hyacinth and Ceslaus receive the habit from his hands: that fresco stands over the very spot where the Apostle of Poland did indeed receive it; and it was in the ancient choir that stretches behind the altar, that those two holy brothers, in their short novitiate of four months, learnt saintliness enough at the feet of Dominic to be sent back at the end of that time to plant the new order in their native land. There, now as then, you may see the Friars-Preachers chanting their evening office. Their habit has known no reforming change; it is the same as the day when B. Reginald received it from the hands of the Queen of Heaven. There they sit, each one like the pictured heads of their own Angelico; and if you stay to the end, you will see what recalls the old times of which we have been speaking in a yet more striking way than aught you have seen beside. The compline psalms are ended, and the brethren rise as if to leave the choir. The old church is arranged in the usual basilica style, and the choir-seats are behind the altar, which divides it from the nave. Separating into two ranks, the younger walking first, they come out on either side the altar, and pass along to the bottom of the nave, singing as they walk. It is the "*Salve* Procession." Every evening after compline in every convent of the order it is thus sung, and to the same sweet and antique strain; for the Friars-Preachers have their own music, like their own prayers. They reach the bottom of the nave, and turning towards the altar, move up till they reach the middle: then, at the words "Eia ergo" all kneel, and the prior, walking through the kneeling ranks, sprinkles each one with holy water, and then returns to his place till the anthem is finished; when they go back in the same order as they came. And as you watch this singular and beautiful procession in the darkened nave of the old church, even if a stranger to the Dominican chronicles, you will be in some way carried back to another age; for nothing in all that meets your eye has the character of our own day. The shaven heads before you might well be those of St. Dominic's first children: they are all young, and with the look on their countenances which devotion and austerity imprint upon a fervent youthfulness; for Santa Sabina is now the Dominican Novitiate, and the centre of the strictest reformed observance. As they pass before you. it is like an old painting come to life; and the whole scene is one which any one may see has a history and an association. It is briefly this: when the great patriarch St. Dominic was called from this world to his eternal reward, he left the order, which had been regularly established only four years previously, possessed of a footing in every country of Christendom. At the Second General Chapter, held at

Bologna just before his death, the order reckoned sixty convents in different parts of the world; and it was found necessary to divide the government into eight large provinces or nations. In short, the Friars-Preachers had taken possession of Christendom. In their first fervour they carried everything before them. Men listened with wonder to the preaching of men whose lives were more marvellous than their words; whether for the austerity and sanctity which they exhibited, or for those extraordinary graces which they were known to enjoy; so that they were said to hold in their convents as familiar intercourse with the blessed spirits as men are accustomed to hold one with another. Such was the familiarity that the brethren had with the blessed angels, says Castiglio, in his history of the order, that oftentimes they saw and conversed with them, with that consolation and happiness which those only who taste the like can understand. Thus, of a certain novice at the Convent of Santa Sabina at Rome it is written, that being awake one night, and lying so on his bed in the dormitory, he heard steps passing that way, and looked out to see the cause. He saw three figures habited like friars; so that he indeed thought them three of the brethren. One of these walked first bearing the cross, another the vessel of holy water, and the third followed sprinkling the beds and the whole dormitory with the water, after a manner customary in the order at that time. As he watched them, one of them spoke, and said to the others, "Brothers, we have now chased away all the demons from this dormitory; who is to be sent to the other parts of the house?" And he who carried the holy water replied, "Our Lord has sent other angels to them; our business was only with this place." Then the novice perceived that they were angels, and not friars; and when their work was done, they all three disappeared.

But the graces which they enjoyed, and which rendered their labours so successful in the conversion of souls, drew down on them the utmost fury of the malignant spirits. If the strange occurrences we find recorded in the early chronicles of the order were related of one convent only, or on the evidence of one or two witnesses, we might be excused for giving them but little attention. But it was far otherwise. At one and the same time, throughout every convent of the order, a storm of temptations and disturbances broke out, of so strange a character, that none could doubt the source from whence it arose. At first these trials, though extraordinary in degree, were not supernatural in their kind; it was only that the brethren were tormented, now with temptations to indiscreet austerity, now with disgusts and weariness of their rule, so that many returned to the world. But very soon there were added to these horrible and alarming apparitions, specially in the two great Convents of Paris and Bologna; where day and night the brethren were harassed, and wellnigh driven to despair, by the incessant assaults of their infernal enemies. The forms of hideous and unclean animals were seen in the dormitories and cells. Shapes of unspeakable horror met them as they went about, and the cries and voices and blasphemies of hell broke the silent hours of the night. Nor was it the young and inexperienced alone who testified to the existence of these things; the oldest and most saintly of the Fathers were those who suffered most. One of these, a man of unimpeachable life, whilst in prayer in the Convent of Bologna, was heard to utter so great and terrible a cry, that the other Fathers ran to his assistance, and found him alive indeed, but without speech or power of motion. When they spoke to him, he did not answer; a trembling like death shook every limb, and his eyes remained ever fixed in one direction. And in this state he continued the whole of that night. In the morning, having a little recovered, the prior questioned him as to the cause. "Father," he replied, "do not ask me what I saw. I saw the devil; but in so horrible a manner, that the marvel is, not that I am as you see me now, but rather that I still live: were I to see that sight again on one hand, and the fiery furnace of hell on the other, I would rather leap alive into the fire, than gaze for one moment on a thing so horrible." These dreadful visitations lasted more than three years, till the strength and courage of the brethren were well-nigh exhausted. Long vigils, and fasts, and many prayers, wore out the vigour of their bodily frames, while constant terror and anxiety weakened their spirits. They watched day and night before the Most Holy Sacrament in uninterrupted prayer; but still the troubles continued, and even increased, till the order seemed threatened with destruction; for none had courage to embrace or persevere in a body which seemed to have become the butt of evil spirits. At length the subject was formally laid before the General Chapter held at Paris in 1224, during the government of B. Jordan of Saxony; and he ordered the procession during the *Salve* to be generally practised in every convent of the order, in the manner in which it has been already described, and has ever since been continued to be performed. The effects which followed on the adoption of this devotion were no less wonderful than the sufferings which gave rise to it. Everywhere the apparitions and other disturbances ceased. It seemed as though Mary had, in answer to her children's cry for help, come in person to chase away the powers of darkness, and to bless their choirs with the sensible manifestations of her own presence and protection. The stories which are related of her appearances in the Dominican churches during the singing of the *Salve* at this period have many of them a peculiar beauty. Nor were they witnessed by the brethren alone. It soon became a popular devotion to attend the singing of the *Salve* in the churches of the Friars-Preachers; and in the great church of St. James, at Paris, crowds met every evening after compline to witness the procession; which, performed as it was with unaffected earnestness and devotion, had so powerful an effect on the spectators, that their sobs and tears were often heard mingling with the voices of the Fathers. And some were rapt in ecstasies, and saw the church crowded with angelic spirits, and Mary in the midst; and watched her as she received the salutation of the brethren, and answered it bowing her head. Once she appeared visibly to the eyes of many, standing in front of the kneeling ranks, and looking down upon them as they sang. And when they came to the words "*Et spes nostra, salve,*" she gravely and sweetly bowed her head. And as they sang those other words, "*Eia ergo advocata nostra*" she turned to the altar, and prostrated herself at her Son's feet, and implored His mercy for her children. And again, as they said "*Illos tuos misericordes oculos ad nos converte*" she answered the prayer by turning her soft and melting glance upon them, smiling with a joyful and benign countenance; so that the hearts of those who saw it were filled with gladness. Then at the last words, "*Et Jesum benedictum fructum ventris tui nobis post hoc exilium ostende,*" she took her Divine Child into her arms; and holding Him before them, she seemed to show Him to them as they had prayed; and so disappeared. At another time she came down on the altar, which suddenly became brightly illuminated and surrounded by a vast number of celestial spirits, among whom she sat enthroned, with the Holy Infant in her arms. She listened as the anthem was sung, and continued to look down upon the brethren as they knelt turning towards her, until its close. Then she rose; and taking the hand of the little Jesus, she made with it the holy sign above their heads and disappeared.

Such are some of the associations connected with the first institution of this singular devotion, rendering it something more than a curious relic of antiquity; for the interest attaching to it is not merely historical, but supernatural. It is not to be doubted that to our fathers, whose eye of faith was clearer than our own, it was often granted to see in visible shape some of those presences which sanctify the house of God. In the next story, we shall see this same devotion of the *Salve* connected with a tale of one of the earliest martyrdoms of the order.

THE
SCHOLAR OF THE
ROSARY

IN a certain district in the south of France, about the time when B. Alan de la Roche was reviving the almost forgotten devotion of the Rosary in the fifteenth century, there lived a noble lady, who governed her household and family in all holy discipline, and who was among the first to join the confraternity in honour of the Mother of God, on its re-establishment in that country. She had an only child, named Bernard; a boy whose disposition was as noble as his birth, although indeed he was rather distinguished for the angelic innocence of his life than for the endowment of his mind. He was sent by his mother to study at a school in the neighbourhood, from whence he was wont to return home every evening, for she could not resolve to trust him away from her own care whilst he was still so young a child. It does not seem that Bernard was in any way deficient in ability; and he even made considerable progress in some of his studies, especially in grammar; but he was wanting in quickness and vivacity of imagination; and the composition of French and Latin verses, which was one of the common school tasks of his class, became an insurmountable difficulty. Many a weary hour did the poor boy spend, striving, by hard labour and toilsome perseverance, to accomplish what many a thoughtless, quick-witted scapegrace had finished in a few minutes; his constant failures and his wretched verses made him the butt of his companions, and were always bringing him into disgrace; and still the more he tried, the harder and more hopeless it seemed to get either ideas or verses out of his dull and tired brain.

One evening, when he returned home, after a day of unusual trouble, he sat down in disconsolate mood on the steps leading into the garden, and leaning his head on his hand, he gave himself up to very sorrowful reflections. He knew how much his mother cared that he should grow up a learned man, and then he was at the bottom of his class, with the reputation of being the dunce of the school; and all because he was not born a poet: it was certainly a little hard. Poets, as all know, are born, not made; and it seemed an unreasonable thing to spend so many a long day in trying to become what nature had not made him. Verses, he thought, were such unnecessary things: he could be a doctor, a soldier, or even a preacher, and still keep to simple prose; he could save his soul and the souls of other people, and never have mastered the scanning of an hexameter: "What can be the use of it all?" he muttered; "if they would but have kept to grammar!" Now, when he had come to this point in his melancholy meditation, he was joined by his mother, whose quick eye had caught a glimpse of her darling, and recognised in his attitude, and the heavy sorrowful way that his head lay on his clasped hands, that something unusual was the matter.

"Bernard," she said,—and at the sound of that gentle voice the poor boy started to his feet—"what is the matter? Your hair is hanging about your eyes, your cap is on the ground, and I see something very like tears on those white cheeks: moreover, this is not the first time that you have come home in the same way; but for many weeks past I have watched you with an aching heart, and with a sore misgiving

lest the trouble should be in your own conscience." Bernard
hung his head, but did not say a word. "Do you not speak,
my child?" continued his mother: "you were never wont to
hide your sorrows thus; or is it, indeed, that you have fallen
into some grievous fault at school, and fear to declare it to
me?" "No, mother," replied Bernard, "they call me dunce,
and fool, and they speak truly: but though now I could cry,
as though my heart would break, it is for no fault that you
would deem a grievous one; it is that I am not a poet." And
with these words, Bernard hid his face on his mother's knee,
and sobbed aloud.

"A poet, child!" said his mother; "is that your only trouble?
Heard you ever that poets were happier or better than other
men, that you should crave a gift that brings little ease, and
ofttimes less of grace: covet the better gifts, Bernard, for
this is hardly worth your tears; a holy heart and a spotless
faith were fitter things to weep after."

"But, mother," replied Bernard, earnestly, "you know not
how the case stands with boys: we have to learn so many
things you would marvel to find the use for; and among
them all there is none so strange to fit a meaning to as the
making of these verses. And yet Master Roland says I am
a dunce if I do not make them; and shall abide as I am,
the laglast of the school, till I better know how to scan my
lines, and have learnt the difference between a trochee and
a spondee; and that," he added, with a heavy sigh, "I shall
never learn."

"And so you are in disgrace with Master Roland because
you write bad verses, is that the case?" said his mother; "perhaps it rather is, that you try not to write them better."

"Oh, mother," exclaimed Bernard, in a pitiful voice,
"you know not what it is. For first there is the toil to find
the words, and that is not so easy; for what sounds brave
enough in plain-speaking prose, will never do for verse:
then there are lines both short and long, and syllables and
feet to be counted on your fingers, and seldom counted

right; moreover, I know not how it is, but when I think I have them in their right number, Master Roland is sure to tell me they are all in the wrong place."

"Bernard," said his mother, "I do not think I can help to mend your verses, but I may chance to be able to mend your courage. It was but the other day that Master Alan de la Roche told me of a student whoso books were as grievous to him as any verses of yours can be, and yet he found the way not only to read them, but to write them too; and died a great doctor and professor in the university."

"And what was his way?" asked Bernard. "Perhaps his books were written in prose; it might have been different if they had been poetry."

"His way was a very simple one," replied his mother; "he asked our dear Lady's help, and every day said the Rosary in her honour. I think there is little to hinder you from doing the same. Master Alan has given you a Rosary, though I see not that you often use it; take it before her altar every morning before you go to school, and say the prayers as he has taught you; and remember that no one ever prayed to Mary without obtaining relief."

Bernard was not slow in following his mother's counsel; and not content with saying part of the Rosary, he every day recited the entire fifteen mysteries on his knees before the image on Our Lady's altar. Nor was it long before a singular change was observed in the boy; not only did his former dulness and heaviness of capacity gradually disappear, but a certain depth of feeling and gracefulness of imagery was displayed in his school-verses, that placed them very far above the ordinary standard of such productions. How, in-deed, should it have been otherwise? His soul was drinking at the very sources of spiritual beauty; and in the mysteries of joy and sorrow and glory which formed his daily occupation, he penetrated to the very depths of that divine life and passion, which supplied him with a profounder pathos than could be caught by the study of any human emotion. Moreover, the gracious names which were thus constantly on his lips sank into his heart, and brought their sweetness with them; the presence of Mary was with him like an unseen companion; and all day long he felt shining on his heart the earnest gaze of those "merciful eyes" he so constantly invoked: it refined his rudeness, and warmed the sluggish intellect with the flame of spiritual love; and whilst others would praise their favourite poets for their airy images and lively fancy, Bernard was happy in the thought that the inspiration of his pen was caught from no phantom of earthly imagination, but from the influence of an abiding Reality.

The masters marvelled at the change, and said many learned things about the development of the understanding; the scholars wondered also, and soon came to beseech Bernard to help them in their tasks; as for the boy himself, the light in his soul had stolen into it with such a soft and quiet gentleness, that he hardly knew the change; and when they praised and questioned him as to whence he drew his thoughts and imagery, he was wont to answer, with a wondering simplicity, that any one might do the same, for he found it all in the Rosary. This reply, which he constantly gave, soon became talked about among the rest, and gained him the title among his companions of the Scholar of the Rosary.

Every one now predicted great things of Bernard; he was the head of his class and of the school; the highest awards of learning, he was told, were now within his grasp; with that delicate and subtle fancy, and that solidity of understanding, he might aspire to any thing; the professor's chair or the doctor's cap would never surely be denied him. But their hopes and expectations were not to be realised; for the Scholar of Mary a higher and very different distinction was in store. One day he came home as usual, and complained of an aching pain in his eyes; before the morning the inflammation had increased to such a degree, that he could not bear the light, and was obliged to keep his bed in a darkened room, where, in spite of every care and remedy which his mother's tenderness could bestow, he suffered the extremity of pain. For two months he lay in this state, whilst the disease gradually assumed a more dangerous character. The physicians desired that every ray of daylight should be excluded from his room, and the utmost care taken to preserve the slightest object from irritating the eye; an order which was strictly obeyed.

Nevertheless, in spite of his pain and increasing weakness, nothing prevented Bernard from fulfilling his customary prayers. Every day, as usual, he recited the fifteen Mysteries of the Rosary, and comforted his mother, when she grieved over the blindness that threatened him, by saying his devotion was one which needed neither book nor daylight to help it, but only the familiar touch of those dear beads that never left his neck. Alas, blindness was before long not the only evil she had to dread: it was soon evident that the malady had reached a fatal form, which no human skill could avail to remedy. Bernard was to die; all the great hopes excited by his newly-displayed talents vanished into thin air; and those whose tongues had been so busy with his precocious genius were now loud in deploring the loss of one from whom so brilliant a career might have been expected. As to his mother, she thought little of such things; and if she mourned her own loss, her grief had its consolation too; for she knew the innocence of his soul, and had the sure hope that she was but trusting him to the arms of a more loving Mother than herself. But there were the last deathbed duties to be performed; the priest was in the house; and before administering the Viaticum and the holy Unction, he was to receive the last confession of the dying child.

His mother entered the room to prepare him for the coming of the priest; and as she did so, she desired the attendant to bring a candle into the still-darkened chamber.

"What need of a candle?" said the boy; "tell them that it

is not wanted."

"It is for the priest, my child," she replied. "You will try and bear the light for a few minutes; for the good Father is come to hear your confession, and he could not see to enter without a light."

"But there is light," he replied; "the room is full of it, and has never been dark to me. I wonder that you do not see it."

"What light?" asked the priest, who was by this time bending over him. "Your mother and I are standing here, but to our eyes the room is darkened still."

"It is from Our Lady," replied the boy; "she is here by my bedside, and the rays are shining from her, and make it day. There has never been darkness here since I have been ill."

The priest felt an awe stealing over him, and involuntarily bowed his head towards the spot indicated by the child.

"And does that light hurt your eyes?" he asked; "you could not bear the daylight."

"It is joy," answered Bernard faintly,—"joy and glory; the sorrow is all gone now!" and the priest saw that in his last words he was still thinking of the Rosary. And so he died; and those whom he left needed not the evidence of miracles to assure them that the Scholar of Mary had been taken to the fulness of that glory, something of whose radiance had thus rested over his dying bed.*

* The substance of the above may be found in the work of Father Girolamo Taix on the Rosary.

THE STORY OF BLESSED SADOC AND THE FORTY-NINE MARTYRS

In the year of grace 1260, the whole country of Poland suffered greatly from the ravages of the barbarous Scythian or Tartar tribes, who then formed the great terror of the Christian countries situated on the northeastern frontier of Europe. Instigated and assisted by the treacherous Russians, they overran the open country; setting fire to villages and convents, and putting all the helpless inhabitants to the sword. Unable to resist their violence in the open country, the Polish nobles, gathering together as many of the fugitive peasantry as had escaped, threw themselves into the strong town of Sandomir; where they gallantly defended themselves against the enemy for a considerable time. The Tartars were but little used to habits of regular warfare; and were about to give up the siege in despair, when the Russian leaders who were in the camp persuaded them to continue the attempt, and laid a plan for overcoming the defenders of the town by a fraudulent device. They presented themselves to the governor of the fortress under the character of ambassadors of peace; and offered to negotiate with the barbarians, and induce them to evacuate the country on payment of a sum of money. The Poles, who never doubted the sincerity of the Russian envoys, agreed to a suspension of arms; and it was arranged that their chiefs should pass to the enemy's camp, under the safe-conduct of the Russians, to arrange the articles of peace. This had been the plan arranged beforehand by the treacherous Russians, in order to seize the persons of the Polish leaders, and in their absence make themselves masters of the city during the suspension of hostilities.

There was at this time in the Convent of Friars-Preachers established at Sandomir a very holy prior named Sadoc, one of the first companions of Blessed Paul, when he was sent from Bologna by the great patriarch Saint Dominic to plant the order of preachers in his native country of Hungary. The apostolic labours of Blessed Paul had already been crowned with martyrdom; and ninety other sons of the same glorious order had suffered death together with him at the hands of the barbarous tribes whom they had laboured to bring to the faith. Sadoc had not been with his brethren, but had been sent on a mission to Poland; where, being appointed prior of the Convent of Sandomir, he governed the brethren in so admirable a manner, that it was commonly said among the people of the town that the Convent of St. Mary Magdalen was inhabited by angels.

On the night when the Polish chiefs left the city for the Tartar camp, the brethren had assembled in their choir as usual for the recital of matins. Matins were now just ended; and all being seated in their places as the custom is, one of the younger novices, standing in the middle of the choir, prepared to read aloud the martyrology for the ensuing day; that is, the names of the saints who were to be commemorated. He opened the heavy clasped book that lay before him; something seemed to perplex and astonish him, for there was a moment's pause. The pages of the book were rich with the gold and painted letters of manuscripts of that day; but it was none of these that caught and riveted his gaze. For an instant he doubted if he saw aright; for there, in characters not of gold but of intense and glorious light, appeared the words, "At Sandomir, the Passion of Forty-nine Martyrs." His hesitation was but momentary; the next instant the passing emotion of surprise was put away; and, faithful to the simple instinct of obedience, he sang in a clear boyish voice the words which seemed to announce to his brethren their own impending fate. The words fell on their astonished ears like a thunderclap: Sadoc rose from his seat and called the novice to his side. "Is this a jest, my child?" he said; "if so, it is but ill-timed. What words are those you have just sung?" "Father," replied the young man, with much simplicity, "I only sang what I saw in the book;" and so saying, he placed the open page before the prior. Then the Divine illumination of the Holy Spirit revealed to Sadoc that these things were written for him and his companions; and turning to them as they sat in wonder what all this might mean, "Fathers, brothers, and dear friends," he said, "the Most High God has sent us blessed tidings to-night. Listen, my children; 'At Sandomir, the Passion of Forty-nine Martyrs;' who should these forty-nine be but ourselves, for we exactly make up that number? Tomorrow, therefore, will see the golden gates of the New Jerusalem open to receive us; and doubtless it will be the swords of the Tartars that are to carve a short way for us to heaven. O blessed death, that shall crown us with the green wreath of the martyrs, and admit us to the embraces of Eternal Love! What can we desire more? God is calling us home from our long exile; we will go there right joyfully, and welcome the blows that shall make our path thither so quick and easy. But our time is very short; and we who have so soon to meet the Bridegroom must see that our lamps are bright and burning, and ourselves ready for His coming. Let the night, therefore, be given to prayer, and the purification of our souls in the holy Bath of Penance; and in the morning we will receive the Bread of Heaven, which will give us the strength and courage of true martyrs." The brethren listened to his words with an extraordinary joy; and that night was spent in solemn preparation for death. Each one confessed his sins to the venerable prior, with the tears and contrition of men whose last hour was at hand; then they remained in silent prayer before the altar, calmly and joyfully awaiting the dawn of that day which they knew was to be their last.

Bright and beautiful was the morning light that streamed through the tall eastern window, and fell over the kneeling forms of that little white-robed army of martyrs. There was no sound of combat or of danger without; the city lay in profound quiet, and nothing seemed to betoken that the glorious summer day which was breaking over the world was to be one of bloodshed and of crime. There was but one Mass said that morning in the convent church; and the few citizens who assisted at the Holy Sacrifice marvelled not a little at the unusual sight they witnessed; for the Mass was celebrated by Sadoc himself, and the entire community received communion together at his hands, a thing which was not customary save at some of the greater festivals of the Church. And then there was nothing more to do but to wait for their executioners. They knew not the hour when they would come; and though possibly they felt something of a holy impatience for their release, the loveliness of religious discipline was never more wonderfully manifested than during the long hours of that day in the Convent of the Magdalen. As if nothing unusual were at hand, each one went to his accustomed office and occupation. The bell rang and called them to refectory and to choir; and no sign of unwonted haste or excited gesture could be marked to break their holy and unruffled tranquillity. Only sometimes sighs and words of fervent desire would burst from their hearts. "Ah, will they never come!" said the young novice to whose eyes the blessed tidings had first been given. "They are long about it; I counted by this time to have been with Jesus and Mary." "Let us go and bid farewell to the holy images and altars," said another; "it will be a happy thing to die before them: or perhaps even God may suffer us to give our blood in defence of the Blessed Sacrament."

But still the day passed on, and everything wore its usual aspect. The convent was situated in a remote part of the city, and surrounded by a garden; so that few of the sounds from the busier streets and more populous quarters reached its quiet cloisters. The friars, too, had been full of their own thoughts; or perhaps they would have heard from time to time the echoed shouts and cries, which showed that a fierce struggle of some kind was going on at no great distance. But, as I have said, they were full of their own thoughts; and their thoughts were now with God. It even seemed to them that the day had a quietness of its own; for the solemnity of their own feelings seemed to cast the stillness of unwonted prayer over all the world around them.

Evening came at last, and the bell for compline summoned the brethren to sing the Divine praises in their choir; the last homage they were to offer to their Creator in this world, before being translated to the celestial choir of the angels. Surely never had the words of that most beautiful service sounded so full of meaning to their hearts, as now when they were fitting themselves for death. First, Sadoc's voice might be heard giving the blessing, as the office began: "May the Almighty God grant us a quiet night and a *perfect end*," Then came another tone, which sang the warning words: "Brethren, be sober and watch; for your adversary the devil as a roaring lion goeth about, seeking whom he may devour; whom resist ye, strong in faith." Then burst forth from the choir the solemn and magnificent chant, swelling through the arched aisles with more than usual power in its tones. What wonderful words were those for dying men to utter! "He that dwelleth in the help of the Most High shall abide under the protection of the God of heaven. His truth shall compass thee as a shield; thou shalt not be afraid for the terror of the night, for the arrow that flieth in the day, or for the assault of the evil one in the noon-day. Forsake us not, O Lord, our God. *In manus tuas. Domine, commendo spiritum meum. Commendo spiritum meum. Gloria Patri et Filio et Spiritui Sancto. Commendo spiritum meum.*"

Already might the Tartar war-cry be heard clear and terrible in the very street beneath them; already too heavy blows were falling thick and fast on the convent-gate: yet still the friars seemed to take no heed. Quietly and in order they formed themselves into rank for the procession, and moved down into the nave, singing the *Salve* with tones so sweet and joyous, that you might have thought their voices were already mingling with the angel choirs. Then they knelt, turning to the altar; and Sadoc walked through the rank, and gave the accustomed sprinkling of holy water. It was at this moment that the door of the church burst open, and a band of the Tartars rushed in: their hands and garments were dripping with blood, and their whole appearance savage and revolting. They advanced tumultuously towards the kneeling friars; but for a moment the scene before them seemed to strike them with awe, and they paused as if under the influence of a supernatural presence. They might well feel it so, as they marked that kneeling row of figures clothed in white garments, whose faces were turned towards the heaven which was about to receive them into its rest, already wearing something of celestial beauty. Not a head was moved, not a voice faltered; you might hear the words of the anthem sung as clearly and as sweetly as ever: "*Et Jesum benedictum fructum ventris tui, nobis post hoc exilium ostende.*" They were the last they were to utter; the barbarians recovered from their momentary astonishment, and with a yell of savage malice rushed on them, and slaughtered them where they knelt. They fell with those words upon their lips, singing as they died. One alone moved from his place, and seemed touched by an emotion of terror. He rose, and turned to fly; but a wonderful sign was given him which restored his courage. "For," says the old chronicle which records this history, "he perceived that the dismembered and mangled bodies of his companions, whose souls were now singing everlasting alleluias with the angels, ceased not to utter in accents of superhuman melody the words of the half-finished anthem; whereupon he also cast away all base and cowardly fear, and offered himself to the swords of the Tartars. So did these heavenly swans fly up to heaven, singing the praises of their great Mother Mary; and very well may we believe that her virgin hands did there crown their brows with the immortal laurels of the martyrs."

In the office granted in their memory by Pope Pius VII., the words which they are recorded to have been singing at the moment of their massacre are introduced into the collect: "*Et Jesum, benedictum fructum ventris tui, nobis post hoc exilium ostende.*" Pope Alexander IV., who filled the Chair of St. Peter at the time of their martyrdom, granted singular privileges to all who in their honour should visit the Church of Sandomir; and their festival is still observed on the scene of their death with extraordinary devotion and splendour.

THE STORY OF BLESSED
EGIDIUS, OR GILES

During the reign of Sancho I., King of Portugal, there lived at the court of that monarch a counsellor of high rank, named Don Rodriguez de Vagliadites. This nobleman had an only son, named Egidius, who displayed from his earliest years every sign of an extraordinary genius. Being sent to the University of Coimbra, the reputation which he there acquired was of so unusual a character as to attract the notice of the king; who, willing to mark his sense of the son's talents and the father's long services, loaded him with several rich benefices—he having chosen the ecclesiastical state. Unhappily, in making this choice Egidius had been guided only by interest. Finding himself whilst still a mere youth his own master, with an enormous revenue at his disposal, and flattered by the proud sense of his own unequalled genius and powers of mind, he used his sacred office only as a means of gratifying his thirst for learning; but neglected all its duties, and gave himself up to a life of unrestrained indulgence and licentiousness. Once having entered on this course, it seemed indeed as if the whole energy of his mind, with all its brilliant and varied attainments, were directed to no other end than to procure the degradation of his soul. His profound science was employed to provide for himself new excitements; and stimulated by a restless and unholy curiosity, he determined to commence the study of medicine; and for this purpose set out for Paris, whose university then enjoyed the highest reputation of any throughout Europe in every department of science.

On his journey thither he was joined by a young man, who fell into conversation with him on the road, and in whose company he continued to travel during the whole of that day. He was of a strangely fascinating and winning address; and almost without being aware of it, Egidius suffered him to read the very secrets of his heart, and revealed to him all the designs and plans which were revolving in his brain. It was, indeed, no other than the great enemy of souls himself, who had taken this disguise in order to complete the ruin of the unhappy Egidius. With many a word of artful eloquence he won his confidence: nothing was concealed; the excessive and unrestrained passion for human science, which, unsanctified by Divine grace, had united itself to a bold and quenchless thirst for the enjoyments of sense, was all laid bare before the keen eye of the stranger; and whilst the latter encouraged him in all his designs, he assured him at the same time that in choosing the study of medicine he had not selected the best means of carrying them into effect. "There is a science," he said, "which will bring you far more quickly to your desired end than any you have yet attempted; it will itself aid you to acquire all sciences. Intellectual power, without bound or limit, and the enjoyment of pleasures which you never pictured to yourself in the wildest moments of your imagination, will it pour out at your feet. Nay more, it will secure you also a fame amongst men, which no mere human science can ever procure; and whilst you enjoy the cup of pleasure to the full, the world will reckon you as her wisest and most renowned master. This science is magic; and if you will trust yourself to my guidance, I can introduce you to a university at Toledo where its profoundest secrets are taught and practised." It was not without a secret thrill of horror that Egidius listened to the suggestions of the fiend: but he hesitated not to stifle the whisperings of conscience; and, dazzled at the thought of acquiring an unbounded possession of all after which his heart longed with so passionate an ardour, he gave a ready consent, and they took the road to Toledo.

Far from every human habitation, on the side of a desolate mountain, yawned the gloomy entrance into two vast subterranean caverns: this was the school of magic of which the fiend had spoken; and it was here that his disciples pursued their dark and unholy studies. As he drew near the spot with his new victim, there came out to meet them several of these unhappy men, accompanied also by demons in human shape, who acted as their masters, and received their new associate with extraordinary joy. He was very soon initiated into the rules and mysteries of this fearful society; he subscribed their laws and statutes, and submitted to the three conditions imposed on him before being suffered to become a member: the first, to renounce obedience to the laws of God; the second, to abjure the faith and his baptismal vows; the third, to become henceforth the pledged bond-slave of Satan. One might well suppose such a contract would have startled the most blind and hardened; but a long course of sin and resistance to inspirations of Divine grace, had rendered the depths of evil neither new nor terrible to Egidius, and he signed the paper without hesitation, and with his own blood.

It is a common saying that the devil gets better served than God. Egidius, the votary of pleasure, who was impatient of a day which did not bring its new excitement and indulgence, consented to spend seven years in these gloomy caverns, severed from the society of all save his unhappy companions, whilst he gave himself up to a painful and weary apprenticeship in the art of magic: "another proof," says his Portuguese chronicler, "that the service of Satan is a harder bondage than the yoke of Christ. They who serve this lord think no labour too hard to attain unto the enjoyment of a pleasure, which, when attained, does but weary and torment."

He left the Caverns of Toledo a master in human, and in more than human, knowledge. The secrets of hell, the hidden and mysterious forces of nature, were all his own. Armed with a power which no rival was ever able to withstand, he now appeared in Paris; and very soon was rewarded for his long labours by a dazzling and universal fame. His cures were little short of miraculous; his skill in every branch of medicine astonished the most learned: but deeper and profounder even than his science was the secret course of unbridled vice to which he gave himself up, and which seemed to penetrate into the very recesses of his degraded being.

Thus dead to grace and sunk in corruption lay the soul of the gifted Egidius. The brilliancy of human intellect and a rich imagination were there indeed; but they were like the fair blossoms which hang around a grave, drawing their nourishment from its deadly contents, and scarce veiling the hideousness that lies beneath. Yet this man, the slave of hell and the outcast of the world, was, in the eternal counsels of God, chosen to be a living monument of His grace. Nor was the manner of his conversion less marvellous than the change it wrought.

It was the dead of night, and Egidius sat alone in his chamber, surrounded by his books. Suddenly the door swung on its hinges, and a terrible and gigantic figure, clad in brazen armour and mounted on a black steed, rode into the apartment. In his hand he bore a lance, with which he threatened the astonished master; then, in a voice so harsh and terrible that it would have shaken the heart of any ordinary man, he cried, "Change thy life, unhappy wretch!"— repeating thrice the words, "Change thy life." For the moment a sensation of fear did indeed pass through the soul of Egidius. He seemed to see hell open to receive him, and the hand of God raised to cast him in. But the feeling was but for an instant,—the next he laughed at his own weakness, at being disturbed at what he resolved to consider nothing but a troublesome dream.

Three days passed away, and again, at the same time and in the same room, he sat as before. And, as before, the door burst open, and the strange horseman once more entered; but this time in a far more terrible manner. He spurred his gigantic horse at full speed right at Egidius; and as the fierce animal raised its brazen hoofs, and seemed about to crush him to the earth, the same voice sounded beneath the closed visor of the helmet, "Change thy life!" and then the raised lance struck on his heart, and he fell senseless to the ground. He awoke from a long and fearful trance, and found himself another man. Like Saul, the first words that rose to his lips were: "Lord, what wilt Thou have me to do?" The pain of his mysterious wound still smarted in his breast; he looked, and found a scar indeed, but perfectly healed and cicatrised; but the blow had struck deep into his heart. His eyes were opened to behold the light, and its first rays discovered to him the darkness that reigned within. Well-nigh did he despair of pardon and salvation, when he remembered the renunciation of his Baptism and the contract which made him the slave of Satan; but the better teaching of childish days returned upon him in that hour of grace, and a thought of the Lord who had died for him was strong enough to save him from despair. There was indeed a bloody compact, which sold him body and soul to the powers of hell; but he remembered another purchase-deed made long before, and now again renewable,—sprinkled over, and signed, and sealed with the precious Blood of Christ. The morning light found him still plunged in these conflicting thoughts: he looked round him, and saw scattered about the room the books of magic which had been his study the night before; and seizing them hastily, as a first sacrifice and token of his returning vassalage to God, he cast them into the flames.

He determined to leave the scene of his sins at once and for ever; and, returning to Spain, to seek admission into some strict order of religious penance. His journey was a sad and painful one; tormented with remorse, his nights were spent without sleep, and his days absorbed in melancholy reflections. Distress of mind so preyed on him that it brought on a low fever; yet he would not rest in his journey till, entering Spain, he arrived at the city of Valencia, where the new Order of Friars-Preachers were just established, and were engaged in the erection of their convent. Egidius, weary and worn out in body and mind, paused by the building and watched the brethren at their work. With modest and humble yet cheerful looks they passed to and fro, carrying stones and mortar,—all busy in raising the walls of their happy retreat. Something in the sight touched his heart; perhaps it contrasted with the unholy labours of his own solitary life. Every tongue was full of the sanctity of the new religious,— of their rigour, their poverty, and their heroic work for God. He made a rapid and wise resolution; and presenting himself to the prior, told him the story of his life in the sacred tribunal of confession. The prior treated him with charity and gentleness, and did not doubt to receive him to absolution; for he saw that his contrition was true and unfeigned. What a weight was lifted from his heart! the chains that had so long bound him fell off, and he saw the happiness of serving God, and the bondage of a life of sin. One day of these new feelings and desires was enough for the impetuous nature of Egidius. He returned to the convent; and casting himself at the feet of the prior, besought him to suffer him to receive the habit. "Yesterday," he said, "you saw at your feet the greatest sinner of the world; I thought to find in you a severe judge; I found only a loving father, whose tears of pity joined with mine to wash away the stains of my guilt. That spirit of love which you breathed over me yesterday has brought me back today to crave a new favour. I have sinned enough; admit me to your angelic brotherhood, and teach me how to sanctify the soul so long drowned in the deep waters of iniquity." The prior embraced him, and promised him his request should be granted; and in a few days Egidius had dismissed his servants and attendants, and, sending word to his father of his change of intention, received the holy habit with sentiments of the deepest fervour and contrition. The Convent of Valencia was then in the early vigour of its foundation. The brethren led a life of incredible mortification and uninterrupted labour: during the day they preached and heard confessions, and assisted in the actual building of their church and convent; whilst the night was given as much to prayer and watching as to sleep. Their food was as coarse and scanty as that of the ancient fathers of the desert.

Prompt obedience, strict silence, charity, peace of soul, and hard work,—such were the elements of the new life to which Egidius found himself so wonderfully called. It was a holy paradise; yet it proved at first a hard struggle to a nature so long accustomed to indulgence and habits of luxury as was his. His conversion was indeed sincere; but the old man is not so quickly laid aside as to render so severe a change at once sweet and supportable. Those seven years of noviceship to Satan had, moreover, to be expiated by long and sore travail of spirit in the service of God. The remembrance of the past was a continual agony; the rigour of the present seemed often more than he could bear. Yet in these struggles of the flesh against the spirit Egidius bore himself well and manfully; with continued labour and hard austerities he quelled the rebellion of the senses, whilst that tongue, so long given to an idle and worldly volubility, was now restrained with so rigorous a law of silence, that B. Humbert, who was afterwards his companion and fellow student, has left it on record in his memoirs, that he never once heard him speak an idle word. He studied how to mortify himself even in ways which his rule did not touch; and refused to exercise or pursue his darling study of medicine, save under obedience; as though he desired to turn his back on every association of his past life.

Having made his profession in 1221, he was soon after sent to the Convent of Santarem, in his native country of Portugal. There he led a life of the same persevering fervour; but the peace of his soul was still wanting. One thought ever preyed on his mind—the recollection of that horrible compact, signed with his own blood, which bound him to Satan as his slave and bond-servant. Many a night did he lie prostrate before the altar, drowned in bitter tears, and imploring the Divine power to deliver him from his servitude to the powers of evil; then sometimes, feeling that prayer from such as he was could not reach the throne of God, he would have recourse to the sure refuge of sinners—the most loving and merciful Mary—and call on her to be his advocate, and to free him by the omnipotence of her intercession. There was in the convent church of Santarem a devout image of the Virgin Mother; and to this spot Egidius would fly for refuge from his own tormenting thoughts. It was the silent witness of his long nights of prayer, of his tears and discipline to blood; and so for many years did the anguish of his soul remain unabated, whilst he wore out in penance the scars of his unforgotten sins. The devil, too, enraged at the loss of his victim, assaulted him with incessant temptations to despair. Often he appeared to him in hideous forms, and claimed him as his own; and the unhappy penitent, so hardly tried, knew no better protection at such times than in the repetition of the blessed Name of Jesus. Yet never once did his faith or constancy fail. Exhausted with bodily and mental suffering, he would drag himself to the foot of the crucifix, and strive to regain strength and courage at the sight and touch of those pierced feet. Thus seven years were spent in one uninterrupted conflict with the exterior assaults of Satan and interior temptations to despair. The time at last came when the vessel, cleansed and purified by so long a fire, was to be filled with the sweet and odoriferous oil of the Holy Spirit. One night he was at his usual post before that image of the Mother of God, whose presence had a power over his soul like the cool mountain breeze as it passes over the dry and parched desert. Infernal voices called in his ears, and told him his prayers were vain, and there was no hope or mercy for him; yet still he knelt and prayed. "Star of hope!" he cried, "it is all true. My sins are heavier than they say; yet they cannot weigh down the Blood which was shed for me on the Cross. Ah, sweet fountain of mercy! take the cause into thine own hands; for I am tired out with these struggles, and can do no more." And, as he lay prostrate and exhausted, an invisible force scattered the hosts of hell, and a clear and horrible voice cried aloud: "There, take with my bitterest curse thy written bond; but know this, that never would I have given it up to thee, had I not been compelled by the power of her who stands on that altar, and whom you call the Mother of God."

Egidius raised his weeping eyes, and saw falling through the opening of the roof where the bell-ropes of the church passed, the paper he had signed at Toledo; whilst through the same opening a strange and hideous form was escaping with a gesture of baffled malice. The paper fell on the pavement at his feet; he grasped it once more in his own hands, and felt he was free,—and free through the intercession and patronage of Mary. Wherefore, kneeling again before her image, he entered into a new compact; and bound himself for the rest of his life as slave to that sweet Mother who had broken the bonds of his servitude and restored his soul to peace. From that hour the darkness and temptation he had so long endured vanished. In his after-life he tasted some of the deepest of those spiritual consolations with which God is wont to favour His chosen servants; and his chronicler, in narrating some of his ecstasies and miracles, and the unearthly rapture into which the very sound of the holy Name of Jesus was wont to cast him, observes: "A stronger magic, surely, were these things, than aught that ever he learned in the caves of Toledo."

He was long Provincial of Spain, and died in the year 1265, being universally considered the greatest man of his order during the time in which he lived. The circumstances of his conversion, as given above, are found in most of the early chronicles; and though omitted by Touron in his biographical notice of his life, yet he assigns no other reason for the omission than the "unlikeliness" of the whole history; an argument which can hardly be admitted as of much weight in treating of the supernatural displays of God's power.

THE STORY OF BLESSED BERNARD AND HIS TWO NOVICES

At the time that the celebrated Egidius was provincial of Spain, he gave the habit of the order to a young Gascon named Bernard, who was received into the Convent of Santarem, and became so distinguished among that saintly community for the holy simplicity of his life, that Andrea of Rosende, in his Chronicle of Portugal, draws a parallel between him and his great namesake the Abbot of Clairvaux, "to whom," he says, "he bore no small resemblance, in a certain dove-like innocence and simplicity of manners." The circumstances attending his death, attested by almost all the writers on the history of the order, are of peculiar beauty.

Bernard filled the office of sacristan in the Convent of Santarem, an office, the exercise of which was peculiarly delightful to him, from the many opportunities it gave him of indulging his devotion unseen by anyone but his Lord, whom he loved to honour by a reverent care of the altar and everything belonging to the Divine mysteries. Besides this employment, his spare time was occupied in the education of two children, the sons of a neighbouring gentleman, who sent them every day to the convent, where they remained until evening, only sleeping at their father's house. These two boys were permitted to wear the novices' habit of the Friars-Preachers, being probably destined for the order, although not as yet received into the community; and their innocence and goodness of disposition rendered them peculiarly dear to Blessed Bernard. It was his custom, when busy in the sacristy, to allow them to remain in a chapel then dedicated to the Holy Kings on the right of the high altar, where they used to sit on the altar-steps, reading, or writing their exercises; spending their time quietly and happily until their master's return. Here also they were accustomed to spread out the dinners which they brought with them from home, which they took together in the same place as soon as they had finished their daily lessons. On the altar of this chapel, which was seldom used for the purpose of saying Mass, there was an image of the Blessed Virgin, holding her Divine Son in her arms; and the two children came to look on the Holy Infant almost as a companion, and were wont to talk to Him, as He seemed to look down on them from His Mother's arms, with the simple familiarity of their age. One day, as they thus sat on the altar-steps, one of them raised his eyes to the image of the little Jesus that was just above him, and said, "Beautiful Child, how is it you never take any dinner as we do, but always remain without moving all day long? Come down and eat some dinner with us,—we will give it to you with all our hearts." And it pleased God to reward the innocence and simple faith of the children by a wonderful miracle; for the carved form of the Holy Child became radiant with life, and coming down from His Mother's arms, He sat with them on the ground before the altar, and took some of their dinner with them. Nor need we wonder at so great a condescension, remembering how he came uninvited to be a guest with Zaccheus who was a sinner, and that the two whom he now consented to treat as His hosts were clothed in that pure robe of baptismal innocence which makes us worthy to receive Him under our roof. Now this happened more than once, so that the neglected chapel became to these two children full of the joy of heaven; and by daily converse with their Divine Lord they grew in such fervent love towards Him, that they wearied for the hour when they might have Him with them; caring for nothing else than this sweet and familiar intercourse with the Lord of heaven. And their parents perceived a change in them, and how their only pleasure was in hastening to the convent, as if it contained a secret source of happiness which had not been revealed before. They therefore questioned them closely; and the children told them everything without reserve. But the tale seemed to those who listened nothing but an idle invention, or perhaps an artifice in order to obtain a larger quantity of food; and they therefore took no notice of what they said beyond reproving them for their folly.

But when they repeated the same story to B. Bernard, he listened with very different feelings; for he knew the holy hearts of his two little disciples; and he felt, moreover, that there was nothing unworthy of belief in the fact that He who, being God, became a little child, should condescend to give a mark of favour to those of whom He Himself has said, that "of such is the kingdom of heaven." When, therefore, after many inquiries, he had satisfied himself of the truth of their tale, he bade them give glory to God for His goodness; and then considered whether there was no way in which these circumstances might be made to serve yet further to the happiness and sanctification of his pupils. And hearing how they, in their childish way, expressed a wonder that, after they had so often invited the Child to eat some of their dinner, He had never brought any food with Him to share with them, he bade them the next time He came ask Him how this was, and whether He would not also ask them some day to dine with Him in His Father's house. The boys were delighted with this idea; and they failed not to do as they were directed the next time that they were alone in the chapel. Then the Child smiled on them graciously, and said, "What you say is very just; within three days I invite you to a banquet in My Father's house and with this answer they returned full of joy to their master. He well knew the meaning of this invitation: the change that had gradually appeared in his two beloved disciples had not been unmarked by him; he had seen them, as it were before their time, growing ripe for heaven; and he understood that it was the Divine pleasure, after thus training them for Himself in a marvellous way, that they should be transplanted to the angelic company, before their hearts had once been touched by the Knowledge of sin or the contamination of the world. Yet he sighed to think that they should thus be granted to pass to Christ in their happy infancy, whilst he, who had grown old in the spiritual warfare, was to be left behind; and resolving to make one more trial of the condescension which had been so bounteously lavished on his pupils, he bade them go back again to the chapel, and tell the Divine Child that since they wore the habit of the Order, it was necessary for them to observe the rules; and that it was never permitted for novices to accept of any invitation, or go to the house of any person, except in their master's company. "Return, then, to your master," said the Holy Child, "and bid him be of the company; and on Thursday morning I will receive you all three together in My Father's house."

Bernard's heart bounded with emotion when he heard these words. It was then the first of the Rogation Days, and the day which had been appointed was therefore Ascension Day. He made every arrangement as for his approaching death, and obtained leave on that day to say the last Mass,—his two disciples serving during the celebration, and receiving Communion from his hands. Doubtless it would be hard for us to realise his feelings of devout and joyful expectation during those moments. And when Mass was ended, he knelt before the same altar with the children, one on either side, and all three commended their souls to God, as though they knew their last hour was come, and the altar-steps were to be their deathbed. And it was even so. An hour after, some of the brethren found them still kneeling thus before the altar, Bernard vested as for Mass, and the two boys in their serving-robes. But they were quite dead: their eyes were closed, and their faces wore a smile of most sweet tranquillity; and it was evident that there had been no death-struggle, but that their souls had passed to the presence of God whilst in the very act of prayer. They were buried in the Chapel of the Holy Kings, which had been the scene of so many of our Lord's visits to the two children; and a picture was hung up over the spot, representing them seated on the altar-step, with the Divine Child between them.

This was the only monument to mark the place of their burial; and in course of years the memory of it was lost, and the chapel became disused and neglected as before. One of the succeeding priors of the convent, wishing to find some further record of the ancient tradition, dug down beneath the spot indicated by the picture; taking care to have two apostolic notaries and the vicar-general of the diocese present, together with other authorities of distinction and credit. At a little distance beneath the surface a carved stone sarcophagus was found, which being opened, the church was immediately filled with an odour of surpassing sweetness, and on removing the clothes that Lay on the top, the remains of three bodies were discovered, which they could not doubt were those of B. Bernard and his novices, for the bones of the middle skeleton were of the size of a grown man, whilst those on either side were small and delicate. From the great number of years that had passed, most of them were reduced to mere dust; but some portions of white cloth showed that they had been buried in the habit of the order. The memory of this history has been preserved even up to our own times; for from the time of this solemn translation of their bodies, a Mass of the Ascension was celebrated every Thursday, in thanksgiving for the graces granted to them, and a confraternity of the Infant Jesus established, to whom the custody of the ancient image was intrusted. Their death is supposed by Sosa to have taken place about the year 1277.*

* Another story occurs in the Dominican annals, whose particulars are almost precisely similar to those narrated above; except that there was but one child to whom the vision of our Lord appeared, and that the scene of the story is laid in Majorca. There is, however, ample evidence that it is not a different version of the same event, as might be supposed, but that they are two distinct and well-authenticated facts. It has not, however, been thought necessary to insert the second in this place, from the strong similarity it bears to that given above. It occurred at the time of the great plague in 1348.

THE
LAKE OF THE APOSTLES

The city of Mons, which owes its origin to the holy St. Vaudra more than to the old Roman camp of Cicero's brother, began to increase in importance in 874. Charlemagne, seventy years before, had raised it to the dignity of an earldom. The last Count of Mons, Albon II. had left his estates to his only daughter Albraide. She was the happy bride of Regnier, surnamed the Long-heeled, a knight celebrated for his bravery no less than for his manly beauty. "Never, never," say the old chronicles, "had there lived a more devoted pair than Albraide and Regnier." Beloved by all their subjects, they were occupied in enlarging and adorning their city, which in those days did not occupy a third of the ground covered by the present beautiful and flourishing town, when a sudden invasion of Normans came upon them.

Many times already since the death of Charlemagne the northern barbarians had appeared like a whirlwind on the coasts of France. Baldwin of the Iron-arm had driven them from Flanders; but now messenger after messenger announced that their sails appeared riding over the waves, and bearing death and misery to France.

Regnier was brave; like Baldwin of the Iron-arm, he was

of noble blood; and like him, he called together his warriors, and armed himself for battle. Albraide, weeping and anxious, hastened to shut herself in a little chapel which she had raised in honour of the Twelve Apostles, and where she spent the remainder of the day in tearful prayers for her country and her knight.

Meanwhile Regnier had advanced to Tournai, which he hoped to defend. But he had only been able to collect a handful of men, and the Normans came in legions. The fleet was headed by Rollo, or Rolf, the fiercest and the most dreaded of all the warriors of the north. Weary of his dangerous and adventurous life, he had vowed to take up his permanent abode in the richest country which earth could offer him; and the conquest of Hainault was one to kindle all his ambition. It was, therefore, with the fury of a baffled demon that Rolf advanced upon Regnier. He fought with desperate courage; he led forth a gigantic army; and the young count was driven back.

But Albraide was praying.

Battle upon battle did Regnier wage; still day by day repulsed, and day by day returning to the charge with renewed courage. Before long, however, he was forced to acknowledge to himself that it was impossible to be victorious in open warfare against Rolf. He retired to the neighbourhood of Condé, and there tried by ambushes and night attacks to harass the enemy.

And Albraide still prayed on.

One day she knelt before the altar of the Apostles, when the sound of a footstep sent her blood to her heart. She turned. A messenger from her husband's camp stood before her. Glad indeed were the tidings which he brought. Regnier had captured Rollo's twelve principal generals. A holiday was proclaimed through all the castle; all hearts, from that of the countess to her lowest serf, beat high with joy. And after reciting together with all her household a fervent *Te Deum*, Albraide retired to rest and to hopeful dreams.

Alas! on the next morning a woeful change had fallen upon the castle; all sounds of joy and triumph had given way to tears and bitter lamentations. A messenger had arrived with early dawn, bringing the news that the young Count of Mons, the hero and the glory of his people, was taken captive.

Long and most bitterly did his young bride weep. But when the first bitterness was past, she consoled herself with the idea, that it would be easy to ransom her husband by setting at liberty the twelve Norman generals. But, by and by, she heard to her dismay that Rollo would not consent to such an exchange; that, knowing well how dearly loved the young count was, he would only surrender such a prize when his country should be given up. And lastly, a messenger arrived with the news that Rollo threatened to cut off the head of his prisoner at once. Then the young countess seemed to lose her presence of mind and her courage. In the restlessness of her agony she flew out of the palace and out of the town, only imploring to be left alone. No one attempted to follow her. There are moments in war when only selfish fears can make themselves heard; and the people of Mons already imagined the savage Northmen in their desecrated homes.

Despair in her heart, and madness in her brain, the wretched Albraide rushed into the open country, and in the direction of a deep lake which lay not far from the city. And now its cold quiet waters lay before her; and her good angel must have trembled for her. Bewildered, miserable, tempted almost beyond her strength, she was already on the brink, and one moment more would have hurried her into eternity. But suddenly, upon the borders of the lake rose up before her a venerable man in flowing antique robes, and leaning on a pilgrim's staff. She turned away to avoid him; another, like him in appearance, again stood before her. Further on, a third appeared, holding rays in his hand; a fourth, leaning on a Greek cross: twelve ancient men, marked by different emblems,—a scythe, a sword, a palm, and a chalice,—surrounded the lake, as if to guard it.

The countess hurried round it again and again, without remarking that the old men were slowly following her; till, at the point where she had first seen the pilgrim with his staff, they all surrounded her, and with one solemn voice addressed her:

"Albraide, God in His mercy saves you from a fearful sin: a thought is in your heart which you have never offered up to Him; but we have not forgotten you, poor suffering child! Send back the twelve generals. Return to Mons: do all which the barbarian demands, and you will see your Regnier again."

A light streamed over the black waters as the vision disappeared: and in its radiance knelt Albraide,—weeping bitterly, indeed, but now with soft and healthful tears. She could not doubt but her preservers from sin and death were no others than the twelve apostles.

She quickly regained her palace, and summoned the twelve prisoners before her.

"You are free," she said; "return to your leader; and may he deal by Regnier as I have dealt by you."

The twelve generals looked one upon the other in surprise. Free from their chains, they returned to their camp, blessing and praising the generous countess.

The people of Mons, however, had already sent to negotiate with Rollo for the liberation of their prince. The barbarian had demanded as ransom, not only the liberty of his twelve generals, but also all the gold and silver in Hainault; and that Albraide should swear by her God, that neither jewels or costly ornaments of any kind remained in her castles nor in her churches. He also demanded a contribution in kind for the maintenance of his troops. Twenty-four hours were given to the people of Mons; and if by that time the ransom was not paid, they might expect, said Rollo, to receive the head of their count.

Rollo had not recovered from his surprise at the return of his generals, when the first wagon containing the gold and silver arrived. The spoils of every palace, church, or castle, followed from hour to hour; and last of all arrived the jewels of the young countess.

Surprised and touched through all his rugged nature, Rollo summoned Regnier to his presence, fell upon his neck, presented him with a horse, and insisted on himself accompanying him home to his wife, to whom he restored all her treasures.

"Duc Regnier," he said, "between you and me there must be perpetual peace and an eternal friendship."

Pressing his hand, he swore to respect for his sake Hainault and Brabant, set sail for the open sea, and hastened off to conquer that part of France which has since been named Normandy.

In memory of the countess's vision, the lake where she had seen the twelve venerable men has ever since been named

The Lake of the Apostles.

OUR LADY OF GALLORO

Of all the retreats scattered up and down along the sides of the Alban and Sabine Hills, in which the Romans and their guests seek shelter from the summer heats, there is none more peaceful and more pleasant than the little village of L'Ariccia. Prettily situated on the summit of one of those knolls, or minor eminences, which form the outskirts of the Alban range where first it begins to rise out of the Campagna, it still retains those ancient characteristics by which it is known to the classical student. As your carriage toils slowly up the steep ascent by which the village is entered from the side of Rome, it is beset by troops of beggars, imploring the same assistance, and using (in many instances) the very same outward gesture as their forefathers did in the days of Juvenal;* when you have reached the top, and penetrated nearly to the end of the one long narrow street of which the village consists, you come to a very unpretending but very comfortable little hotel, which might serve as the genuine representative of that "*hospitium modicum*" wherein Horace† took his first night's rest in his celebrated journey from Rome to Brindisi; and if you go on but a few paces further, and pass under the archway at the other extremity of the village, you find yourself at once in that thick

* Sat. iv. 117-8.
† 1 Sat v. 2.

dark wood, that "*Nemus Aricinum,*" through which many an ancient worshipper of Jupiter Latialis must often have passed on his way to or from the solemn assemblies that were wont to be held on the summit of Monte Cavi. It is not, however, with the classical associations of this little village that we are now concerned, but with a shrine in its immediate neighbourhood dedicated to the Holy Mother of God, to which the inhabitants have a very special devotion, and which is continually visited by all strangers who happen to have taken up their abode for the summer months in any of the adjacent villages.

It was in the early spring of the year 1621, that a boy, named Santi Bevilacqua, a native of Tuscany, but then living with his uncle (a carpenter) at L'Ariccia, was out in this wood on some boyish quest after wild fruits or flowers; and in the course of his rambles, he chanced to spy what seemed to him to be a piece of high wall or broken rock, thickly surrounded with brambles and all sorts of underwood. Impelled by an idle curiosity, or by some other motive of which we have no account, he peered more closely into this dense mass of wild tangled vegetation, until he fancied that he saw against the face of the rock something shining and coloured. Having removed, as well as he was able, all the impediments in his way, he discovered, to his great delight, that there was a picture there of our Blessed Lady holding the Divine Infant in her arms, for which, with the true instinct of a Catholic child, he immediately conceived a very lively devotion; and falling on his knees, spent a considerable time in prayer and meditation before it. For some time the boy took a great pride in keeping his discovery a profound secret from all his companions; and every day, as he left school, he used to steal away as secretly as he could, and pay a solitary visit to his dear Madonna. He had no other means of finding his way to the spot than by faithfully following the course he had chanced to pursue on the day of the original discovery; yet this, he was well aware, was needlessly long and circuitous. He set about, therefore, to make a more direct path for himself; but as this proved to be a task beyond his strength, he was obliged to call to his assistance some of his older schoolfellows. These went to work with admirable diligence, and managed to force a passage through a great deal of brushwood, until they had nearly arrived at the object of their desires. But here the wood grew thicker and more stout, and no force which this band of juvenile workmen could command would make any impression upon it. Day after day they renewed their attempts, but always failed. At last one of them suggested a brilliant idea, which, with the characteristic thoughtlessness of their age, they immediately proceeded to carry into execution. It was no other than to set fire to the obnoxious impediments; and, wonderful to relate, they succeeded in their purpose without doing any mischief to other parts of the wood. When once this feat had been accomplished, the picture of our Lady in the wood became a favourite resort of all the children who were aware of its existence; they made daily pilgrimages to it, offering their little nosegays of wild flowers or anything else they could get, by way of ornament; and although some of the good villagers of L'Ariccia did not quite approve of such a troop of children continually passing to and fro in what they conceived to be very dangerous proximity to their vineyards and gardens, yet the pious practice could not be checked, but only grew more and more general.

It was in the designs of Divine Providence, however, that this picture should receive a still greater celebrity, and become an object of devotion to a more extensive circle; and the child Santi was selected to be the occasion of this, as he had also been of its first discovery. One day, being somewhat weary on his return from the wood, he lay down in his uncle's shop, leaning his head against a heap of boards which were ranged along the wall. During his sleep, all these planks fell, and of course the child was buried under them.

The carpenter, hearing the noise, ran to the spot to see what was the matter; other neighbours also were soon gathered together to the scene of the accident. At first they lamented over the child as dead; but on hearing his voice calling from beneath the timber, they lost no time in removing it, and, to their great amazement, they found the boy not only alive, but absolutely unhurt. Nothing was now to be heard but cries on all sides of "*Miracolo! miracolo! Madre di Dio! Maria santissima!*" and other such exclamations; and the boy was called upon to give an account of his extraordinary escape. This was soon done; for all that he could say about it was, that as soon as he felt the planks were moving, he instantly invoked the Madonna of Vallericcia, and that he had never ceased to do so ever since. This led of course to a rehearsal of the whole story above, of the way in which the picture had first been brought to light, and how the juvenile pilgrims had been constantly honouring it ever since; whereupon the older inhabitants of the village called to mind, that in their younger days they had often heard talk of this picture; they could not, indeed, give any accurate account of who it was that had painted it, nor how old it was; but it was generally supposed that it was the work of one of the Basilian monks of Grotta Ferrata, who had once owned some property in that neighbourhood, and whose zeal for religious painting was so notorious; any how, they could remember when there had been a great devotion to this Madonna; even as late as the year 1594, the Princess Artemisia Savelli (whose family then occupied the palace and lands in L'Ariccia now belonging to the Chigi family) had attributed her own unexpected recovery from some dangerous malady to a vow which she made with reference to this very picture; and she had afterwards been very anxious to build a little chapel for it, only unfortunately there was some dispute between the prince and the ecclesiastical authorities of the village as to the right of property in this portion of the wood; hence the whole scheme had fallen to the ground, and the public devotion received a check, which ended, as we have seen, in the total neglect of the picture, and indeed absolute forgetfulness of its existence. Now, however, news of the miracle being everywhere noised abroad, people naturally flocked together to go and visit the place; and since it only needs for a Catholic to show special devotion to our Blessed Lady in order to receive special benefits from her intercession, it follows, as a matter of course, that other wonderful cures and other favours, both temporal and spiritual, were soon received at the same spot. What has been before now said of troubles and sorrows, and what is indeed a common proverb in the mouth of everybody, even in matters of this world, may be still more truly said of any outpouring of wonderful gifts and graces at the hand of Mary: *they do not come singly*. "That one hailstone falls is a proof, not that no more will come, but that others are coming surely; when we feel the first, we say, 'it *begins* to hail,'—we do not argue that it is over, but that it is to come." Just so is it with these miracles wrought by the intercession of Mary; where we hear of one, immediately we look for another; it continues, because it has begun; its beginning marks its presence; and it goes on for months or years, or even for whole generations, according to the good pleasure of Almighty God.

The *grazia*, then, that had been received by the boy Bevilacqua, was followed by innumerable others of various kinds, bestowed upon persons who came to offer up their prayers, and to call upon our Blessed Lady for help, in the presence of this ancient picture, until at length one of the priests of L'Ariccia, by name Polidori, a native of Frascati, determined on erecting an altar there, and enclosing it in a little oratory. He also built a cottage adjoining, as a residence for someone to take care of the sanctuary; and in addition to this person, Santi also went and lived there, to serve the Masses, and perform all the other offices of a sacristan. The chapel was opened on the 3d of May, 1623, the whole population of the neighbourhood assisting at a grand procession; and it was soon so much frequented, that fourteen or fifteen Masses were said there nearly every day. Offerings too of various kinds were given in such abundance, that it was proposed to erect a church of greater pretensions, capable of accommodating the continually increasing number of pilgrims. The Cardinal Bishop of Albano and Prince Savelli having consented to this proposal, and upwards of 8000 *lire* having been contributed for the purpose, the foundation-stone was laid on the 15th of August, 1624, on a little platform of land which almost overhangs the site of the more humble oratory and the place where the picture was first discovered. It was several years before the building was completed, more especially since it was determined to erect a convent also, adjoining the new church; and the funds which had been collected proved inadequate to this extension of the original plan. At length, however, the whole work was accomplished, and on the 15th of May, 1633, the church was solemnly dedicated to our Blessed Lady, under the title of her Immaculate Conception, and at the same time religious of the congregation of Vallambrosa took possession of the new monastery. Early on the following day (which in that year was Whit-Monday) upwards of thirty thousand persons might be seen flocking together from all the neighbouring villages, and even from Rome itself, anxious to assist at the ceremony of removing the picture from its original position in the wood to the place that was now prepared for it over the high altar in the church. Canon Pofidori's little oratory had merely enclosed the rock on whose surface the image of our Lady was painted, he had not attempted to detach the painting from the rock itself; and indeed this would have been impossible, the coat of plaster on which it stood being too thin and delicate to bear removal. But now they had sawn off that portion of the rock which they wished to preserve; and this fragment being placed on a wooden frame, highly ornamented with flowers and lights, and otherwise prepared for the purpose, they proceeded to carry up the hill, and to deposit it in its new resting-place. This was done by bodies of ten men at a time, continually relieving one another, and moving onwards amid the solemn prayers, and hymns and psalms of thanksgiving of the assembled multitudes. Many miracles, it is said, were wrought both during its progress and after it was placed in the church, where it was exposed to the veneration of the faithful on a platform near the high altar until the end of the month; and similar blessings have been renewed from time to time ever since, of which the inhabitants of L'Ariccia retain a most grateful remembrance.

The plague in 1656 and the cholera in 1837 had spread far and wide through central Italy and the States of the Church; it had even reached as far as the little town of Albano, scarcely half a mile distant from the village of which we are speaking; but the faithful inhabitants flocked together to pay their vows at the shrine of Galloro; old men and children, young men and maidens, princes, priests, and beggars, all might then be seen wending their way through the shady wood to the little chapel, which was crowded from morning till night; the petitioners told their beads as they went along, or they recited psalms, or they sang hymns and litanies, and many of them walked barefooted: in a word, they were pilgrims and humble clients of Mary; and Mary received their prayers, the plague was stayed, and not a single inhabitant of the village fell a victim on either occasion.

Equally remarkable was the deliverance of this village, not indeed from all molestation and alarm, yet from all plunder and violence on the part of the republican troops of France at the close of the last century. The sanctuary itself had been sacrilegiously stripped of all that was costly and valuable in the way of precious stones or metals; the religious had been driven from their home, and the monastery, with all its furniture, was sold; the church, therefore, was necessarily closed, and all public devotion to the picture suspended. Yet, day after day, many a peasant might be seen kneeling on the bare ground without the door, invoking the assistance and protection of their ancient patron; and by and by the picture itself was removed to L'Ariccia, and even the altar which had stood below it; and after this translation, the inhabitants both felt and found themselves safe from the lawless depredations of their enemies.

A combination of circumstances, such as the world calls chance, but in which religion never fails to recognise the finger of God, served to protect them from all those further injuries by which their less favoured neighbours were so grievously oppressed. Their grateful devotion for this mercy rendered them extremely unwilling to restore the picture to Galloro, when the Vallambrosian monks returned to take possession of the monastery; indeed, the religious were obliged to call for the interference of the Pope, before they could recover it. Ten years afterwards saw Napoleon master of Rome, and all the religious communities dispersed. Galloro, however, was not this time altogether abandoned. Although the Vallambrosians were obliged to withdraw, they left two American priests—ex-Jesuits, who had been staying with them for some time since the dissolution of their own society—to serve the church during their absence; and when, on the restoration of Pope Pius VII. to his throne, and of the various religious orders to their homes, the Vallambrosians, in consequence of an insufficiency of numbers, were no longer in a condition to resume their residence here, the Holy Father, who had just then re-established the Society of Jesus, appointed these Fathers in their stead, and they have retained it ever since. Only three or four Jesuits are in constant residence here; its healthy situation, however, and the quiet retirement of the place, cause it to be constantly visited by Fathers from other parts who have been overworked, and stand in need of rest; hence the functions in the church are frequent and good, and the devotion to the sanctuary is probably as great at the present day as it has ever been, excepting perhaps on certain special occasions immediately after some notorious miracle. At one time, for a period of two months or more, we enjoyed the opportunity of visiting it ourselves almost daily, and can testify to the number and devotion of those who worship there. We have already said that the church stands on the side of a hill, without any habitations nearer to it than the villages of L'Ariccia on the one side, and of Genzano on the other (the former being a little more than half a mile off perhaps, the latter at more than double that distance); yet the number of communions that were made there in a single year (1846) were upwards of 7060, being an average of nearly twenty pilgrims a day.[*] There can be no doubt but that the Romans and foreigners who make their summer retreat in the neighbourhood contribute something to this number; we observe, however, that in the very depth of winter the average number of communions is not less than 500 a month: thus, in December 512, in January 464, in February 633, &c. These details may enable the reader in some degree to realise to himself the habit which prevails among the people, of having recourse to this shrine on all occasions of special devotion during the time of any public or private trial; in a word, when they wish to be more earnest in their prayers, and to draw nearer, as it were, to the throne of grace and the fount of mercy.

---

[*] The number of Easter communicants in L'Ariccia is about 900; that in Genzano we do not accurately know; it it probably three times as much.

THE
CHILDREN OF THE
JUSTINIANI

In glancing over the pages of any history, it is curious to remark how capriciously the associations of historical interest seem to change localities. At one time some particular country is chosen out, and into its limits are crowded all the life and greatness of the period; and if we look at it at another time, perhaps in the very next age, we find it forgotten; the light that rested over it for a moment has passed on, and is illuminating some other spot, leaving it again, in its turn, to fall into its former insignificance. All the classic regions of antiquity may be said to be illustrations of this remark, and none more so than the Isles of Greece; their interest in the map of Europe at the present day is limited to their names. Yet not to speak only of times of distant antiquity, scarcely more than three hundred years ago these islands played a distinguished part in the long struggle maintained by Christian Europe against the power of the infidels. In the present weakened and contemptible state of the Turkish empire, it is difficult for us to realise a time, and that not so very long ago, when the very name of the Turks was a word of terror to Christendom. Yet during the whole of the sixteenth century (until, under the patronage of Mary the

Help of Christians, their naval power was utterly destroyed at Lepanto) we find Europe lying almost at their mercy. Among the many tales which may be found of touching interest in connection with their cruel incursions on the shores of the Mediterranean and Levant, the following is told concerning the illustrious family of the Justiniani.

The original stock of this noble house was settled at Venice; but a branch had long been fixed in the isle of Scio, of which island they were indeed the lords, though in the beginning of the sixteenth century they had become tributary to the Turks. A noble devotedness in resistance to the infidel, and in the protection of Christendom, was hereditary among them. In every account of the armament sent by Venice against the forces of the Turks, we may be almost sure to find a prince of the Justiniani family at their head, or dying gallantly in the struggle. There was also another hereditary feeling among them, and this was their attachment to the Order of St. Dominic. They have given no less than nine bishops to the Order, one of whom (Vincent Justiniani) was Master General during the pontificate of St. Pius V.

At the time of the circumstances we are about to relate, Timothy Justiniani, a member of the same illustrious order, was bishop of his native island of Scio, and his cousin Antony, also a Dominican, archbishop of the neighbouring island of Naxia. It was the year 1566; the Council of Trent was just over, and the Bishop of Scio, who had assisted at its deliberations, had returned to his diocese. There had been a short lull in the fierce desultory warfare which had been carried on for many years with the Turks. The inhabitants paid their tribute to the infidels regularly and exactly, and a treaty had been solemnly granted them, by which peace and quiet seemed to be assured to them in return for this pledge of their submission. And indeed there seemed the less chance of this treaty being broken, for the Turkish general, Mustapha, had just been repulsed from Malta with shame and loss by the gallant Grand Master La Valetta, and had been forced to carry back the shattered remains of his forces, without having gained the slightest advantage over the Christians.

The Scian islanders, therefore, laid aside the fear of a descent of the infidels, which was the perpetual bugbear, if we may so say, of those days, and prepared to celebrate the festival of Easter with unusual joy and solemnity. Everything this year contributed to make this peculiarly a holiday of rejoicing. The return of their bishop after his long labours at the Council, and the termination of the Council itself, settling and confirming as it had done the faith of the Church, and fixing the adamant barriers of its definitions against the distractions and heresies of the time, gave a special gladness to the feelings with which all flocked to the churches on the 14th of April (on which day the Paschal festival fell that year). It was the moment chosen by the Turks to come upon them with a powerful fleet, which landing its forces before the Scians were aware of its approach, took them utterly by surprise; so that the entire island fell into their hands almost without resistance. The Bishop was in the cathedral engaged in the celebration of the Holy Mysteries, when a large body of the infidels entered the church. In their hatred to the Christian faith, they made every kind of profanation and sacrilege one of the express objects of their depredatory attacks. Justiniani, therefore, well knew what would follow; and turning from the altar to meet his enemies, he used every entreaty, and offered the riches of the entire island, if only he might be suffered to preserve the holy sanctuaries unprofaned. Their answer was a rush towards the altar, headed by their chief, Pasha Piali. This man, rudely pushing aside the Bishop, laid his hands on the ciborium, and cried contemptuously, "Is this the God of the Christians?" "It is Himself," replied the Bishop; "I will never deny Him;" and perhaps he hoped this answer might strike some awe into the minds of the Turks. But Piali with a sneer cast the vessel to the ground, and would have trampled on its contents, if the Bishop had not thrown himself in the way. "Strike me to death, if you will," he exclaimed; "the Sacred Mysteries shall never be trampled under your feet;" and so saying, resisting with extraordinary coolness and courage the attempts of all those who stood round to prevent him, he on his knees carefully and reverently gathered together every one of the Sacred Hosts, even to the smallest particle.

Whether, indeed, his courage and devotion inspired them with some respect, we cannot say; but the infidels spared his life. Every church, however, throughout the island was destroyed, save that of the Dominican convent, which was turned into a mosque. The next care of the Turks was, if possible, to destroy the family whose enmity they had so much cause to dread. Every member of the Justiniani family was carefully sought for, and taken captive. Some were carried to the Crimea, others to Constantinople, and different parts of the empire. Their property was seized, and the few who escaped captivity took refuge in Italy in a state of absolute destitution. A few of them sent into banishment recovered their liberty, being ransomed through the interest of the Pope and the French king; but they never recovered their former power and distinction. Not one of these, however, but bore himself in this fall and ruin of his house with the spirit of a hero; and the Christian gallantry which they held as a birthright was nowhere more nobly displayed than in some young children, whose fate was peculiarly melancholy. With a refinement of cruelty, the Turks had chosen the youngest children of the family to the number of about twenty, and separating them from their parents, carried them to Constantinople, where they were placed among the pages of the court of Solyman II. They doubtless hoped that at their tender age (for they were not above ten years old) it would be easy to make them forget the teaching of their fathers, and bring them up in the Mussulman religion; and they were well aware no agony and no humiliation could be greater to the princes of the hated Justiniani, than to know that their sons were living renegades to their faith. If this was their hope, they had little calculated the temper of those with whom they had to do. Neither the luxury of an eastern court nor the threats of cruel punishment could tempt one of these children to disgrace his faith as a Christian, or prove unworthy of the name of a Justiniani. Like Daniel and his companions in the court of Nebuchodonozor, they stood equally firm against threats and allurements. The Turks for a while contented themselves with endeavouring to tempt them from their allegiance with the flattering seductions of the senses; but finding all their efforts in vain, they savagely condemned them to be whipped to death. This torture was inflicted with unusual barbarity, for the infidels were piqued to see themselves defied and baffled by a little company of children. Not one gave way; in the midst of unspeakable torments they all showed the same constancy, and encouraged one another to suffer yet more for Jesus Christ. As one of these little martyrs was dying under the lash, a Turk who stood by approached, and bade him only lift his finger as a sign that he renounced Christianity, and he should be released. The noble child, unable to speak, confessed his faith by signs; for raising the hand to which the Turk pointed as he spoke, he clenched the fingers together so tightly, that no force was able to open them, and they remained firmly locked together even after his death. The Pasha himself came to the spot, and addressing another, who had as yet survived the punishment, said he should be thrown from the top of a high tower if he still refused to embrace the faith of Mahomet. "I am not worthy to be a martyr for Jesus Christ, like my brothers," replied the boy; "but all I desire in this world is to die for Him." On this he was shut up in prison, with the idea of wearying out his constancy. He knelt down on the floor, and addressing himself to God in words of childish simplicity and confidence, prayed for constancy and courage to die in the faith. After spending three whole days in this manner, he died of his wounds and exhaustion.

St. Pius V. is said to have been touched with an extraordinary emotion of grief on hearing of these circumstances. As a Dominican, the Justiniani were like his religious brethren; and he gave the only testimony that lay in his power to do honour to these heroic children. In the Consistory held at St. Mark's in the September of the same year, he narrated the story of their martyrdom. Nor was their melancholy fate without its influence in the events which followed. The treacherous attack on Scio, with the revengeful ruin of this illustrious house, and, above all, the cruelty practised on their children, were felt to call for a severe chastisement; and when, five years afterwards, the Christian fleet lay opposite to the overwhelming armament of the infidels in the Gulf of Lepanto, many a heart was nerved to heroism by a thought of the devoted courage of the martyred children of the Justiniani.

THE DELIVERANCE OF ANTWERP

In the year 1622, the Prince of Orange, Maurice of Nassau, determined on besieging Antwerp, reckoning on the secret intelligence which he maintained with the heretics inside the town, and relying also on the number of his soldiers and engines of war. With this design he embarked, together with twelve thousand men, eight thousand of whom were musketeers; and passing by Dordrecht, took from thence twenty-four cannon and other pieces of artillery. Thirty-six long ships had been built on purpose for this expedition; and in these he placed two hundred and seventy horses and several instruments of war, such as had never before been known in the Dutch armies. As the fleet left Dordrecht, the wind was in their favour: Maurice had just held a review of his army, and at the sight of this formidable force, with the certainty moreover of meeting with none but a very feeble resistance, he cried out that he was sure of success; that he had nothing to fear from the power of man, and that God alone could hinder him.

Meanwhile, in the city thus threatened, there dwelt a certain holy nun named Anne of St. Bartholomew, a Teresian Carmelite from Spain, who had been trained under St. Teresa herself in the convent of St. Joseph of Avila, and had made such progress in the way of perfection, that her holy superior said of her, "I have the name of a saint, but Anne does the works of one." It was in her arms that the saint died; and soon afterwards she was called into France, and chosen superior of the convent of Pontoise, and afterwards of that of Paris; and in 1611, at the request of the Archduke Albert, she founded the convent of Carmelites in the city of Antwerp; and it was by her assistance that the first convent of English Teresian nuns was founded a few years later (on the 1st May, 1619) in the very same city. On the very night when Maurice and his army embarked, as we have seen, at Dordrecht, this holy nun suddenly awoke, and called up her religious for prayer with such extreme earnestness, that all thought she had received intimation of some treason, which she was imploring the assistance of God to defeat. She declared, however, that it was not so; that she only knew that God was calling her inwardly to pray, and to cause them to pray also. At two o'clock in the morning, her fervour redoubled; with her hands raised to heaven, she cried again and again for mercy, and that with such effort, that her frame seemed to be sinking with fatigue. In the morning, she told one of the nuns that she was as weary as though her whole body had been bruised: "There must be some great treason afoot," she said; "for I feel as if I had been fighting all night. I have been forced to pray when I wished to rest, being quite exhausted; and when my arms, which I was holding stretched out towards God, dropped for very lassitude, I heard a voice within me, Pray on, pray on. If I had been fighting against a whole army, I could not have felt more utterly worn out."

Two hours after this, the effect of her prayer was known. Tidings then reached Antwerp, that at the very moment when Anne had begun to pray, the wind had changed; and that by the time the prince had reached a town called Gresboo, a dreadful tempest had arisen: it had hailed with such violence as to cut to pieces or otherwise spoil the cordage of his vessels; and he himself, with a few gentle-men, had thrown themselves into a boat, and with difficulty escaped to Willemstad.

On another occasion, a few years later, when a night-attack was unexpectedly made on the citadel of Antwerp, Anne was again awakened by a cry, which she found on inquiry had proceeded from no one in the house, and which she therefore regarded as a summons to prayer, feeling certain that the city must be in some danger. Her apprehensions were fully verified; for it soon became known that the enemy had attempted the citadel, but had suddenly withdrawn, leaving many of their guns and other instruments of war behind them.

So high an opinion of the efficacy of Anne's prayers was held among her contemporaries, that the Infanta Isabel of Spain declared to Inigo Borgia, the governor of the citadel of Antwerp, that she had no fears for the safety of that fortress, nor of the town of Antwerp, so long as it should contain within its walls the Mother Anne of St. Bartholomew, "who," she said, "inspired her with more confidence than a numerous army."

OUR LADY OF
GOOD COUNSEL AT
GENAZZANO

In the little town of Genazzano, a town pleasantly situated on the side of a range of hills skirting one of the high roads from Rome to Naples, there lived, not quite four hundred years ago, a very devout old woman, named Petruccia de Jeneo. She was a native of the place, and a member of the Third Order of St. Augustine, living in the world. She had had a little property of her own, but at the time of our narrative it was all spent, and spent too in a somewhat singular way. She had a great devotion to the principal church of the place, which was dedicated to our Lady under the title of Mother of Good Counsel. It was but a small and poor building, and Petruccia determined to rebuild it on a scale of great magnificence. Her means were quite unequal to the task. Nevertheless, such as they were, she devoted them entirely to the work. She went and sold all that she had, and the undertaking was begun. Her friends and neighbours laughed her to scorn, as one who had begun to build without "having first set down and reckoned the charges that were necessary, whether she had wherewithal to finish it." Her relations—not without some suspicion of a selfish regard to their own interests as the motive of their interference—rebuked her sharply for her improvidence, in thus voluntarily depriving herself of those means of support with which God had blessed her, in the time of her greatest necessity. She was old and infirm, they said; and who would undertake the burden of her support, since her impoverishment had been the result of a foolish indulgence of her own fancy? Her answer to these objections was always the same: "The work will be finished, and that right soon, because it is not my work, but God's; our Blessed Lady and St. Augustine will do it before I die and she continually repeated, with an air of exulting confidence, what seemed like the ravings of madness to those who heard her: "Oh, what a *gran signora*, what a noble lady, will soon come and take possession of this place!"

Meanwhile the work proceeded, and the walls had already risen to some height above the ground, close to the old church which they were intended to enclose. But by and by the builders ceased; Petruccia's funds were all spent, and there were no means of procuring any more. For the good woman had publicly declared that she had begun the undertaking, and was encouraged to persevere with it, mainly in reliance upon some secret inspiration, vision, or revelation (it does not clearly appear which), that she believed herself to have received from God, whereas the Church, in order to guard against abuses which had sometimes arisen from giving heed to pretended supernatural messages of this kind, had issued a law forbidding such things to be attended to, unless they were corroborated by some other external and independent testimony; the mere assertion of a dream, a vision, or a revelation, was on no account to be obeyed.* Petruccia's work, therefore, was not only suspended for want of means, it was also canonically prohibited; that is to say, her own substance had been entirely exhausted, and

* Quæ per somnia et inanes revelationes quorumlibet hominum ubicumque constituuntur altaria, omnino reprobentur.—Conc. Afric. A.D. 424: De Consecr. Dist. 1. Can. 26.

an appeal to the assistance of others could not be sanctioned by the ecclesiastical authorities. Matters were in this state in the spring of 1467, when the following miraculous event at once justified and completed the whole undertaking.

From time immemorial, the feast of St. Mark the Evangelist had been celebrated in Genazzano as a very special holiday. Tradition records that this was the consequence of some decree of the holy Pontiff of that name, who lived in the middle of the fourth century, and who hoped thereby to abolish certain impure and superstitious practices by which the heathen had been wont to pollute that day. Any how the fact is certain, that the 26th of April was always the principal day of the great fair or market of the year in that town. Accordingly it was being celebrated in the usual manner in the year already mentioned; the town was full of strangers; crowds of persons had passed and repassed the old church, and the imperfect walls of the new. Some had jeered and mocked, saying, "This woman had begun to build, and was not able to finish;" but others were sorry to see so good a work unfinished. Evening was now fast approaching, the gayest, brightest hour of the fair, when, business being ended, the pleasure of the day began: all were devoting themselves to amusement, each in his own way, when suddenly some who stood on the public piazza, or square, in front of the church, saw something like a thin cloud floating in the air, and then settling on one of the walls of the unfinished building. Here the cloud seemed to divide and disappear, and there remained upon the wall a picture of our Blessed Lady and the Holy Child Jesus, which had not been there before,—a picture which was new to all the bystanders, and which they could not in any way account for. At the same moment the bells of the church and of all the other churches in the town began to sound, yet no human hand could be seen to touch them. People ran from their houses to ask the cause of this general commotion; and indistinct rumours spread rapidly among them, that something wonderful had happened in the Piazza della Madonna. Those who were nearest to the spot arrived just in time to see the aged Petruccia come out, like the rest, from the church to inquire what had happened. As soon as she saw the picture she threw herself on her knees, and saluted it with outstretched arms; then rising and turning round to the people, she told them, with a voice half-choked by the violence of her emotions of joy and gratitude, that this was the gran signora whom she had so long expected; that she was now come to take possession of the church that ought to have been ready for her, and that the bells were being rung in this miraculous way only to do her honour. At this intelligence the people fell upon their knees, and began to pour forth their prayers before this marvellous painting, which they knew not how otherwise to designate than as the *Madonna del Paradiso*, or our Lady from Heaven.

Meanwhile, the inhabitants of the adjacent villages, alarmed by the unusual sound of the bells, accompanied (as is still the custom in many parts of Italy on all festive occasions) by the discharge of numerous firearms, imagined that some disturbance must have broken out in the city— no unlikely circumstance in those days of violence—and began to feel great anxiety for those of their relations and friends who were absent at the fair. Some, indeed, had already returned, but these were as much at a loss as the rest; for when they came away they had seen no symptoms of a riot, neither had they heard of any extraordinary cause of rejoicing. Others, again, had left the city, and were in the act of returning homewards, when their steps were arrested by these unaccountable sounds; and of these some, whose discretion was stronger than their curiosity, only hurried home the faster, whilst others turned back to investigate the cause. These, however, tarried so long to gaze at the wondrous sight, to hear its history, and to see the marvellous effects that followed, that the public anxiety of the neighbourhood still remained unrelieved. At length, at a very late hour of the night, some few stragglers returned, and told so strange a tale, that long before daybreak on the following morning, multitudes of the country people might be seen taking advantage of the day of rest (it was the fourth Sunday after Easter), and hurrying towards the town to hear and see for themselves. And not only the hale and the active, but even the aged and infirm, the blind, the lame, the maimed, and many others, came or were brought to this new pool of Bethsaida; for it was part of the intelligence which reached them, that persons were being miraculously healed of their infirmities in the presence of this strange picture. And the faith of many of these simple-hearted pilgrims received the reward they looked for: the blind received their sight; the ears of the deaf were opened, and the tongue of the dumb was loosed; the lame walked; nay, in one or two instances, the very dead were restored to life again; and during the next two or three months we have authentic evidence of nearly 200 miracles that were wrought on this favoured spot.

But whence had this picture really come? and how had it been brought? The people of Genazzano thought that it had come straight from heaven, and had been brought by angels, as tradition says that the picture of Sta. Maria in Portico was once brought to St. Galla in Rome. So they called it, as we have seen, the Madonna del Paradiso; and were not a little annoyed when, a few days after its first appearance, two strangers arrived from Rome, and said that they knew the picture well, and could tell all about its history. One of these strangers was a Sclavonian, the other an Albanian; and the story which they told was this:

They had been resident together in Scutari, a city of Albania, now called Iscodar, situated on the eastern coast of the Adriatic, and distant about five-and-twenty miles from the sea. On a little hill outside this city, not half a mile beyond the gates, there was a church in which this Madonna, painted upon the wall, was much venerated as the *Madonna* *del Buon Officio*. It was a picture to which there had always been a very great devotion, they said; but latterly, in the disturbed miserable condition of the country, the inhabitants had been more than usually frequent in their visits to it, entreating the Madonna's interference to defend them from their dangerous enemies, the Turks, who, they had reason to apprehend, were meditating a fresh invasion, and who, as a matter of fact, did, not many years afterwards, lay waste the whole country, and destroy many cities with fire and sword. Numbers of the citizens had already fled from the impending calamity, and taken refuge (as contemporary historians tell us) some in Venice, others in different cities of Romagna. Amongst the rest, our two strangers at length determined to expatriate themselves like their neighbours; but before doing so, they went out to bid a last farewell to their favourite shrine, and to pray the Mother of God, that, as she with her Divine Son had once been forced to flee from the face of one of the kings of the earth, who was plotting mischief against them, so she would mercifully vouchsafe to accompany, to guide, and protect these her humble clients in their no less compulsory flight. They said that, whilst they were yet praying, the picture disappeared from their sight, and in its stead a white cloud seemed to detach itself from the wall, to float through the air, and to pass out through the doors of the church. Attracted by an impulse which they could not account for, yet were unable to resist, they rose from their knees and followed; presently, they found themselves caught up in some mysterious manner along with it, and carried forward in its company. The manner of their transit they could not explain; they only knew that, as the angel of the Lord once set Habacuc in Babylon over the lions' den where Daniel was imprisoned, "in the force of his Spirit," and then presently set him again in his own place in Judea;* and as, when Philip and the eunuch were come up out of

* Dan. xiv. 35-38

the water, "the Spirit of the Lord took away Philip, and the eunuch saw him no more: And *he* went on his way rejoicing, but Philip was found at Azotus;"* so they too had been miraculously transported through the air by some invisible hand from one place to another; first to the sea coast; then across the Adriatic, whose waves had borne them up, as the sea of Galilee had borne St. Peter, when Jesus bade him come to Him upon the waters; then, that, as evening drew on, that which had seemed a pillar of a cloud by day became as it were a pillar of fire; and that, finally, when they had been brought to the gates of Rome, it entirely disappeared.

Entered into the Eternal City, the travellers had sought diligently for traces of their lost guide; they went from one church to another, inquiring for the picture which they had watched so long, and then so suddenly lost sight of; but all their inquiries were in vain. At length, at the end of two or three days, they heard of a picture having appeared in a strange way at Genazzano, and that its appearance was followed by many miracles. Immediately they set out to visit it; and as soon as they had arrived, they recognised and proclaimed its identity.

The people of Genazzano lent no willing ear to this strange history; it detracted somewhat from the heavenly origin which they would fain have assigned to their newly-gotten treasure; and it gave them some uneasiness too as to the ultimate security of their possession of it; for, should this story be authenticated, the picture might one day be reclaimed and carried away. In the course of a few days, however, as the story got noised abroad, other Albanians, who were scattered up and down in different parts of Italy, came to see it; and these too confirmed its identity. And many years afterwards, when people who took an interest in the

---

* Acts viii.39

matter, had the opportunity of going to Scutari and examining for themselves, they testified upon oath that they had found a blank space in the plaster of the walls of the church described; that its size and form corresponded exactly to that of the picture; and that the colouring and style of art exhibited in the picture were precisely the same with that which characterised all the other parts of the church. For it must be remembered, that this was no painting executed upon board or canvas, and thus capable of easy removal, and leaving no trace behind it; it was a mere fresco upon a very thin coating of plaster, which no human skill could have detached from the wall in a single piece, still less have transported from one place to another without injury.

Of course it was impossible that so marvellous a story, circulated in the immediate neighbourhood of the Holy See—for Genazzano is not more than thirty miles from Rome—should fail to attract the attention of that ever-watchful, jealous tribunal. The translation of the picture is said to have taken place late on the evening of the 25th of April; and before the middle of July, Pope Paul II. sent two bishops to examine, upon the very spot, into all the circumstances of the case. Cardinal Cortin, the Bishop of Palestrina, in whose diocese Genazzano is situated, was absent at this time at Avignon, the Pope therefore appointed a friend of his in his stead, Monsignor Gaucer, Bishop of Gap in Dauphiny, and with him he associated Monsignor Nicolo de Cruci, Bishop of Lesina, one of the islands in the Adriatic, near the coast of Dalmatia, whose familiarity as well with the language of the strangers as with the localities from which they professed to have come, could not fail to be of the utmost service in the investigation. The result of their inquiries was most satisfactory, and placed the truth of the narrative we have given beyond all reasonable doubt; Petruccia's unfinished building was immediately resumed;

and a handsome church, together with a large monastery attached to it, were completed in less than three years; the two strangers settled in the town, determined never more to abandon their heavenly guide, and the descendants of one of them (the Albanian De Giorgis) still remain there; and the Sanctuary of our Lady of Good Counsel was henceforth established for ever.

THE CONVENT OF
SAINT CECILY

One day, towards the close of the sixteenth century, when the iconoclasts or image-breakers were all-powerful in the Netherlands, there met four brothers in the town of Aix-la-Chapelle. Three of them were students from Wittemberg, and the fourth held the situation of preacher in Antwerp; and they had come to Aix-la-Chapelle to take possession of a property that had been left them by an uncle lately deceased. Not having any acquaintances in the place, they took up their quarters at an hotel. Here they lived very pleasantly for a few days, the preacher entertaining them with an account of all the wonderful changes that had recently been made in the country from which he came in matters of religion.

Now it happened that the Feast of Corpus Christi was at hand; and the four brothers, inflamed by fanaticism, youth, and the evil example of so many others in other parts of the country, determined to give Aix-la-Chapelle also a sample of their dexterity in the art of image-breaking. The preacher, who had more than once headed such enterprises, collected on the evening before the feast a number of young men, sons of merchants and students devoted to the new doctrine, who spent the night carousing in the tavern; and at break of day, having provided themselves with crowbars and other instruments of destruction, they proceeded to the Convent of St. Cecily, which was outside the gates of the town, and which they had chosen as the scene of their reckless operations. A signal was agreed upon, at which the assault should be begun upon the stained-glass windows, rich with stories from the sacred Scriptures; and assured of finding many adherents amongst the crowd, they determined to proceed with the work of destruction till there was not left one stone upon another.

The abbess, who even before dawn had received information of the danger which threatened the convent, sent to the imperial officer then commanding in the town, requesting a guard for its protection. But he was one of those who secretly favoured the new school; and he refused the guard, on the plea that they were ghosts which had frightened her, and that there was not even a shadow of danger for her convent. Meanwhile the hour appointed for the commencement of the ceremonies was approaching, and the nuns prepared for Mass with much prayer, and under a painful apprehension of all that might probably happen. They could count upon no defender save an old steward of the convent, now past seventy, who planted himself at the entrance of the church, with a few young boys whom he had armed for the occasion.

To add to the troubles and anxieties of the nuns on this memorable morning, it so happened that the leader and mistress of the choir, Sister Antonia, had been attacked by a violent nervous fever a few days before; so that, besides their alarm at the four sacrilegious brothers, who might already be seen wrapped up in their large mantles, waiting behind the pillars of the church, the convent was in the greatest embarrassment as to the due performance of the music appropriate to so high a festival. The abbess on the previous evening had ordered a Mass, the production of an old Italian master whose name is unknown, which was remarkable for the peculiar tone of sanctity and grandeur which breathed through its composition, and now anxiously sent to make new inquiries for Sister Antonia; but the nun, who went to see her, brought back word that their dear sister was in a state of absolute insensibility, so that it was useless to expect that she could by any possibility conduct the performance.

Meanwhile some alarming scenes had already taken place in the church, now filled with more than a hundred men of all ranks and ages, armed with axes and crowbars, and a variety of other similar instruments; they had spoken in the most unseemly manner to the persons stationed at the porches of the church, and made use of language the most insolent and shameless towards the nuns, who now and then glided through the aisles on some pious errand. Matters indeed had gone so far, that the old steward hastened to the sacristy, and there on his knees implored the abbess to postpone the festival, and to take refuge in the town under the protection of the commandant. But the abbess continued inflexible in her resolution, that this festival, ordained for the honour and glory of God, should at all hazards be celebrated; she reminded the steward of his duty to protect with life and limb the High Mass and solemn procession about to be held in the church; and as the bell was then tolling, ordered the nuns, who surrounded her in fear and trembling, to select any music, however inferior, so they might commence without delay.

The nuns were taking their places; the parts of a Mass which they had frequently sung before had just been distributed, when suddenly Sister Antonia, in sound and perfect health, though somewhat pale, appeared slowly ascending the stairs, carrying under her arm the Mass of that old Italian master, for the performance of which the abbess had expressed so great an anxiety. "No matter, sisters, no matter!" was her reply to the inquiries of the astonished nuns as to the secret of her wonderful recovery; and giving to each their several parts, she seated herself at the organ.

No sooner had she commenced, than the pious sisters felt in their breasts a most heavenly and miraculous feeling of consolation; the very anxiety which they felt only helped to waft their souls, as on wings, still higher and higher. The Mass was performed with the utmost dignity and grandeur. Not a breath was heard in the aisles or nave throughout the entire service; during the "Kyrie" especially, and yet more at the "Gloria," it seemed as though the whole congregation had been stricken dead; even the dust on the pavement remained unstirred by the wind, as if in defiance of the four sacrilegious brothers and their followers.

******

Six years afterwards, when this event had been long forgotten, the mother of these four young men arrived from the Hague, and instituted inquiries, with the aid of the magistrates, as to what road they had taken on leaving Aix-la-Chapelle; for that they had never since been heard of. The last accounts received of them in the Netherlands came, she said, in a letter written by the preacher to his friend, a schoolmaster in Antwerp, on the eve of the Festival of Corpus Christi, six years before; and in it he had given a detailed description of an enterprise they had projected against the Convent of St. Cecily, but of which she would not now communicate any further particulars.

After many vain efforts to discover the objects of her search, the magistrates recollected that many years before, about the period she mentioned, four young men, whose country and parentage were unknown, had been confined in the lunatic asylum recently founded by the emperor. But as they were suffering from religious derangement, and, as the magistrate seemed to imply from obscure report, of such a character as to lead to the impression that they were Catholics, the description so little answered the well-known disposition of her sons, that the unhappy woman paid little or no heed to the information. At length, however, being struck by many of the particulars given, she went one day, accompanied by an officer of the court, to the asylum, and begged to be permitted to see the four unfortunate lunatics.

They were seated, in long black mantles, at a table, on which stood a crucifix. They appeared to be praying before it in silence, their folded hands resting on the table. The unfortunate mother, recognising her sons, sank powerless on a chair. To her inquiries as to the nature of their insanity, the governor replied that they were simply engaged in the adoration of the Redeemer, imagining that they had a clearer conception than others of His divinity as the true Son of the one living God. He said that they had now led this ascetic life for more than six years; that they slept little, ate little, never opened their lips, and never rose from their seats save at midnight, and then only for the purpose of intoning the *Gloria in excelsis*, which they did with a voice loud enough to shatter the very windows of the house. He concluded by assuring her, that notwithstanding all this, these patients enjoyed perfect health, and even a certain degree of cheerfulness, though of a somewhat grave and solemn character; that whenever anyone pronounced them deranged, they compassionately shrugged their shoulders, and more than once exclaimed, that if the good town of Aix-la-Chapelle were only to know as much as they did, every one of its inhabitants would leave his business, kneel down round the crucifix, and employ his time in singing the *Gloria in excelsis*, like themselves.

The wretched woman, no longer able to endure the painful sight, at length allowed herself to be conducted home; and on the following morning, hoping to gain some information as to the cause which had produced this extraordinary effect, she sought the house of Herr Veit Gotthelf, a wealthy cloth-merchant of the town, who had been mentioned in the letter written by the preacher as one who took an active part in the project for the destruction of the Convent of St. Cecily. Veit Gotthelf received the stranger with much courtesy; but on learning her business, he bolted the door, and after requesting her to be seated, he cautiously began his narrative in the following words:—

"My good lady, provided you promise not to implicate me, who some six years since was in habits of close intimacy with your sons, in any judicial investigations which may hereafter arise out of this affair, I will deal frankly with you, and tell you all I know without reserve. It is quite true that we harboured the intention spoken of in the letter you refer to; and by what means this project, planned and arranged with admirable precision and sagacity, came to be frustrated in the execution, I have never been able to discover; heaven itself seems to have taken the convent of these good women under its holy protection. All I know is, that, as a preliminary to more decided measures, your sons had already indulged in many wanton pranks, disturbing the divine service; and that upwards of three hundred miscreants, armed with crowbars and torches, only awaited the signal of the preacher to raze the church to the ground. But instead of this, at the first sound of the music, your sons simultaneously took off their hats with an air of reverence that struck us all with surprise; then, by degrees, they buried their faces in their hands, as though in some strange access of deep and speechless emotion; and after awhile the preacher, turning round suddenly, called on us all, in a loud and terrible voice, to do as they had done, and to uncover our heads. In vain did some of the party touch his arm, and beg of him in a whisper to give the preconcerted signal. Instead of answering, the preacher crossed his hands on his breast, dropped on his knees, and, together with his three brothers, bowing his head with fervour to the very ground, recited in an under-tone those very prayers at which the moment before he had been openly scoffing. Utterly perplexed at such a spectacle, the crowd of fanatics, deprived of their leader, remained standing, undecided and inactive, until the conclusion of the wonderful musical composition that had just been performed by the choir; then, as several of those who had committed the disturbances were seized and taken off by a guard, the miserable gang had no alternative but to retire from the church and disperse. That evening, after many fruitless inquiries at the hotel for your sons, who had not yet returned, I went back with a few friends in a great state of alarm to the convent, with the view of obtaining further information from the door-keepers, who had been actively engaged in assisting the imperial guard. But how can I describe my horror, madam, on beholding these men transformed, as it were, into stone, lying prostrate, with folded hands, before the altar, and kissing the ground with most enthusiastic fervour! It was in vain that the convent steward pulled their cloaks and shook them by the arm, begging of them to leave the church, which was already quite dark. They heeded neither threat nor entreaty, but half rose up as if in a dream, until the steward, with some of his servants, laid hold of them, and led them out of the church. Then only did they consent to follow us to the town; though not without heavy sighs, and constantly looking round, as if their hearts were breaking at this parting from the church. We repeatedly asked them what had happened, thus thoroughly to change their whole being; but they made no other reply than by pressing our hands, looking at us kindly, then gazing on the ground, and wiping from time to time the tears from their eyes, with an expression, the remembrance of which still to this very day deeply affects me. Arrived at their lodgings, they very ingeniously made a cross of birch-rods; and setting it upon a little mound of wax, placed it on the large table in the centre of the room, between two lights; and then, as if their senses were closed to everything else in the world, they seated themselves at the table, and commenced with folded hands their acts of silent adoration; whilst their friends, who came crowding to see them in increasing numbers, stood round in separate groups, wringing their hands in unutterable anguish at witnessing such strange and ghostlike behaviour. They refused to partake of the dinner which they had ordered for the entertainment of their accomplices, nor would they at a later hour retire to the beds that had been prepared for them in the adjoining chamber. By and by, at the hour of midnight, your four sons, after listening for a moment to the dull striking of the clock, rose abruptly with one accord from their seats, and began to intone the *Gloria in excelsis* with a voice as terrible as the howling of wolves and leopards in the icy winter season. I assure you, the very pillars of the house shook again, and the windows gave forth a sound as though handfuls of sand had been thrown against them. We rushed out without cloaks or hats through the neighbouring streets, which soon became filled with crowds of people, roused suddenly from their slumbers. The mob, breaking through the house-door, reached up stairs to the hall in search of the cause of all this clamour; yet your sons still continued their dreadful chant, without paying the least attention to the anger of the landlord, or the exclamations of the surrounding multitude. At length, when the clock struck one, they suddenly stopped, wiped from their foreheads the perspiration which was falling in large drops on the table, and spreading out their cloaks, laid them down on the hard floor to take an hour's repose. With the first crowing of the cock, they rose again, resumed their seats round the table, with the crucifix in the midst, and recommenced their melancholy mode of existence, which exhaustion alone had forced them for a moment to interrupt. They would take no advice or assistance from the landlord; they only begged him to deny them to such of their friends as might come as usual to visit them in the morning, asked for some bread and water, and a little straw for their bed at night; in short, they conducted themselves in such a manner, that the landlord felt bound to notify the case to the magistrates, and beg them to assist him in getting rid of his lodgers, who were doubtless possessed by some evil spirit. They were subjected to medical inspection; and being declared deranged, were lodged in the lunatic asylum, where you have seen them."

Three days afterwards, the poor mother set out with a female friend to the convent, for the melancholy purpose of viewing with her own eyes the spot where God had so smitten her sons to the earth, as if with invisible lightning. The lady abbess having heard of her arrival, requested she might be sent for to her own room, where they entered into very earnest conversation on the subject of the melancholy history in which they were both so deeply interested. On a desk, by the side of the abbess, lay a piece of music, the scores of a Mass; and the lady timidly asked if this were the same composition which had been performed on that fearful day. On receiving an answer in the affirmative, she rose in a state of great excitement, and examined the unknown and magical signs, which seemed to her like the mysterious work of some fearful spirit; and on finding the page opened at the *Gloria in excelsis*, was on the point of sinking to the ground. It seemed to her as though the same mysterious power which had crushed the intellects of her children was now rushing with equal force on her own devoted head; she feared that she was about to lose her own senses also from the mere sight; and after having hastily pressed her lips to the page, with an intense feeling of humility and resignation to the Divine Will, she resumed her seat. "It was God, my dear lady," said the abbess, "who protected our convent on that extraordinary day against the contemplated violence of your children, now so heavily afflicted. No one has the least idea who it was that in the confusion and distress of that dreadful hour, when the image-breakers were on the point of rushing in upon us, sat calmly and quietly at the organ, and directed the execution of that composition you see lying before you. It is certain that Sister Antonia, who was the only member of our community capable of doing it, lay on her sick-bed during the whole period of its performance, devoid of all consciousness, and deprived of the use of all her limbs. The sister who had been selected to attend her did not once quit her bedside the whole of that forenoon during the celebration of the Festival of Corpus Christi; and, in fact, Sister Antonia never recovered from the state of insensibility in which she was on the morning of that day, but died that very same evening. The Archbishop of Trêves does not hesitate to say that he believes it to have been St. Cecilia herself who wrought this fearful yet glorious miracle, and I have just received a brief from his Holiness the Pope expressing the same opinion."

The lady returned to the Hague, and was received the following year into the bosom of the Catholic Church. Her sons passed in a good old age to a calm and peaceful death, after intoning once more, according to their custom, the *Gloria in excelsis*.

ZULIMA,
THE MOORISH MAIDEN

The tents of Ferdinand and Isabella spread far and wide before the walls of Grenada; inclosed within which, and hoping in vain for succour, the cowardly Boabdil, whom his people named in derision the little king, found no consolation for his calamities but in the cruelties which he practised more and more ferociously from day to day. But while discouragement and despair gradually took possession of the troops and people of Grenada, the hope of triumph and zeal for battle animated the warriors of Spain. They made as yet no general assault, but contented themselves with firing on the ramparts, and forcing back further and further the outworks of the besieged. These little skirmishes were more like joyous tournaments than bloody battles; and even the death of the Christian heroes who fell in them served but to raise the courage of their brethren; for their obsequies were celebrated with all the splendour the Church could throw around them, as of martyrs for the faith.

In the midst of the camp, Isabella had caused to be erected a wooden building, crowned with towers, on the loftiest of which floated the sacred banner of the cross. The interior was so arranged as to serve for a cloister and a church, where Benedictine nuns sang their holy office daily; and every morning the queen, accompanied by her attendant ladies and a company of knights, came there to hear Mass said by her confessor, at which a choir of nuns assisted.

One morning Isabella distinguished a voice among them, the beautiful quality of which made it heard through all the others; and the manner in which it pronounced the words was so singular, that she could not doubt but that it was joining for the first time in the holy service. The queen looked around her, and perceiving that her attendants participated in her astonishment, began to suspect some strange adventure, when her eyes fell on her brave General Aguilar, who was placed not far from her, and who, kneeling on his chair, his hands joined, and his eyes glistening with earnestness, was gazing fixedly at the grating of the choir. When Mass was ended, Isabella went to the apartment of Donna Maria, the Superior, and asked who this strange singer was.

"You may remember, O queen," said Donna Maria, in answer, "that, a month ago, Don Aguilar had formed the project of attacking one of the enemy's outworks, which supports a magnificent terrace, used by the Moors as a public promenade. That night the songs of the pagans resounded in our camp like the voices of syrens; and the brave Aguilar chose it intentionally, on purpose to destroy the haunt of the unbelievers. Already the outwork was carried, and the women taken prisoners and borne away, when an unexpected reinforcement obliged the conqueror to retire to the camp; where, however, the enemy dared not pursue him, so that the prisoners remained in the hands of our people. Among them was one woman whose despair excited the attention of Don Aguilar. He drew near to her; she was veiled, and, as if her grief could find no other expression but in song, she took the lute, which was hung round her neck by a ribbon of gold, and after having struck a few chords, she began to pour forth, in the form of a ballad, a pathetic lament on the forcible separation of two lovers. Aguilar, deeply moved by her sorrow, resolved to send her back into

Grenada; and in gratitude she threw herself at his feet, and raised her veil. 'Art thou not Zulima, the pearl of all the singing-maidens of Grenada?' cried Aguilar; and it was in fact Zulima, whom he had seen once before when he was on a mission at the court of King Boabdil; 'I will give thee thy liberty,' he continued. But at that moment the reverend Father Agostino Sanchez, who had come to the Spanish camp, the crucifix in ins hand, and was standing near, interrupted him, suggesting that it was no kindness to the captive to send her back into a camp of misbelievers; and that perhaps, if she remained among Christians, the grace of God might enlighten her, and bring her back into the fold of the faithful. In consequence of this representation, Aguilar determined that she should remain a month among us, and that if at the end of that time she should not be awakened to the faith, she should then return to Grenada. It was thus, O Queen," continued the Superior, "that Zulima came among us in this our cloister. At first she gave herself up to unmeasured grief, and filled the cloister with songs, now wild and fearful, now soft and plaintive; her ringing voice was heard everywhere. One night, as we were all gathered together in the choir of the church, singing our holy office by the light of the waxen tapers, I discerned Zulima standing by the open door of the choir, gazing at us with a grave and meditative aspect; and when we left the chapel, walking two and two, I saw Zulima kneeling near an image of our Blessed Lady. The following day she sang no Moorish songs; but passed it in silence and reflection: and soon we heard her trying on her lute the chants which we had sang in church; and afterwards endeavouring, in a low voice, to sing them herself, and even to imitate the sacred words, which sounded strangely in her mouth.

"I felt that the grace of God was manifesting itself in this song, and therefore I sent Sister Emanuela, our choir-mistress, to the Moorish maiden, that she might keep alive the sacred spark which seemed to be kindled within her; and in truth, in the midst of the holy psalms which they sang to-gether, her heart awakened to faith. Zulima has not yet been received into the bosom of the Church by the Sacrament of Baptism; but it has been permitted her to join us in praising the Lord, and in raising her wonderful voice for the glory of our holy religion."

The queen rejoiced greatly in the conversion of Zulima, who some days after was baptised, and received the name of Julia, the queen herself, and the Marquis of Cadiz, Henry of Gusman, standing as her sponsors. After her baptism, how-ever, a singular change seemed to come over her: she would sometimes trouble the service of the church by strange sounds, while the low murmurs of her lute were like the moanings of a distant storm. She herself became more and more restless, and even sometimes interrupted the Latin hymns with Moorish words. The choir-mistress, Emanuela, admonished her to resist this temptation; but Julia, far from following her council, would often, to the great scandal of the sisters, sing Moorish songs at the very time when the chants of the Church were echoing through the cloisters, touching at the same time on her instrument,—a light flute-like accompaniment, which formed a singular con-trast to the solemn chords of the religious music.

One day, when the queen, accompanied by the chief cap-tains of her army, went as usual to hear Mass at the chapel of the Benedictine nuns, a beggar covered with rags was standing at the principal gate, who, when the guards wished to drag him away, rushed from side to side like a madman, and even struck against the queen. Aguilar, irritated by this, was about to strike him with his sword, when the beggar, drawing a lute from under his mantle, drew from it such wild notes as startled all around. The guards at last succeed-ed in leading him away, and it was told the queen that he was a Moorish prisoner who had lost his wits, and who was allowed to run up and down the camp to amuse the sol-diers by his songs. The queen entered the church, and the

Mass began. The sisters of the choir intoned the Sanctus; but at the moment when Julia began with a powerful voice Pleni sunt cœli et terra gloria tua, the notes of a lute rung through the church, and the young convert, closing her books, prepared to leave the choir. The Superior strove in vain to detain her. "Do you not hear," she said wildly, "the master's splendid chords? I must go to sing with him." But Donna Emanuela, holding her by the arm, said in a solemn voice: "Sinner, who thus forsakest the service of thy Lord, and whose heart is full of worldly thoughts, fly from this place; but know that thy voice shall fail thee, and the tones which the Lord has lent thee to praise Him shall be hushed for ever." Julia turned her head in silence, and disappeared.

At the hour of matins, when the nuns were just assembling in the church, a thick cloud of smoke rose to its roof; and very soon the crackling flames burst through its wooden walls, and communicated to the cloister, so that it was with great difficulty that the lives of the nuns were saved. The trumpet was immediately sounded through the camp, to rouse the soldiers from their sleep; and Aguilar was seen to rush among them, scorched, and in wild disorder. He had sought in vain to save Julia from the midst of the flames: she had disappeared. In a short time the whole of Isabella's camp was a heap of ruins; and the Moors, taking advantage of the tumult, made an attack on the Christian army. But the Spaniards displayed on this occasion a valour even more brilliant than usual; and when the enemy was driven back within their entrenchments, the Queen Isabella, assembling her chiefs, gave orders to build a town on the spot which her camp had occupied, thereby announcing to the Moors that the siege would never be raised.

During the building of this town, the Moors were continually harassing the Spaniards, and many bloody conflicts took place, in which the valour of Aguilar was particularly distinguished. Returning one day from a skirmish, he left his squadron near a wood of myrtles, and continued his solitary way absorbed in thought. The image of Julia was continually before his eyes; even during the combat he had seemed several times to hear her voice, and in this moment, he fancied that in the far distance he could distinguish singular sounds, a mixture as it were of Moorish modulations with ecclesiastical chants. While straining his ear to catch these distant sounds, the clang of armour echoed near him: he turned, and saw a Moorish horseman mounted on a light Arab horse gallop rapidly by, while at the same time a javelin whizzed past his ear. He rushed after his assailant; but a second javelin pierced the chest of his horse, who reared with pain and rage, and threw his rider into the dust. He rose quickly; but the Moor was already upon him, standing in his stirrups, and with his scymitar raised. In the twinkling of an eye, however, Aguilar was on his feet; and, straining his opponent in his arms, threw him violently on the ground, and kneeling on his breast, pointed his poignard at his throat. He was on the point of stabbing him, when he heard the Moor with a sigh pronounce the name of Zulima.

"What name is that," exclaimed Aguilar, "that thou darest to pronounce in my presence?"

"Strike, strike!" said the Moor; "strike him who has vowed thy death! Learn, Christian, that Hichem is the last of the race of Alhamar, and that it was he who snatched Zulima from thee. I am the beggar who burnt thy church on purpose to carry off the soul of my thoughts. Strike, then, and end my life, since I have not been able to take thine."

"Zulima still lives!" exclaimed Aguilar.

"She lives," answered the Moor, with a bitter laugh; "but your idol has smitten her with a magic curse, and our fairest flower has withered in your hands: her melodious voice has ceased to sound, and her life is ready to forsake her with her gift of song. Strike then, Christian, for you have already bereft me of more than life."

Aguilar rose slowly. "Hichem," he said, "Zulima was my prisoner by the laws of war: enlightened by Divine grace, she has forsaken the religion of Mahomet: do not then name the soul of thy thoughts, her who is become my lady, or prepare to meet me in fair combat. Resume thy arms."

Hichem hastily resumed his buckler and scymitar; but, instead of rushing upon Aguilar, he set spurs to his horse, and disappeared with the swiftness of lightning.

After a time the Moors, continually repulsed in their sallies, and worn by famine, found themselves forced to capitulate, and to open their gates to Ferdinand and Isabella, who made their triumphal entry into Grenada. The grand mosque was blest by the priests, and converted into a cathedral, when there was sung a solemn *Te Deum* in thanksgiving to the God of armies. The rage and fury of the Moors being well known, bands of soldiers were placed in all the neighbouring streets to protect the procession, and Aguilar, who commanded one of these bands, was advancing towards the cathedral, when he felt himself wounded in the left shoulder by an arrow. At the same moment, a troop of Moors rushed out of a narrow street, and attacked the Christians with inconceivable fury. Hichem was at their head; and Aguilar, immediately recognising him, joined in fight with him hand to hand, and did not leave him till he had plunged his sword deep in his heart. After this, the Spaniards pursued the Moors into a large stone house, whose gates opened to admit them, and then reclosed on them immediately; an instant after, a cloud of arrows from the windows of this house wounded many of Aguilar's soldiers, and he commanded that torches should be brought and the house set on fire. This order was executed, and already the flames were mounting even to the roof, when a wonderful voice made itself heard from the midst of the burning building, chanting, Sanctus, sanctus, sanctus Dominus Deus Sabaoth.

"Julia, O Julia!" cried Aguilar, in despair; and immediately the doors were flung open, and Julia, dressed as a Benedictine nun, came forth, still singing Sanctus, sanctus, sanctus; while behind her marched a long file of Moors, their heads cast down, and their hands crossed on their breast. The Spaniards drew back involuntarily; and Julia, followed by the Moors, advanced through their ranks to the cathedral, on entering which she intoned, *Benedictus qui venit in nomine Domini.*

The people fell on their knees; and Julia, her eyes turned towards heaven, walked with a firm step up to the high altar, where Ferdinand and Isabella were engaged in assisting at the holy function; and as soon as the last strophe, Dona nobis pacem, was concluded, fell lifeless into the arms of the queen. All the Moors who had followed her received that same day the holy Sacrament of Baptism.

THE STORY OF THE ABBEY OF EINSIEDELN

(INTRODUCTION)

It is now some years ago since I made a tour on foot through Switzerland. Having visited Chamouny and the upper district of Berne, I came at length to the lesser cantons. There the deepened solitude of the valleys, the more gently sloping Alps stripped of their horrors of precipice and avalanche, and the wood-girdled villages, guiltless of inns and tourists, brought refreshment to me on my way. I stopped some days at Lucerne; and then anxious to exhaust everything remarkable in these parts, I began to think of going towards the Grisons, for the sake of the new scenery promised by their mountains, when an excursion of an altogether different nature turned me for a time aside.

In my walks to the Righi, to Schwytz, and to the funereal vale of Goldau, I had frequently met troops of poor folks, their bundles on their backs, as if they had come from a distance, asking neither alms nor employment, but with a calm indifference to people and things, going on their way in companies, telling their beads or repeating litanies, kneeling before the wayside crosses which guard the Catholic cantons, greeting travellers as they went with a friendly bow or a pious word, and invariably answering when I asked them whither they were bound, "For Einsiedeln."

On referring to my guide-book I found Einsiedeln was a large Abbey of Benedictines, celebrated for its church and as a place of pilgrimage. Nothing more was necessary to excite my interest warmly, I immediately took the road thither, and after crossing one or two mountains, and passing a large town made up of inns and completely behung with signs, I found myself before the convent of our Lady of Hermits.

Situated at the extremity of a long valley, and shadowed by mountains covered with firs, the buildings of the monastery, which nearly a century ago were rebuilt after a conflagration, present an imposing mass, with a regular and majestic façade; between two wings, inhabited by the monks, rises the church with its two towers, each bearing a double cross, and separated by a large open square from the village, which is dependent on the convent for its origin and prosperity. In the centre of this square is the fountain of Saint Meinrad, crowned by a beautiful image of the Blessed Virgin, and pouring from twelve ever-flowing jets its cool pure water. All round the galleries form a circle of shops, where rosaries, images, and medals are exposed for sale. Behind the façade the edifice stretches out into wings, which conceal the court and gardens of the convent.

On entering the church one is struck by the richness of its ornaments, and the profusion of statues, frescoes, and paintings. The whole history of Christianity is depicted beneath these vaulted roofs, angels, saints, the mysteries, and the life of Jesus, from Bethlehem to Calvary. The touching recollections of the Old and New Testament revive here under the brash of the painter and the chisel of the statuary. The choir and the sanctuary are masterpieces, every chapel bears witness to the miracles of its patron, and every altar rests upon the ashes of a saint.

A few steps within the entrance, in the middle of the nave, rises a little dome, supported on pillars of black marble.

The bas-reliefs which ornament it are all in honour of the Mother of God, and represent her sojourn on this earth and her Assumption into heaven. Beneath this dome, an altar serves as pedestal to a black statue, from which stream golden rays, and the pale reflections of a single lamp show it to be that of the Virgin and her divine Child. The stones around this little chapel are more deeply worn than any others, for it is here all come to shed their tears and pour forth their prayers; this is the object of so many a pilgrimage; this is the image (as we shall see in the sequel) before which the holy Meinrad used to pray.

When for the first time I ascended the lofty steps which lead to the church, many families of pilgrims had just arrived. Sinking under the burden of heat and fatigue, they had nevertheless passed through the village without a moment's pause. I watched them stoop to drink at the sacred fountain, then climb the steps with slow and weary feet, and go to cast themselves on their knees within that holy chapel, before a thought of rest or food came near them. There was no anxiety about a place of shelter or a morsel of bread; the fulfilment of their vow seemed to be all that occupied their hearts.

I knelt amongst the pilgrims, and mingled my voice with their litanies; and forgetful for a moment that I was a traveller, who came to make his observations on the habits of another people, I thought only of God and of the absent ones at home. I now understood the nature of a pilgrimage,—that pious custom of our forefathers,—I understood its promises and its hopes,—the religious feelings it must inspire,—the confidence which sustains one through its toils.

It seemed as if a new source of consolation was revealed to me at the foot of this altar, as if a protecting power was discovered, hitherto unknown, against the evils of the future,—a refuge to which, in times of desolation, I should not appeal in vain.

While thus plunged in meditation, a hymn to the Blessed Virgin re-echoed through the church. It was sung by fifty pilgrims from the mountains of the Tyrol; they had but just arrived, and hastened to raise, in clear harmonious voices, a hymn in honour of the Mother of Angels. The next day they were to return to their home filled with blessings from the Virgin of Einsiedeln. The sole object of this long and fatiguing journey had been to kneel at the foot of her sacred image, recite the rosary, and pour forth a canticle of praise. The shades of evening revealed but dimly the bold, manly forms of the Tyrolese hunters, in their picturesque costume, and the pious devotion of the women and children, who, in their holy faith alone could have found the strength suffi-cient for such a journey. Some old men, whose enfeebled limbs were exhausted by the efforts they had made, blended deep sighs with these pure sonorous tones, and the voice of more than one mother, who had left perhaps her child languishing upon a bed of sickness, gave more plaintive and tender melody to the hymn of joy. As for me, I could join only by my tears.

The next day I begged permission to see the abbey, which being granted, a Benedictine showed me, besides the cells, a fine library, with several ancient manuscripts, a collection of philosophical instruments, and one of mineralogical specimens.

He also told me the history of the abbey, the ravages it had endured from fire and revolutions, and how, rising once more from its ashes, it now beheld the number and the piety of its pilgrims year by year increase. He told me of wonders that had been accomplished in this spot by the intercession of Mary, and described to me the rule of the Benedictines, who divide their days between prayer, study, and their sacred ministry.

It was thus he related the origin of the abbey:

The Story

In the ninth century, Meinrad, the son of Prince Berthold of Hohenzollern, in Swabia, allied by his illustrious birth to the noblest families in Europe, resigned the wealth and honours to which he was entitled, and entering a monastery, became a Benedictine. But even here, the reverence with which he was regarded for the sacrifice he had made, savoured too nearly of human respect and worldly glory to leave Meinrad satisfied with his choice. He resolved to become a hermit; and building secretly with his own hands a little hut amongst the solitary hollows of a mountain near the monastery, he went out one day, as if for a ramble, and took up his abode there. This mountain, named Mount Etzel, separates the Lake of Zurich from the valley of Einsiedeln, and here, for seven years, dwelt Meinrad, practising all the austerities the most rigid penance could suggest. But even here the world discovered his retreat. Crowds of anxious penitents sought out the holy recluse of the mountain, and wearing into beaten paths its hitherto untrodden tracks, came day by day to beg counsel, or consolation, or pardon of their sins from one who lived so near to God. In those days it was the custom for all who had doubts and difficulties to refer themselves with unhesitating confidence to the advice of solitaries such as Meinrad. The more, certainly, they were separated from the world, the more surely did their words breathe inspiration from on high. Rich and poor, labourers and noblemen, the priest, the lord, the old man and the child, the humble monk and the prince-bishop, all took their way to the hermit Meinrad, and received the same cordial welcome, advice, and tender consolation.

But often, when the poor man went home to his cottage with joy, lightened of all his troubles, the rich one returned sorrowful to his palace, disquiet in his soul, and shame upon his forehead. For Meinrad, like a true servant of God, spoke faithfully to all, fearing not man, and determined to do justice.

However, these crowds of visitors distracted him sorely. He yearned to give himself wholly to prayer and meditation; and having, discovered at the foot of the mountain in a wilder region a pine-forest, so thick and lonely that the hunters themselves dreaded to explore its shades, and known even in this land of gloomy woods as the "Dark Forest," he resolved to fly thither, and hide himself securely. Unknown to all, he effected his departure, taking with him nothing but an image of the Blessed Virgin; but it was impossible so transcendent a light could be completely buried even in these forest depths. The sad and the repentant followed him still. Resisting no more the evident will of God concerning him, Meinrad received all who braved the terrors of the forest, and even suffered them to build him a cell which should shelter him from storms, and a simple oratory, where he could set up the holy image of the Mother of Mercy. To her feet, where he himself knelt almost unceasingly, Meinrad brought his penitents, and none went away without a blessing. Nor was it only human visitants he welcomed there. At midnight, once, a religious from the convent of Reichenau, who occasionally paid the hermit a visit, followed him at a distance to the little chapel, whither he went to say the evening office, when suddenly the whole chapel became illuminated, and as the monk drew near, he beheld upon the altar-steps, where Meinrad knelt, a young child of celestial aspect, who recited the office with him.

Thirty-three years had passed away since Meinrad retired from the world, twenty-six of which had been passed in the Dark Forest, when two miserable men came one day, as if to beg hospitality from the holy hermit. He read their deadly purpose in their souls, and said to them: "You should have come a little sooner, that you might have assisted at my Mass, and prayed the saints to show you mercy at your last hour. You shall receive my blessing and forgiveness before you kill me; and when I am dead, light, I charge you, these two candles, one at the head and the other at the foot of my couch. After this, fly for your lives, lest you should be denounced by those who come to visit me."

Notwithstanding this address, the simple piety of which would have been sufficient to disarm most ruffians, the hope of plunder induced these wretches to kill the hermit: they found nothing, however, but his penitential hair-shirt. They forgot to light the candles as he charged them; but beheld them, says the German tradition, miraculously kindled by invisible hands. Fleeing in terror and remorse, they escaped unseen by human eye, and took refuge in an inn at Zurich. But Meinrad had made friends with the birds of the air; and two tame crows, with whom he had been accustomed to share his bread, followed the murderers, crying after them, and striking at them with their beaks, as far as the inn, from which one of the servants vainly endeavoured to chase them away. This circumstance attracted the attention of some people of Wolrau, who having found the hermit dead, had instantly set forth in quest of the assassins, and recognising the birds as those of Meinrad, felt little doubt they had pursued the guilty men. The two miserable creatures, when arrested, confessed their crime and suffered its penalty; the birds, adds the tradition, still hovering above the scaffold. The inn where this occurred bears to this very day the motto of "The two faithful Crows," and they are introduced into the arms of the abbey.

Thus died the holy Meinrad, January 21, 863; but to his empty cell crowds of pilgrims still travelled. And before it had quite crumbled into decay, Bennon, or Benoit, a royal prince, and canon of Strasbourg, renouncing all his worldly wealth, came to the Dark Forest, and raised around the hut of Meinrad many little wooden cells, wherein he and other holy men might dwell. This was the origin of the abbey. The forest lost its solitude and gloom, and the place took the name of "Einsiedeln," which has been rendered into Latin thus by chroniclers: *Eremus, eremus Deiparæ, eremitarum cœnobium.*

By St. Eberhard these humble cells were afterwards improved into a fine monastery, and the chapel became a magnificent church. Under the third abbot, the title of "Prince of the Holy Empire" was given for ever to the Abbot of Einsiedeln. Princes poured in their wealth, and the sanctity of its inmates bestowed a higher dignity upon the monastery. It became the centre of intelligence, activity, and labour in those parts, the school for young nobles, a well-spring of general civilisation.*

Century after century rolled away, and still the glory of Einsiedeln did but increase. Saints and learned men came and went within its walls, and countless communities drew from its sanctity and wisdom the beginning of their strength.

But a time of persecution and of darkness succeeded to centuries of increasing prosperity. The impiety of a French army, and the envy of an ungrateful populace, devastated

---

* An ancient tradition affirms that the consecration of this church was performed in a miraculous manner; and this is the belief of no less a person than St. Charles Borromeo. Conrad Bishop of Constance, Ulric, Bishop of Augsburg, and other prelates, came in the year 949 to celebrate the rite of dedication in the usual manner; but on the eve of the day appointed, whilst Conrad was praying at midnight, on a sudden he saw the new sanctuary lighted up, and the consecration performed by angelic bands, our Lord Himself and His apostles appearing in the midst. In the morning all assembled for the ceremony; but on seeking out Conrad, they were informed by him of the prodigy which had taken place. So marvellous did the circumstance appear, that they at first treated it as an illusion, and were about to proceed to the dedication, when a voice was thrice heard from the sanctuary, declaring that the church was consecrated. It may be added that several other churches lay claim to a similar privilege: among others, those of St. Denis, near Paris, and the Cathedral of Rheims. We have already mentioned the testimony of St. Charles Borromeo. We may also add a bull of Pope Leo VIII., to the same effect; and the following sentence of the angelic doctor in his *Summa*: "*Quædam templa dicuntur angelico ministerio consecrata*—Some churches are said to have been consecrated by the ministry of angels."

and well-nigh destroyed this sacred edifice. An attempt was even made to carry off the venerated Image to which Meinrad had knelt in the solitude of the Dark Forest. But the pious care of the good monks prevented this sacrilege; and whilst a similar one was taken to Paris, the true relic was securely guarded, and now once more adorns the restored monastery.

Again, the praises of God resound where first the venerable saint upraised his holy hands; and pilgrims still throng thither, as almost a thousand years ago they crowded to the recluse of the mountain.

THE MADONNA DELLA GROTTA, NAPLES

Catholic travellers, who, after visiting the shrine of St. Alphonso at Pagani, and the ancient Baptistery of St. Mary Major's at Nocera, go on to the shrines of St. Matthew and St. Gregory VII. at Salerno, not unfrequently make a little *détour* from the high road, as soon as they have passed La Cava, that they may visit the famous Benedictine monastery of La Trinità. The road by which the ascent to this monastery is generally made passes a little to the right of the sanctuary of Santa Maria della Grotta, and hides from the unconscious traveller the very beautiful scenery which is so near him; but if he turned aside to the left, soon after having passed the village of San Cesareo, two minutes' walk would suffice to bring him to the edge of a long deep narrow and precipitous ravine, clothed with wood down to the brink of the stream which rushes along the bottom, and crowned on either side with a chapel of the Madonna. At present there is a very safe and commodious path, leading to the mill which is a little farther up the valley, and a bridge whereby we may cross from one side to the other. But two hundred years ago, at which time our history begins, this path was neither safe nor convenient; it had a very bad name, and was said to be infested by evil spirits. One day, in the year 1654, as a certain Don Federigo, a priest of La Cava, was going along by this way to St. Pietro a Dragonea, one of the hamlets belonging to the parish of San Cesareo, he had an encounter with some of these spirits, just at the mouth of one of those grottoes or natural caverns in the rock, which are so frequent in that neighbourhood, and from whence La Cava itself is supposed to have derived its name. On his return home, this good priest determined to place so dangerous a cavern under the immediate protection of the Madonna; but not having sufficient means to procure a statue or painting for this purpose, he was obliged to content himself with fastening to the rock a little print, which he happened to have, representing the Blessed Virgin, with the Dove and the Cherubim over her head, holding the child Jesus in her arms, and having St. Paul, the first hermit, on her right hand, and St. Onofrius on her left. The title of this picture was the Advocate of Sinners; and as the print remained there, uninjured by time and by the damp, during a period of forty-eight years, the cave gradually lost its old name of the *Grotta de Sportiglioni* (or, of the bats), and received in its stead that of the *Avvocatella.*

Doubtless it had been saluted with many an Ave by the devotion of the passers-by during this half century; and at length, in the year 1702, Fra Angiolo Maria di Majuri, a lay brother of one of the Franciscan convents in La Cava, remarkable for his devotion to the Blessed Virgin, caused a copy of the engraving to be executed in fresco, in a little niche which he had prepared for it in the rock. At the same time he exhorted the neighbours to burn a lamp before it, and frequently repeated, in the presence of the parish priests and others, that that grotto, which had once been the abode of infernal spirits, would ere long become the house of God, and that the Mother of God would dispense from thence the treasures of her power and goodness with a most liberal hand. Of course, the first part of this prophecy, so to call it, had a natural tendency to bring about its own fulfilment.

One of the priests, who had often listened to Fra Angiolo's confident assurances on this subject, caused an altar to be raised before the painting, a lamp to be kept burning, and the litanies and other devotional exercises to be frequently repeated there.

It happened on Saturday, the 19th of May, in the following year, that as a poor man, named Antonio Casaburi, accompanied by his son, a boy of six years old, was driving along this path a donkey laden with corn, the animal went too near the edge of the precipice and rolled over, carrying the boy along with him. The depth of the rock in this place was about 120 feet, so that the poor father expected nothing else than to see his son dashed to pieces at the bottom; nevertheless, with the natural instinct of a Catholic, he called loudly upon Santa Maria dell' Avvocata, whose shrine was at his side, to assist him in this hour of danger; and when, in company with two or three others who had been witnesses of the accident, or whom he had called from the mill to assist him, he arrived at the spot, he found the animal quietly grazing, the boy busily collecting the scattered grain, and both perfectly uninjured.

The fame of this miracle, which was attested by three competent witnesses, besides the father and the child themselves, drew such multitudes of persons to the grotto, that the crowd passing to and fro in so narrow a place became quite dangerous, and leave was obtained from the proper ecclesiastical authorities to erect a spacious chapel there. The building was carried on briskly, through the liberal almsgiving of those who came to ask for *grazie* here, and but few of whom were "sent empty away," but in the meanwhile a new bishop had been appointed to the see of Cava, who determined to take those precautions enjoined by the Council of Trent, and to inform himself, by means of a congregation of theologians, and by the juridical examination of witnesses, of the exact truth of the marvellous reports which were in circulation. The painting was boarded up, and all access to it forbidden whilst this examination was pending; but it soon appeared that the proofs were too distinct and too numerous to admit of doubt; and after fifteen days the people were once more gladdened with the sight of their *Avvocata,* and the former episcopal sanction was renewed to the undertaking in hand. On the 7th of September, 1704, the first Mass was celebrated in the new church by one of the parish priests, a man whose span of life had already exceeded "the threescore years and ten," and who, having himself received a signal *grazia* at the hands of this *Advocate,* consecrated the last years of his life to celebrating her glories, and, by order of the bishop, published an account of them.

It would be too long to enumerate or even make a selection from them. Suffice it to say, that every year, as the principal festa, which is in the month of May, comes round, persons crowd to visit the sanctuary, not only from Nocera and Salerno, but also from Castellamare, Sorrento, and even Naples itself; and at all times of the year, simple peasants from the adjoining villages, groups of women, members of the same family, or neighbours in the same village, suffering under some common affliction, may be seen wending their way through the chestnut-groves of La Cava, with bare feet and dishevelled hair, alternately telling their beads and reciting the litanies until they reach this Church of the Grotta; here they kneel for a while to repeat their devotions in the presence of the picture itself, and to make some little offering of flowers, or oil, or candles, after which they return to their homes, bearing with them some portion of the oil from the lamp that has been burning before the shrine, nothing doubting that, if it be God's will, the sick will receive the same benefits from the application of this oil, as we know from the testimony of St. Chrysostom, the Christians of his days often experienced from the same remedy.

THE MONKS OF LERINS

The deep silence of night was yet unbroken except by the rustling of the foliage in the fresh sea-breeze, when the bell of the monastery of Lerins began to ring for Matins, and its sound re-echoed through the whole of the little island. At the holy summons, more than 500 monks left their hard pallets to meet in the church, and sing the praises of Him to whom they had vowed their lives, and of His blessed Mother, whose assumption into Heaven they were about that day to celebrate. The altars were lighted up with a thousand waxen tapers, and the whole church wreathed with green garlands, mixed with flowers, gathered in the gardens of the monastery, whose bright colours formed a pleasant contrast to the dark habits of the religious.

Scarcely had the bell given its second signal before the Fathers, with noiseless steps, had gained the choir. One alone seemed deaf to the accustomed summons: it was the abbot, who, standing at the window of his cell, looked out into the pale moonlight, and fixed his eyes with melancholy intentness on the mainland opposite the southern coast of France, as if he sought to discern some object in the distance. Sometimes, too, he seemed straining his ear as if to catch a remote sound; but all was still, except the gentle murmur of the waves as they rippled to the shore of his own island, or broke against its cliffs. At last, rousing himself from his mournful reverie, he prostrated himself on the ground, and with clasped hands, and eyes raised to heaven, exclaimed thrice, "Thy holy will be done, O my God!" As soon as he had pronounced these words, his countenance resumed its accustomed serenity; and, at the third and last summons of the bell, he rose, and went to the choir, where his brethren were awaiting him in some anxiety; for their abbot was ever wont to be first, not last, at the midnight office.

As soon as he had taken his place, the cantors intoned the invitatory: "Oh, come, let us adore the King of kings, whose Virgin Mother was this day taken up into heaven!" and all the religious repeated in chorus, "Oh, come, let us adore the King of kings, whose Virgin Mother was this day taken up into heaven!" "Oh, come," resumed the cantors, "let us rejoice before the Lord; let us praise God our Saviour; let us come into His presence with songs of gladness, and sing hymns to His glory!" And again the choir repeated, "Oh, come, let us adore the King of kings, whose Virgin Mother was this day taken up into heaven!"

When matins were ended, the abbot robed himself in the sacerdotal vestments, and began to offer the Holy Sacrifice of the Mass, which the choir accompanied with sacred chants, now of penitence, and now of joy.

One by one, their arms crossed on their breasts, the religious advanced towards the altar, to place themselves in fitting order to receive the Holy Communion. Then the abbot, holding aloft the vessel containing the Sacred Hosts, thus addressed his children: "My well-beloved brethren in Christ Jesus, this God who has already given His blood for you on Calvary, is now going to give you Himself. After such generosity, can you refuse Him anything? Nay, even if he should demand from each one of you the last drop of your blood, which of you would dare withhold the gift? Which of you would not burn to exchange this perishable life against the crown of immortality? In this holy solitude, you have learnt to renounce not only things external to yourselves, but even those very selves; day by day you have been learning by practice how to sacrifice yourselves to Him who has just sacrificed Himself for you. Well, my dear children, now is the moment come when it will be required from at least the larger number among you to consummate this sacrifice; and the holy bread you are about to receive will serve as your viaticum. Be of good cheer, my children; the sun which is now about to rise shall never set for you; but its light will be succeeded by the eternal brightness of the Sun of Righteousness. Your palms are ready, your crowns are even now woven. Before the bell rung for matins this night, I was transported in spirit into this very church. You were all here with me, my children; and the guardian angel of these isles, robed in a vestment of crimson, but his brow radiant with joy, was here among us; and I saw him give first to me and then to another a branch of palm, at the same time crowning your brows with a resplendent garland. Some few only were left out, reserved, no doubt, by the providence of God, for further conflicts. You already know, my brethren, that the Saracens have invaded Provence; their next prey will be this island of ours; be strong then, and remember that they can only reach your bodies, that your souls are treasured up for eternity. But let none among you be self-confident, and then none will be apostates. To suffer for a moment, and to enjoy for ever, such is your blessed destiny. The God whom you see here hidden for love of you, will soon manifest Himself to you in all the brightness of His glory. Come, then, unite yourselves to Him; and love shall lighten all the anguish that you may be called upon to bear."

This address, so far from saddening the hearts of the brethren, only made their festival more joyous; and blissful tears stole down their pale cheeks. Two and two they came forward to receive Holy Communion from the hands of their abbot, from the eldest to the youngest; and the Holy Sacrifice was scarcely completed when the sun appeared above the horizon; then they sang Lauds with more fervour than ever before; and then, at the command of their abbot, they set themselves to meditate on the Passion of Christ, and so to nerve their souls with courage to meet the coming trial.

At the same time the abbot offered to conduct to a place of safety any one among them who feared death, and called to him the youngest of the monks, to the number of thirty-six, together with some children whom they had in the monastery as pensioners, and placing them on board two barks, he sent them towards the coast of Italy, after tenderly embracing them, and giving them his last benediction. They all wept bitterly, and implored permission to stay and die with the rest; but religious obedience constrained them, and they departed, long looking back with regretful eyes to their beloved abode, where they would so gladly have remained to earn the martyr's crown.

Meanwhile, the monks who were left behind busied themselves in securing, as far as they could, against pillage and destruction the objects they considered most valuable. They dug pits in the remotest corners of the island to hide the sacred vessels, the relics of the saints, the sacerdotal vestments, and all that could be profaned by the barbarians. After this, they betook themselves to their ordinary occupations on festival days; some gave themselves to their books, others guided their flocks to the pasture-grounds, and others, again, in the scriptorium, went on with the works they had begun copying. No one seeing them thus employed, in such perfect peace and serenity, could have supposed that they were in the immediate expectation of death.

Soon, however, a number of barks were discerned in the distance, making rapid way towards the island; and, as they came nearer, there resounded from them loud cries of "Death to the Christians!" while at the same time a forest of Damascus blades glittered in the sun. At last they drew to land, and a throng of Saracens, armed to the teeth, leapt on shore, and pressed on towards the monastery.

The religious, as we have said, in obedience to their abbot's commands, were silently engaged in their respective occupations, and the approach of the Saracens only shed a gleam of joy over their countenances; two of them, and no more, named Eleutherius and Colombo, overcome with fear, fled away and hid themselves in a grotto situated in the midst of a wood which skirted the eastern shore of the island.

The Saracens had no sooner landed than they thronged into the narrow path which led to the monastery, at the gate of which knelt the abbot, in tranquil expectation, holding the cross in his hands, and praying to the Lord to give both to him and his numerous children strength to confess His holy name in the presence of His enemies, and to suffer the extremity of pain rather than renounce the faith.

At the sight of the humble attitude and undisturbed serenity of the holy man, the Moors drew back astonished; but fury in a few moments took the place of amazement; they seized him and dragged him forcibly into the midst of the cloister, to make him the chief victim of their rage against the religion of Christ. Very soon they had spread themselves through church and corridors, halls and gardens, and the monks were dragged to the side of their abbot, and there guarded with drawn sabres, while the work of devastation was accomplished.

Then indeed did this abode of silence resound with the clang of arms, with cries of fury, and with the confused noise of destruction; for everything that could not conveniently be carried off was broken,—seats, tables, books, crosses, earthen vessels, were thrown in heaps out of the window's; and the rage of the invaders was inflamed by finding no rich booty,—nothing in any part of the monastery but poverty and simplicity.

At last the chief of the Saracens, snatching the cross from the hands of the abbot, held it up to him, and commanded him to spit on it, and acknowledge Mahomet on pain of instant death.

"Nay, rather," answered the abbot meekly, "give me that holy symbol, that I may cover it with kisses, too happy to die for Him who died for me."

At that same moment the raised scymitar fell, and severed his head from his body, which was the signal for a frightful carnage; and all would have perished in an instant if the chief had not interposed, commanded his soldiers to separate the young from the old, that if they could find no booty, they might at least carry off a good number of slaves. Immediately about a hundred of the younger monks were put aside, and all the others massacred before their eyes, in the hope that they might thus be induced by terror to abjure the more readily the Christian religion. Then the chief thus addressed them:

"See, now you are *free* from those old watch-dogs who guarded you; they had done with life, which has no attractions at their age, and therefore they despised it; but your brows are yet unwrinkled, now is your time for enjoyment, and I offer you the means of attaining it. Renounce the religion of Christ, and embrace that of Mahomet. See Moussa, my lieutenant, was once a Christian like you, and I swear to you by the Crescent that I will treat you as I have treated him; and now I give you your choice between the turban and death."

"Death, death!" they all cried with one voice, and immediately began a song of thanksgiving. The chief commanded their immediate slaughter, and so they all ascended together to claim their crown, four only being reserved, whom the chief kept back for slavery. These were of lofty stature, and so beautiful that they might have been taken for angels rather than men.

Meanwhile, Eleutherius and Colombo remained hidden in their grotto, fancying every moment they heard the Saracens approaching, when suddenly a brilliant light shone before them, and a delicious melody rung in their ears, tokens, as they could not doubt, of their brethren having won at that moment the martyr's crown; for, lifting their eyes, they saw, though the sun was now high in heaven, a number of brilliant stars disappearing one by one in the depths of the sky. Then Colombo said to Eleutherius, "Cowardly soldiers of Christ are we, who have fled before the enemy; and, therefore, now that our brethren have reached the port, we are still here below tossing about in the storm, and in danger of shipwreck. The thought of the eternal prize nerves my heart against the terrors of death; I will seek the Saracen; slavery or martyrdom, whichever be my lot, can nothing avail to shake my faith: I will go and try to bury my brethren; in order to pay them this last duty, I ought to risk my life."

"My brother," answered Eleutherius, "while the Saracens are in the island it will be useless to think of burying our brethren: to attempt it will be to incur certain death. But, however, if you believe that your inspiration is of heaven, follow it, and the Lord will be your helper, covering you with brazen armour, so that you will be invincible; but for myself, I am yet too weak thus to present myself to death with deliberate purpose. The holy will of God be done."

Accordingly, after giving the farewell kiss, Colombo left the grotto, and made his way through the thickets to a narrow path which led to a gate of the convent-garden. He expected to find the Saracens there, and therefore armed himself by prayer before entering; but he met no one, though threatening cries warned him that he had been seen from the windows of the monastery; and he reached the cloister without interruption. There a fearful sight met his eye,—heaps of dead bodies, rivulets of blood, heads separated from their trunks, limbs scattered about here and there, and in the midst, fixed on a pike, the head of the venerable abbot. At this sight he threw himself on his face sobbing; but one blow from the scymitar of a Saracen sent him to join his brethren in heaven.

How long and sad for Eleutherius was the night which followed this day of slaughter! All was profoundly still; and knowing by the silence that the Saracens must have departed, he left his grotto in the middle of the night, and made his way to the monastery. There, thrilled with terror and grief, he stumbled every moment over the bodies of his brethren; and being unable to procure anything to make a light, was constrained to endure the additional horror of darkness for several hours, which he spent in prayer, kneeling on the sod made holy by the blood of so many martyrs. At first, his soul was wrapt in sadness at the thought that he alone was left behind, while his brethren were in glory; but afterwards, he felt a blessed consolation in knowing that they were all interceding in his behalf.

"O my brethren!" he said to them, "I fled, it is true, before the face of the enemy; but I have not denied my faith, therefore you still love me—I dare to hope it, and you will not forget in heaven him who is still left on the battle-field exposed to the darts of his foe. The remembrance of your triumph will sustain my faith, strengthen my hope, and increase the fervour of my charity."

Thus he passed the night in tears and prayer; and at last a ray of joy seemed to pierce the depths of his soul, and he burst forth involuntarily into songs of praise.

His next thought was of his own present duty; and, after some reflection, he resolved to go into Italy and seek the young religious whom the holy abbot had sent thither, in order to bring them back and reestablish the monastery; for he hoped that the Saracens would speedily abandon the coasts of Provence. He was absorbed in these thoughts, when he heard the distant step of a man slowly advancing by the cloister wall. His first impulse was to fly; but he remembered the holy ground on which he stood, and determined not to be again guilty of cowardice. "Let him come," he said to himself, "Mussulman though he be; the blood which surrounds me shall support my courage;" and he threw himself once more on his knees to seek for strength in prayer. Meanwhile, the step grew more and more distinct, though in the twilight he could not distinguish who it was that was approaching him; but in a few moments a Moor stood beside him, and spoke.

"Fear nothing, my brother," he said, "I am no longer thine enemy. I was once a Christian; I became a renegade, but now I would return to the faith of my fathers. Now rise, and hear my story. I was born at Tauroento, a hundred miles from hence, on the shores of the Mediterranean; and I was hardly thirteen when the town was taken and sacked by the Moors. My father, a fervent Christian and a valiant soldier, put himself at the head of the population, and held out during a siege of several months; but at last he fell under the steel of the Mussulman; and his wife Cecilia, my mother, I saw massacred before my eyes while kneeling in prayer; and I myself, seized by her murderers, was thrown, with a great number of companions in misfortune, into a vessel bound for Africa; there, exposed in the market like a beast of burden, I was sold to a zealous Mahometan. For two years, he treated me, if not with kindness, at least without severity; and though several times he proposed to me to change my religion, yet on my refusing he left me in peace. But when I reached the age of sixteen, he attacked me more vigorously; and by dint sometimes of seducing promises, sometimes of harsh treatment, he succeeded in overcoming my resistance."

At this avowal his speech was interrupted by sobs, and the wasted cheeks of the monk were also bathed in tears.

"Alas!" he continued, "why did I not practise the constancy of these noble martyrs, and sacrifice my life rather than my faith! At the moment of accepting the turban I ceased to be a slave, and from that time began to live what is called a life of pleasure, but with a bitter sorrow in the depths of my heart. Some time after this, Abdal Malek set forth from Africa with an army to fight against Charles Martel, who had defeated the Mussulmans at Poitiers, and I accompanied him. From this time I have added crime to crime; under the name of Moussa, I have led the Saracens on to fire, to murder, and to pillage, respecting neither age nor sex,—pillaging churches, devastating monasteries, so that my crimes rather than my valour have raised me to the rank of lieutenant to the chief, Boalkier. O holy monk," he continued, throwing himself at the feet of Eleutherius, "pray for me! I dare not myself address my prayers to heaven; it would be deaf to my voice. How can I hope pardon from a God whom I have so outraged!"

"O my brother," replied Eleutherius, "the mercy of God is greater than even your crimes. The Divine ray which has just pierced the darkness of your heart, has no doubt been obtained for you by the prayers of those whose blood you have shed, and who, imitating their Divine Saviour, have prayed for their murderers. Therefore, let hope spring up in your soul, together with repentance, and penance shall restore peace and felicity to your heart."

By this time the day had dawned, and they both occupied themselves in burying the bodies of the holy martyrs. In a few days, Eleutherius set off for Italy, to bring back the brethren whom the abbot had sent there; but the bark which bore them had been captured in the Gulf of Genoa by African pirates, who had carried them into Spain, where they had been sold as slaves.

Moussa, the converted renegade, was thus left sole guardian of Lerins. He laid aside his Mahometan costume, which he burnt in the midst of the garden, and put on a monk's dress, which he had found in one of the cells. From that time he devoted himself to works of penance, intending to await the re-establishment of the monastery, and to pass therein the rest of his days with the monks whom Eleutherius had gone to seek, and whom he hoped one day to see return to the convent.

The Saracens, meanwhile, after their day of slaughter at Lerins, pursued the work of devastation far and near, sacking and burning towns, villages, and churches. One day, after the destruction of a church in which the whole population of a village had taken refuge, and were buried under its ruins, the chief, Boalkier, remarked, for the first time, the absence of his lieutenant, Moussa, whom he had not seen since the day at Lerins, and inquired for him of his attendants; but none could give any account of him, for he had not communicated his design to any; so that the chief, becoming impatient, commissioned two of his soldiers to go and make inquiries concerning him. For this service he selected two renegades, who, knowing the country, were best able to help him in his search. They were both robbers by profession, one of whom had escaped from the public prisons, and the other was pursued by justice in consequence of a murder which he had committed; and both had joined the Saracens in order to shield themselves from the vengeance of the law; the declaration of apostasy being to them a mere formula, which they pronounced without any thought or conviction one way or the other. After taking counsel together, they agreed to explore first the Isle of Lerins, as it was there that they had last seen Moussa. Accordingly, they took a boat, and rowed towards the monastery.

As they approached the island, serious reflections began, in spite of themselves, to arise in their minds, when they contrasted the savage fury of the Saracens, which they had witnessed, with the meek endurance of the holy monks; and when they landed on the island, even yet reeking with the blood of the martyrs, an emotion to which they had long been strangers stirred the very depths of their hearts, so long hardened by crime. After they had landed, they fastened their boat to a tree in silence, and ascended the narrow path leading to the cloister. The bodies of the martyrs were no longer to be seen; but in a recess in the sanctuary was a monk praying.

"Here is a man," said one, "who has had a narrow escape; what are we to do with him?" The other made no answer.

When they came up to the monk, they saw that his eyes were bathed with tears.

"Well, brother," said they, "you seem to have had a visit from the Saracens; and you must think yourself lucky to be still standing on your feet, and with your head on your shoulders. It is one of these same Saracens that we are seeking: Moussa is his name. Have you met with him?"

"Moussa!" answered the seeming monk: "I am he; or rather I am he who once bore that name. Do you not recognise me? Who you are, I know well; and I know also that I am more guilty than you, because I led you on to crime by word and by example; but since the goodness of God gives me the opportunity of retrieving my sin so far as it is retrievable, I implore you also to leave the ways of wickedness; for there is yet time for you as well as for me. His mercy is infinite, as I am experiencing; but His wrath will indeed be dreadful if you continue in sin."

The two renegades looked one upon another almost stupified with astonishment. They felt as though they were dreaming, and dared not break the silence.

"What are we to do?" at last asked one of them.

"What?" answered Moussa; "do as I do myself, weep and pray, and bow before the just judgment of God. Unworthy as I am, I have taken on myself this holy habit: if you too would wear it, we may be companions in penance, as we have hitherto been in sin."

"But have we not to fear the anger of our chief? He may return to this place."

"Let him return," answered Moussa; "too happy should I be if I might mingle my blood with that which I myself shed on this holy sod."

After a moment's hesitation the two apostates determined to remain in the island with Moussa; and thus did the blood of the martyrs prove, as it ever has done, the "seed of the Church."

THE
STORY OF PLACIDUS

During the reign of the Emperor Trajan, a man of great and distinguished virtue and renown, named Placidus, led the Roman armies victoriously against their Parthian foes. Possessing the grateful confidence of his royal master, Placidus, in his public character, was honoured and esteemed; whilst rich in the gentler virtues of domestic life, he was dear to all who mingled with him in private relationship.

He had a wife named Trojana, and two young sons, with whom, when a return of peace enabled him to leave the army, he retired to a country-house at some little distance from Rome.

There, in the enjoyment of boundless wealth and luxury, Placidus lived content. His home contained all that was necessary to fill up his measure of happiness,— riches, honour, earthly love; what more could be desired to satisfy a heathen soul? And Placidus was a heathen; not one of those joining inveterately in the cry of persecution, which, even in the days of Trajan the Merciful, arose from time to time against the infant Church of Christ; nay, from his natural benevolence, Placidus would have deprecated any act of violence against the Christians, just because they were poor and unprotected; but still he was a heathen, and shared avowedly in the universal feeling of contempt with which the immediate successors of the Apostles and their scattered followers were regarded. Who can tell, however, whether amidst his universal charities, some cup of cold water to a stray disciple, may not have been poured forth from a motive acceptable to the Searcher of hearts; or whether a fervent prayer, uttered in a moment of thankfulness by some Christian rescued from destruction, may have brought down upon Placidus the merciful regard of God? Who shall attempt to limit His grace, or ascribe motives to His providence? Suffice it that a wonderful hour was at hand for Placidus, which is thus recorded by ancient chroniclers.

He had a passion for the chase, and attended by numerous retainers and friends was accustomed to spend much of his time in the forests; finding in pursuit of stags and other game a recreation particularly acceptable to one so long accustomed to the activity of service in the field of battle.

One day, when Placidus and all his gallant company rode out as usual to the chase, a herd of deer was started; and dogs and horses bounded forwards gladly in pursuit. One stag, larger and fleeter than the rest, attracted Placidus. He observed it separate from the herd; and it irresistibly drew him from his company. They followed the flying herd far away into the depths of the forest; whilst he, with an impetuosity that had even to himself something supernatural in it, tracked, closely as his panting horse could bear him, the footsteps of the majestic stag. Sometimes in one direction, sometimes in another, up steep ascents, and through precipitous and narrow thorny ways, it led him on. For a moment he seemed about to capture it; but again it was beyond his reach. On and on he went, forgetful of the time, the distance, the closing hour of the day.

He saw nothing but the stag; he must gain it at last. Suddenly they had passed the thicket, and a bare hill was before them. The stag bounded to its summit, and turning, faced the astonished Placidus. Motionless it stood; and between its branching antlers, dimly discerned against the evening sky, arose a cross, encircled by a ring of light, piercing and dazzling, as no ray of sun or moon could kindle.

A voice of infinite tenderness then called him by his name. Touched in that moment to the very soul, Placidus sank upon his knees, and exclaimed, "Who art thou, Lord?" "Why persecutest thou Me, Placidus?" the voice replied. "I am the God thou ignorantly worshippest; Jesus, thy Lord. Thine alms and prayers have gone up before Me, and therefore am I come. As thou dost hunt this stag, so henceforward will I hunt thee." "Tell me Thy will, O Lord," cried Placidus, "that I may believe and perform it." The voice replied, "I am the Son of the living God. I created heaven and earth, and divided the light from the darkness. I appointed days, and seasons, and years. I formed man out of the dust of the ground; and for his sake took upon Me his own form. Crucified and buried, on the third day I arose again. "This I believe, O Lord," replied Placidus; "yea, and that thou art He who bringest back sinners to the way of peace." "If thou believest," returned the voice, "go into the city and be baptised. And return hither tomorrow, that thou mayest know of thy future life." Long wrapt in silent awe, Placidus remained upon that hallowed spot. Then, lighted by the moon, now high in the heavens, he pursued his way to the city, which he discerned at no great distance.

In those days of secret adherence to the faith of Christ, when a moment's delay might risk alike the conversion or the life of an applicant, no hour was too late for gaining admittance to the Christian bishop; and Placidus was therefore immediately ushered into his presence. Having related his wonderful adventure to the venerable man, and repeated his profession of faith, he was baptised by the name of Eustace; and returned before daybreak to the scene of his miraculous conversion. Then kneeling in prayer, he awaited the message of the mysterious voice. And thus it spoke to him: "Blessed art thou, Eustace, in that thou hast been washed with the laver of My grace, and thereby overcome the devil. Now hast thou trodden him to dust, who beguiled thee. Now will thy fidelity be shown; for he whom thou hast forsaken will rage continually against thee. Many things must thou undergo for My sake. Thou must become another Job; fear not, persevere; My grace is sufficient for thee. In the end thou shalt conquer; choose, then, whether thou wilt experience thy trials in thine old age, or forthwith."

And Eustace, with his new-born self-distrust, replied, "Even as Thou willest, Lord; yet, if it may be so, try me now, and help me in my trial." "Be bold, Eustace," spake the voice, for the last time. "Be bold; My grace can bear thee up." The wife and sons of Eustace, on hearing from his lips the wonderful things which had befallen him, were ready on the instant to believe in the Saviour who had manifested Himself so mysteriously, and were baptised that very day by the names of Theosbyta, Theosbytus, and Agapetus.

But a very short time passed by before Eustace became conscious of an extraordinary change in all his worldly prospects; and had not his faith risen triumphantly over all his pagan superstitions, he might have thought himself persecuted by the gods of his former worship for having treacherously abandoned them. But, enlightened by Divine wisdom, Eustace recognised with joy that his portion was no longer in this world; and that it was through a narrow way, unencumbered and single-hearted, that he was to follow his heavenly Guide.

One by one his treasures dropped away. Disease consumed his flocks and herds; his servants and retainers became faithless; friends looked coldly upon him. His house was plundered and destroyed; his possessions ravaged; he and his family gradually became destitute and homeless. In this state he resolved, for the sake of his family, to apply to Trajan; but the news of his conversion had already gone abroad, and even the emperor forgot his heavy obligations, and shunned his faithful servant.

Eustace then resolved on leaving his native land, and seeking in some distant country a new home, where he might peaceably bring up his children in the true faith. Journeying in this spirit to the sea-shore, he found a vessel about to embark, and entreated to be received amongst the passengers. From his appearance, the captain was about hastily to refuse, convinced that he had no means of paying for the voyage; but on perceiving the beauty of Theosbyta, his wife, a diabolical scheme entered his mind; he consented, and the Christian family set sail from Italy. No sooner had they reached Africa than the captain demanded payment; in vain Eustace pleaded his having been taken on board out of charity; the captain was resolute in pressing his claim; and on being assured by Eustace that he had nothing wherewith to satisfy it, he immediately seized Theosbyta, declaring he would sell her as a slave. Remonstrances and tears were vain; and lest the boys also should attract the cupidity of the heartless Roman, Eustace was compelled to land with them, and leave his beloved Theosbyta in his power. She herself even urged him to save himself and the children; willing herself to endure whatever trials might be appointed for her, so that they were spared.

So parted Eustace and his wife. His children now were all remaining to him in this world, once a treasure-house of joys. Silent and musing on the mysterious ways of God, but still without a murmur, Eustace, clasping the hands of his children on each side, walked forward, through the desert country wherein he found himself. He had no longer an object consciously before him; and for miles he still went on, until the failing footsteps of his young companions recalled his attention to their wants. He must now be father and mother both; where could he find food and shelter for them in the wilderness? They were now at the brink of a wide river, and on the other side Eustace perceived a group of trees which promised both nourishment and shade. Unable to swim with both the children at once, he first crossed the stream with Theosbytus, and placed him in safety on the other side; returning for Agapetus, what was the horror of the father, midway in the river, to hear despairing cries for help from both his sons at once. A lion had already seized Theosbytus, and the childish feet of Agapetus gave way beneath him as he turned to rush from an enormous wolf which sprung out of some hushes by the river side. By the time Eustace had struggled to the nearest shore both children had been carried out of sight. "Be it so, O my God!" cried Eustace, flinging himself face downwards on the ground. "Thy will be done; henceforward I am alone with thee!" And there for hours in silence and in prayer he lay immovable, and the sun scorched his uncovered head, and the cold dews of evening fell upon his exhausted limbs, and he was unconscious of all except the presence of an unseen angel that came and comforted him. When human nature had wept its full, and divine consolations had strengthened and cleared his mind, Eustace arose once more, and journeyed on.

That night, on lying down to sleep desolate and homeless on the bare ground, a vision sent by God came like balm into his tortured heart. He seemed to see his children sporting with the ferocious beasts that had torn them from his side. Suddenly the scene changed, grown into young men and wearing the dress of soldiers, noble and in angel beauty they stood before him, their mother beautiful and calm drew near,—all were restored to him in that blessed moment; and when the vision had faded from before him, and the melancholy cry of the night-birds hovering above him, recalled Eustace to a sense of his bereavement, he still felt that tender comfort lingering in his mind,—he felt that he should yet meet with his beloved ones again in the land beyond the grave.

To find Theosbyta was the first object the returning

faculties of Eustace entertained, when the sort of stupefaction which had followed his late trials began to subside; and every effort a man so poor and destitute of friends could make, he tried for long, but constantly without success. Hopeless at last, he committed the future to God, and settled himself down as the hired servant of a humble peasant. Here, a patient labourer, he toiled for years; never was a word of impatience or regret heard to fall from the lips of the once princely Eustace; he remembered the days of his former magnificence and luxury, but it was only to bow himself more willingly beneath the hand of God. "Thou doest all things well!" he whispered in his heart, and humbled himself literally to the dust. So fifteen years passed away; none knew the story of the silent and obedient labourer; he was more unwearied at his tasks, more faithful to his trust, more forgetful of himself than others; no one knew more than this; he never spoke but of necessity, and then never of himself.

In fifteen years his master died, and appreciating the patient fidelity of Eustace, bequeathed to him the humble cottage where he had served him so long; here then he still dwelt on, without a wish to change his life. Meantime peace no longer reigned in Rome, enemies were at her very gates. Trajan vainly thought upon the noble Placidus, who had ruled his armies with so powerful a spell, and led them on to victory with a resistless arm. Where was the general who had been so honoured and exalted in the moment of triumph, so carelessly discarded at a leisure hour? Oh, that Placidus were at Rome once more! An emperor's wishes are readily divined, more readily accomplished. There were few who would not gladly have undertaken to restore the forgotten Placidus had it but been possible. He was above their envy, he had been trusted, and was now wanted by all. Where could he have hidden himself? Several anxious to please the emperor, some trembling for the fate of their country, and a few from affectionate remembrance of the long-lost Placidus, immediately set forth in search of the absent commander; but there was no clue to his retreat; none knew when, or why, or how he had departed; and disappointment met the expectant emperor as party after party returned desponding from their unsuccessful search.

At length two former comrades of the hero, pushing in their generous zeal beyond the others, arrived one day, footsore and weary, before the cottage-door of Eustace, who hospitably bade them welcome, and hastened to offer them refreshment. Their uniform was a passport to his heart; it was fifteen years since he had seen a soldier. The men made inquiries of their host as to the fate of Placidus. Eustace started, but concealing his emotion, evaded their questions, for he had no desire to brave once more the dangers and temptations of the imperial city; but when he heard the anxious inquiries that had been made for him by his royal master, and the affection with which his name was still remembered at Rome, his heart was touched, and he hastily left the room. During his absence, the soldiers conferred together on his appearance, which reminded them strongly of the commander they were sent to seek; and remembering an old sword-mark which had honourably distinguished Placidus, they agreed to look for it in their host. On his re-entering the room, they accordingly glanced immediately at the back of his neck, and found the identical scar. Convinced that they had now discovered the object of their search, they laid aside all reserve, and spoke so earnestly with Eustace on the dependence that was placed on his generalship at Rome, and the dangers that threatened their country, that the determination of Eustace was gradually shaken, and he consented to return to his former master, and if possible serve him once again. The soldiers could scarcely realise that the once great and magnificent Placidus stood before them disguised in peasant's clothes. When last they saw him, he had reigned like a prince over the hearts of thousands. His palace had been like that of a king, his wealth boundless, his prosperity unclouded. They wept when they heard of his misfortunes and his trials, of his loss of Theosbyta and of his children.

The next day Eustace arose to leave the solitude where he had dwelt so long. Gladly would he have spent there the remainder of his life; he shrunk from the thought of Rome, the pagan city, rich in idol shrines and this world's luxury, underneath all which, in silence and concealment, bowed itself secretly the Church of God; but fearing that in this unwillingness to return there lingered more of selfishness and wilfulness than any better feeling, Eustace braced himself for the departure, and committing his future to the care of God, quitted his lonely dwelling with his guests.

As they journeyed towards the gates of Rome, the news that Placidus was found flew before them to the emperor's throne; he rose, thanked his gods for such a blessing, and came out himself to meet and welcome the returning hero; shouts and acclamations resounded on every side; amid the triumph of the people and their own more deeply-felt emotions, the emperor and his faithful servant entered Rome together. And now returned for Eustace the warlike days of Placidus; the army greeted him with rapture; a victory was now no longer doubted, joy and confidence filled every heart; thousands poured in to swell the imperial forces; there was nothing but glory in joining an army headed by Eustace.

Amongst the youths who crowded contending for this honour, two particularly attracted the attention of the general: he thought of his sons, his lost Theosbytus and Agapetus; had they lived, they would have been the ages of these striplings. Eustace placed them honourably, as they deserved, by all report, in his forces, and kept his eye upon them. The march began, and was continued until the army had advanced within sight of the invading enemy, who lay encamped within but a short distance of that melancholy coast where Eustace had been landed by the treacherous captain.

Night was stealing silently over the hushed camp; the soldiers slept, secure in the vigilance of their guardian sentinels, and Mars their patron deity. The two young strangers, however, still kept watch; and when all their preparations for the morrow were complete, they went out together to find some lonely spot where they might offer up their souls in prayer to God, for they were Christians. Unconsciously they took the very path which had led Eustace and his sons fifteen years before, and paused beneath the same group of trees which had allured him to cross the fatal river, on whose banks they stood. The young men hastened to throw themselves prostrate; but they started on perceiving that they were not alone—another worshipper knelt there—a woman, pale and bowed, and looking in the dim evening twilight so shadowy and motionless, that a sense of awe, as if in the presence of some supernatural being, mingled with the instinctive reverence that stayed the young men's noiseless footsteps on the grass: she saw them not, her eyes were fixed immovably; and words, whose tones had utterance of a sorrow deeper than goes forth in tears, fell slowly from her lips. In the profound stillness of the spot each word was distinctly heard: "My Eustace! my Theosbytus! my Agapetus!" They started at the words so suddenly that the woman turned her head and rose, but not in terror; she seemed like one who has nothing any longer to fear or hope. The young men knew already they were brothers, for they had long since told each other the wonderful tale of their preservation; and now, at the words of the kneeling woman, they doubted no longer they had found their long-lost mother. "Your name?" they gasped in one breath. "Theosbyta," she answered, scarcely looking at them. "Mother!" burst forth in one wild cry, as they threw themselves impetuously towards her. She shuddered at the name so long unheard, and sunk fainting to the ground, but joy in that instant had gone like healing balm into her wounded heart; and when her sons with tender care had poured water from the river on her brow, she once more opened her eyes, and gazed upon them with a rapture that withheld the power of speech. Meanwhile Eustace also sought the grove of trees, which he had already seemed to recognise: it would ease his heart to pour it forth in prayer for his Theosbyta before the day of battle; as for his sons, he doubted not they were already angels, gone in their baptismal innocence before the throne of God, to plead for him and their unhappy mother. The little group upon the grass attracted his attention, and as he quietly came onwards, the words "Theosbytus! my Agapetus!" from the reviving mother, struck on his ear. He paused: the remembrance of his former vision on this very spot came freshly back upon him, and for an instant a thought of spiritual visitations glanced over his mind; but on one of the young men looking up, he recognised the face of his young captain, who started on perceiving his commander; he knew not yet that Eustace, the leader of the Roman armies, was a Christian. Making a sign to his brother, Theosbytus rose upon his feet, and attempted to explain to the general that he and his brother had been just now miraculously restored to their long-lost mother; but Eustace heard him not; the names and the remembrance of his vision still filled his thoughts, and gazing intently on the pale Theosbyta, his faithful eye pierced through the veil that time and grief had wrought over her features, and in a stifled voice he asked, as just before her sons had done, "Your name?" "Theosbyta," she answered. "I am your husband," he replied, and folded her to his heart. "Father, our father!" cried the youths, and Eustace sunk upon his knees at the sound: "My wife, my sons! O God, Thou hast restored me all; how shall we glorify Thy name!" "The end must now be near," murmured Theosbyta; "remember, suffering was to be the portion of thy Christian life." "The will of God be done in all things," replied Eustace; and an "Amen!" echoed by his wife and sons brought peace into their hearts, almost too deeply moved by joy.

Then they prayed till morning's dawn, and then Theosbyta related to her husband how she had been kept as a slave by the wicked captain for many years of anxious misery, but that God had guarded her; and when, after her master's death, she became once more free, she had laboured and maintained herself, ever hoping that the day might arrive when her husband and her children might return to claim her. "And you, my sons," said Eustace, "by what miracle do I find you, whom I thought already torn to pieces by wild beasts?" Then Theosbytus told his father that the lion which had seized him, being pursued by hunters before it had time to do him any serious injury, dropped him to defend itself, whereupon he was taken home by some humane villagers, who healed his wounds and taught him to become a hunter; that some months after, he accidentally met with his brother, who had been rescued by shepherds from the jaws of the wolf; and that hopeless of recovering either of their parents, they had remained many years with the friendly villagers, until able to carry arms; when both becoming soldiers, they had risen rapidly in the army, and been chosen to bear honourable part in it when commanded to rally under Eustace.

The night rapidly wore away in such discourse; and with the dawn of day, kneeling together for a while in prayer, they embraced and parted.

Joy spread through all the ranks when it was known that Eustace had recovered his sons in the two brave young captains. That day the Romans fought victoriously; the presence of their leader inspired every man with confidence and courage, and news was sent to Rome that filled the emperor with delight. But the return of the army was for some time delayed; pursuing his conquest, Eustace followed his retreating foes until he had driven them completely from the country, and then prepared to return to the imperial city. But meanwhile Trajan was no more; Adrian, his successor, filled the throne, and ordered every honour to be paid to the victorious general, that he might enter the city in triumph, as was wont on such occasions.

A day of feasting and rejoicing was proclaimed; and the emperor himself resolved to give it all the splendour that his presence could bestow, by presiding himself at the banquet. "But first," said he to Eustace, "we must satisfy the gods; let us hasten to the Temple of Mars, and make the offerings he has so richly merited at our hands." "My thanks," said Eustace, proudly, "have been already offered to the God I serve, nor can I bow my knee within a heathen temple." The emperor guessed not the meaning of this speech at first, but those who stood around him knew its purport well. "A Christian!" they murmured; "Eustace a Christian!" Adrian caught the word. "Art thou a Christian?" he demanded fiercely. "I am," said Eustace. "I am sorry for thee," was the reply; "but wilt thou not come and offer with us at the shrine of Mars?" "It is but to cast a little incense on his altar," whispered a friendly voice. "I will die first!" cried Eustace, kindling at the whisper, for he knew it to be that of one whom terror had long since won back to heathenism,—who had treacherously deserted the faith of Jesus, rather than die worthy of a martyr's portion. "Then die thou shalt!" cried Adrian furiously, fancying somewhat of insult in the unwonted energy of Eustace's decision. "I also am a Christian," "And I, O emperor!" cried out the manly voices of Theosbytus and Agapetus, whilst their father turned upon them a look half proud, half sorrowful, and then glanced upwards with a smile. Theosbyta was not far off; she heard and understood it all. "I also am a Christian," she said, as firmly as her trembling lips could utter the words, determined now to share the fate of her beloved ones, whatever that might be. Her words did not reach the emperor's ears, but they were taken up by those who stood around, and echoed from one to another till he heard and understood them. "There is but one fate for you all," he answered; "take them to the lions' den."

"Another and a better festival than that they had appointed for us is now provided, my beloved ones," said Eustace, as he gazed inquiringly on the faces of his wife and sons. But not a quiver of emotion was discernible; a holy smile of triumph and of joy lit up each countenance. "We shall be martyrs for Jesus Christ!" It was all they uttered as they were hurried away.

Crowds followed to behold the unexpected sight.

The amphitheatre was thronged to excess. So little sympathy was felt with Christians that even Eustace, on proclaiming himself one, had lost at once all title to their esteem. His victories were forgotten, or ascribed to arts of magic. Already the Christian family were exposed before the raging beasts; but not one would open its mouth against them. Calm and motionless, their hands folded on their breasts, they stood, and the hungry lions came and licked their feet.

This was attributed to some charm: "They have a charm against the teeth of beasts!" was echoed round the amphitheatre. "Away with them to the brazen ox!" the emperor answered; "they cannot quench his fury."

This was an enormous figure, made resembling an ox, and when heated by a fire underneath was used as an instrument of torturing execution to those victims who were placed within it. The fire was kindled, and the door in the side of the figure opened. One by one the martyrs ascended the ladder, entered the brazen ox, and lay down as if to sleep. The door was closed upon them, and the flames roared hotter and more fiercely upwards, whilst the immense multitude held their breath as one man, and a shudder of irrepressible horror ran through the heathen crowd. But not a cry or sound of anguish came from that fearful sepulchre; and the people remembered the wonderful smiles that had made radiant the faces of Eustace and his family as they disappeared one by one within its cavity, and looking on each other they marvelled how these Christians should go so lovingly to death. Then games and processions in honour of the victory went on, and they bowed themselves before the shrine of Mars, and Eustace the Christian was forgotten; but three days afterwards the brazen ox was once more opened. There lay the martyrs calmly, side by side; the same smile was on their faces, no change or smell of fire had passed over them. God had given His beloved sleep.

The martyred family still lives in the memory of the Church; and the Catholic traveller will recall their affecting story as he visits the stately churches which bear the name of St. Eustachius.

THE SANCTUARY
OF OUR LADY OF
THE THORNS

Not far from the highest peak of Jura there is still seen a heap of ruins, which belonged to the church and monastery of *Notre Dame des Epines Fleuries*. It lies at the very extremity of a narrow and deep gorge, but somewhat sheltered on the north, and so produces every year the rarest flowers of that region. At about the distance of half a league, the opposite extremity affords a view of the ruins of an old seignorial manor, long since gone, like the house of God. All that is known now is, that it was the mansion of an illustrious family, that signalised themselves in arms; and that the last who bore the name of that band of noble knights died fighting for the recovery of the Holy Land, without leaving an heir to hand down the name to posterity. The disconsolate widow did not fly from, but remained about the old grounds which so much afforded food to her melancholy; and the report of her piety and charitable deeds extended far and wide, so that her memory has been handed down to, and respected by, Christian generations. The people, who have forgotten all her other titles, still call her *the blessed one*.

On one of these days, at the close of winter, when the rigour of the season relaxes under the influence of a genial sky, the saint was taking her usual exercise, by walking along the avenue of her château, her mind occupied with pious thoughts. Having arrived at the thorny thicket terminating the avenue, she was not a little surprised at seeing that one of the bushes was already charged with all the decorations of spring. She quickened her steps, to assure herself that this appearance was not produced by any remains of the winter's snow; and, overjoyed at seeing it in reality crowned with a great number of beautiful small stars, she carefully removed one of its branches for the purpose of suspending it in her oratory, before an image of the Blessed Virgin, to which, from the days of her childhood, she was devoutly attached; and then returned, her heart surcharged with joy at being the bearer of this simple offering.

Whether it was that this feeble tribute was really pleasing to the Divine Mother of Jesus, or that a peculiar, undefinable pleasure is reserved for the slightest effusion of a tender heart towards the object of its love, the soul of the lady of the manor never experienced more thrilling delight than on that charming evening. With heartfelt joy, she promised to return every day to the blossomed bush, and from it to bring back daily a fresh garland. That she remained faithful to her engagement who can doubt? One day, however, when the care of the sick and indigent had detained her longer than usual, she was obliged to quicken her steps, to gain her wild shrubbery before nightfall. Her haste was vain, for darkness overtook her; and it is said that she began to regret having entered so far into this dreary wild, when a clear and softened light, like that preceding the rising sun, displayed at once before her eyes all the thorns in blossom. She arrested her steps for a moment, thinking that this light might proceed from the halting-place of brigands: for that it could be produced by myriads of glow-worms, brought out before their proper time, could not with any possibility be imagined; the season was still too far removed from the calm and close nights of summer.

Nevertheless, the obligation, self-imposed, presenting itself to her mind, and somewhat giving her courage, she advanced slowly with bated breath, took hold with a trembling hand of a branch,—which of itself seemed to drop into her fingers, so slight was the resistance offered,—and re-entered the way to the manor, without once looking behind her.

During all that night the lady reflected on the phenomenon, and yet could find no satisfactory explanation; and as she was determined to unravel the mystery, on the following day, at the same hour in the evening, she repaired to the thicket, accompanied by a faithful servant, and by her old chaplain. The same delicious softened light played about it as on the previous evening, and seemed to become, the nearer they approached, more bright and radiant. They stopped and placed themselves on their knees, for it seemed to them that this light emanated from heaven; then the aged priest arose, alone advanced respectfully towards the flowery thorns, chanting at the same time a church hymn, and removed them aside without the slightest effort. The spectacle then presented to their view so filled them with admiration, gratitude, and joy, that they remained a long time motionless. It was an image of the Blessed Virgin, rudely carved in wood, painted in rather lively colours by an unskilled hand, and dressed in simple attire; and from that it was that the miraculous light, with which the place was filled, emanated. "Hail Mary, full of grace!" said at length the prostrate chaplain; and the sound of harmony which arose in every part of the wood, when he had pronounced these words, would have induced one to imagine that they were repeated by the angelic choirs. He then solemnly recited those admirable litanies in which faith expresses itself, though unconsciously, in the highest style of poetry; and after renewed acts of adoration, he raised the image between his hands to bear it to the château, where he could find a sanctuary more worthy of it. As he moved on, the lady and her faithful domestic, their hands joined and their heads bowed, followed him slowly, offering up their prayers in union with his.

It is unnecessary to add, that the marvellous image was placed in an elegant niche, that lights blazed around it, that incense curled about its head, on which a superb crown was placed, and that even until midnight the chanting of the faithful offered it their greetings. But, strange to say, on the following morning no image could be seen, and no little alarm was felt by those Christians who experienced such unalloyed happiness at finding it. What unknown sin could have brought down this disgrace on the mansion of "the saint?" Why had the celestial Virgin quitted it? What new resting-place had she selected? There could be little difficulty in solving the mystery. The Blessed Mother of Jesus had preferred the modest retirement of her favourite bushes to the grandeur of a worldly dwelling. She returned to the coolness and freshness of the grove, there to taste the peace of her solitude and the sweet odour of her flowers. All the inmates of the château repaired there in the evening, and found it there, shining with even greater splendour than on the previous eve. They fell down on their knees in respectful silence.

"Powerful Queen of Angels," said the aged chaplain, "this, then, is the temple that you prefer. Your will be done."

And in a little time after, a temple gorgeous and rich—a temple such as could be erected only by the architects of those grand and glorious times—was raised to cover the revered image. The great ones of the earth enriched it with costly presents; kings endowed it with a tabernacle of the purest gold. The fame of the miracles wrought through it extended far and wide through the Christian world, and induced a great many pious women to fix their abode in the valley, and place themselves under monastic rules. The saintly widow, more touched now than ever with the lights of grace, could not refuse her assent to her appointment of superioress; and after a life of good works and edifying examples, which, like odoriferous incense, ascended at the foot of the altar of the Virgin, she died there full of days.

Such, according to the old records of the province, is the origin of the Church and Convent of Notre Dame des Epines Fleuries.

THE STORY OF THE
LORD OF CREQUY

Consolatrix afflictorum—Consoler of the afflicted

LOUIS the Young, King of France, having, at the command of St. Bernard, engaged in the crusade, in 1147, no brave man could hesitate to follow his banner. Dukes and counts, barons and knights, all the young nobles assembled with their vassals, and an army of eighty thousand men were soon on the move towards the Holy Land.

Among the knights who then took the cross, "vowing to defend the tomb of Jesus Christ," Sir Raoul de Crequy was conspicuous as well by his illustrious name and noble origin, as by his handsome person and military air. His father, Gerard, Count of Ternoy, was still living. He had shone amid the staff of Godfrey of Bouillon, and his spirit seemed revived in his young son Raoul.

In this very year, and about six months before the time we write of, Raoul de Crequy had married a Breton lady of sweet and amiable disposition. She was *enceinte* when the baron enrolled himself under the banner of the cross without her consent, *which was contrary to use and to custom.* She was so afflicted on learning this, that nothing could alleviate her distress. Her noble husband endeavoured in vain to persuade her to consent to his departure. His aged father said to her,

"I also, when I was young, crossed the seas. I took the cross without the knowledge of my father, and my good mother was sorely distressed at it. Still both were rejoiced when I returned home, covered with honours. Surely, lady, your husband could not see his sovereign lead this expedition and remain behind. Is he not thirty years of age? the time for every man to distinguish himself. Why then should you wish him to remain on this estate to reap nothing but shame and dishonour?"

The good lady at length gave way, and agreed to the departure of her lord. He took with him his two brothers, Roger and Godfrey, and twenty-seven esquires followed in their suite.

When the terrible moment of separation arrived, the lady could not refrain from weeping bitterly, as Raoul, with emotion, swore to be true and constant to her. He took from her finger the nuptial ring, which she had received with such joy; and, breaking it in two, gave one part to his bride, keeping the other himself.

"This half of the ring which was blessed at our marriage," said he, "I will always keep as a true and loyal husband, and when I return from my pilgrimage I will give you back this pledge of my constancy."

He held his lady by the hand, and leading her to his aged father, besought him to love and cherish her as his own daughter. The old count promised to do so, and embraced the weeping lady. The knight then knelt before him, and said,

"Dear sir, and father, that my days may be happy, bless me; and let your prayers and good wishes accompany me in my journey."

The old man, spreading his hands over his son's head, invoked the blessing of God upon him.

"Almighty Lord," said he, "bless my son in this war, which

he undertakes in your holy name. And you, dearest Virgin, our Sovereign Lady, be his guardian; protect him from danger, and bring him back without blemish to his native land,"

The good old man then blessed his other sons, and embraced them, as well as the esquires who accompanied them.

The lord of Crequy and his companions leaped on their chargers; at the sound of clarions and trumpets the noble troop set forth on their way, preceded by a herald who bore the standard of the cross. They made such haste, that they soon joined the main army, which was in advance by several days' march. "Never," say the ballads of the day, "was seen such a host of noble, gentle, and valiant youths." The record of their deeds would fill a large volume; we have here only to deal with those which relate to the lord of Crequy.

He had left a wife and father in deep sorrow; and in those days the pang of separation could not be alleviated by frequent correspondence. In due time the Countess of Crequy gave birth to a child —a sweet boy, in whom she found some consolation for the absence of her husband. The old count was quite overjoyed, and felt himself young again at the sight of his grandson. A special messenger was dispatched to carry the joyful news to his son, who was found at the port of Satalia.

Raoul de Crequy made great rejoicings with his friends on this occasion. But his happiness was, alas! soon to be changed into sorrow.

An engagement shortly afterwards took place between the Crusaders and the Saracens. Raoul and his companions led the van of the army. Carried away by his ardour, he entered a narrow pass, followed only by two small troops, led by the lords of Breteuil and Varennes. These three companies formed but a hundred lances. The Saracens held possession of the heights overlooking this perilous pass. They let fall a rain of arrows upon the Christians, who fought manfully to gain a passage. Roger and Godfrey, the count's brothers, with twenty of the esquires, fell mortally wounded. But the Christians did not retire. Although they saw nothing but death before them, they earnestly pressed forward. In the encounter, besides the two brothers before mentioned, the lords of Breteuil, Varennes, Montjoy, Maumey, Brimen, Bauraing, Esseike, Mesgrigny, Sempey, and Suresnes perished; and many a beardless youth lay stretched in the dust.

The Lord of Crequy, as a man of high and undaunted valour, would not retire; but continued to fight, invoking our Lady's aid, till, exhausted by the number of his wounds, he at length fell to the earth.

When the seven knights, who alone remained, saw their leader slain, they fled precipitately to the camp, and announced their sad disaster. The enemies, remaining masters of the field, began to strip the dead, when they perceived that the Lord of Crequy still moved; and it was determined not to dispatch him, but to endeavour to heal his wounds and preserve his life, for the sake of the ransom which so noble a knight would fetch.

He was gently carried to the Saracen camp, where it was discovered that his wounds, though dangerous, were not mortal. They were skilfully dressed. But so weakened was he by the loss of blood, that Raoul remained for some time in an inanimate state. His youth, however, was in his favour, and he soon recovered his strength.

But how bitter were his first thoughts in finding himself a slave of the Saracens, and that he had fallen into the hands of one who was inclined to show him no favour? The Saracen gave him his hand to kiss. This the knight did so cheerfully, that he had courage to ask for a small relic—the half of a ring, of which he had been plundered. This, to his great joy, was restored to him.

As soon as he was convalescent, profiting of the offer of his master to accept two hundred pieces of gold for his ransom, Raoul sent a messenger to the Christian camp. This man chanced to arrive at the time that the Crusaders were attacking and massacring the Saracen army, and he

was slain with the others. The Saracens, completely routed in this encounter, retired to the very spot where Raoul
was confined, and who lay in hopes that his brethren in
arms would soon break his chains, and receive him with
joy again into their ranks. But his master waited not their
arrival, but hastily fled, carrying his prisoner with him, and
did not stop, so great was his terror, until he had reached the
boundary of Syria.

In proportion as he was farther from the Christian camp,
Raoul found his captivity more galling. He wrote many letters, none of which reached the king or France. All the army
believed him dead; and the first couriers sent to France were
commissioned to announce their loss to his father and wife.
The latter, on hearing the fatal news, swooned. "Never from
that instant," says the old ballad, "did his father enjoy an
hour's health." He lingered and died. Lady de Crequy would
have envied his lot, had not her son required her life; but she
wept day and night. The youngest of the brothers, Baudoin,
who had remained in France, seized upon the territories,
and assumed the title of Lord of Crequy and other places, in
injury to his brother's child. The lady's father was a powerful
noble of Brittany; and being aged, and at a distance, was unable to assert and defend his grandson's rights. But, seeing
his daughter a widow and unprotected, he advised her to
marry the Lord of Renty, a nobleman, who, charmed with
her amiable qualities, sought her in marriage. She, however,
refused, notwithstanding her trials and defenceless state, to
enter again into the bonds of wedlock, still lamenting her
first spouse, and flattering herself with faint hopes of his
returning to her.

Many years thus passed—long and bitter ones for the
lady, hard and painful for the knight. His master made him
wait on and serve him until he should be ransomed. His
occupation consisted in watching the flocks, under the direction of the first shepherd, who had the management of
the cattle. Hourly did he pray to God while engaged in the

fields, and besought our Blessed Lady to obtain his deliverance from his durance; still he supported with resignation the state to which he fancied the neglect of his friends had reduced him.

Seven years had elapsed since his captivity, when his master died. He was then led to the market and sold with the other slaves. He fetched a good price on account of his great height and strength. The probability also of his being one day ransomed added to his value. He fell to the lot of a severe master, who hated the Christians; and he immediately commenced a series of persecutions on the person of the captive knight.

"You see," said his master to him one day, "that your country has abandoned you; deny your faith, invoke our prophet, and I will give you some land, money, and a wife."

But the Lord of Crequy would rather have suffered any outrage, or death itself, rather than renounce his faith and his plighted love to his dear spouse.

Hoping to reduce him to compliance with his wishes, his master confined him in an old tower, loaded him with chains, and inflicted many other hardships and tortures upon him.

This half-ruined tower had no roof. The sun darted its fiercest rays into the captive's cell. His hands and feet were linked together, and his body attached to the wall by a chain. He received every morning a handful of rice, a piece of black bread, and a jug of water.

His master often came to urge him to change his religion; and on his persevering in his faith, caused him to be whipped till the blood streamed down his body. These persecutions were continued at intervals during three years, without effecting in the least the knight's confidence in God.

After ten years' captivity, abandoning all hope of regaining his liberty, he ardently desired death. Not long after his master said to him, "Well, as it does not seem likely you will be ransomed, and you are obstinate in adhering to your faith, I shall have you strangled tomorrow."

A feeling of satisfaction came over him; but it was soon changed into one of regret, when he thought of his home, his aged father, and above all his dear spouse and young son, whom he was never to behold. However, he said, with firmness, his evening prayers, and recommended his soul into the hands of his Creator; begging of our dear Lady, that since he could no more see those beloved beings, to take them into her special care and protection. He recommended his child, soon to be an orphan, to the patronage of St. Nicholas, the tutelar saint of Christian children. And, placing himself for life or death into the hands of our Blessed Lady, he stretched himself on his hard couch, and soon fell into a deep sleep.

In his sleep he saw an unknown lady, whose features he thought he remembered in the chapel of Crequy. She bent over him, and seemed to free him from his chains and fetters. The delight this caused him awakened him. He then discovered that he was in very deed freed from his chains. Yet he still fancied he was under the influence of a dream, for he was out of prison and walked about in the air. The sun shone forth brightly, but did not oppress him by its heat.

He looked around him, and surprise following surprise, he found himself in a wood.

His first impulse was to fall on his knees and thank God and our Lady for his deliverance, and for the delightful sensations he now felt.

These feelings were so delicious, that he doubted whether or not he had been strangled in the night, and was now in paradise.

But the singing of the birds, the trees waving in the wind, the animals who grazed in the verdant meadows, everything around tended to convince him that he was still on this earth, though the air he breathed was milder than that to which he had been accustomed; and he was free. Yes, free!

he had been delivered from his captivity by some unknown hand. Whose could it be but that of Mary? But was he quite safe from his master's pursuit? How far was he from his abode? How should he be able to return to Europe?

These questions, and other apprehensions, were beginning to excite some misgivings in his mind, when he saw, at the end of the pathway, a peasant cutting wood. He ran towards him. But no sooner did the poor man perceive him, than, taking him for a spectre, he threw down his hatchet, and ran for his life. The knight had not had time to reflect on his personal appearance.

Reduced almost to a state of emaciation, and darkened by the heats of the African sun, with no clothing but a piece of coarse sacking only partially covering the upper part of his body, with a long beard, a shaven head, and dark skin, he certainly presented a most extraordinary appearance. He, however, managed to reach the woodman; and seizing hold of him, asked him, in Syriac, the way out of the wood. The man, hearing him speak, a faculty which he thought was denied to spectres, changed his opinion concerning him, and now took him for one of those Saracen slaves who were sometimes brought by Crusaders into Europe. He answered him in French,

"I do not understand what you say."

At this moment Raoul de Crequy was experiencing the same sensations as did the three knights of Eppe on a like occasion, as before narrated.

"My good man," said he, in French, and breathing hard at each syllable, "tell me whether I am dreaming or under some delusion? Tell me, where am I? I am lost, and know no one in this country."

"This wood is called the forest of Crequy," replied the woodman: "it is on the borders of Flanders. But tell me who you are? Poor man, I suppose you are a Christian captive, who have escaped from some ship which has been wrecked on the neighbouring coasts?"

But the knight heard him not. After he had learnt that he was in his own country and native place, he had fallen on the ground; and, extending his hands in the form of a cross, he exclaimed,

"O Almighty God! O most holy Virgin! my sweet Protectress, my help, and my deliverer, by what miracle have you brought me hither?"

He then rose and asked the woodman, who was regarding him compassionately, whether the aged lord was still alive, and whether the young countess and her son were living, and in good health?

"What, you know them?" said the man: "it is many years since the old count died of grief, bewailing the loss of his three eldest sons. His youngest, Baudoin, has endeavoured to take possession of the title and estate, and has behaved ill to his brother's widow and child. But the lady's father, who still lives, is now with her. He came expressly from his distant home in Brittany to endeavour to persuade his daughter to marry again, in order to secure her son's inheritance. For the Lord of Renty has promised to protect his rights, and to cherish him as the son of his dear friend, our late Lord Raoul, to whose soul God grant rest! He is a rich and powerful lord, and our lady cannot do better than accept his hand. But she had hitherto continually refused to listen to any project of marriage until within the last few days, when she consented, for the sake of her dear son; and today she is to be led to the altar by the Lord of Renty at the hour of six. There will be a grand *fête* and rejoicing at the castle, and all will be welcome; and you, too, poor man, will, I trust, receive some alms on the occasion."

The knight replied not, but followed the woodman to the castle gate, which he recognised with joy. The attendants who surrounded it, seeing the miserable plight of the pilgrim, would not allow him to pass.

"What do you want?" asked they: "whence come you, to be in that wretched state? Are you some prisoner escaped from slavery?"

"I am a pilgrim from the Holy Land," answered the knight, "and wish to see the Lady of Crequy on business of great importance."

"A man in your condition cannot enter the castle; besides, no one can speak to our lady today; she is even now being vested in her nuptial garments. You can step on one side and see her pass."

The count waited in silence; and shortly the Lady of Crequy, richly dressed, and seated on a highly-decorated mare, led by the Count of Renty, and followed by her father, son, and relatives, who had been invited to attend the ceremony, came forth from the castle on her way to the neighbouring abbey, in the church of which she was to be married. She bore the marks of sadness and of tears upon her pale face; and the frequent looks of love she gave her son showed that she was seeking his interest and welfare, and not her own.

Raoul, mastering his emotions, stopped the countess, and said:

"I come, noble lady, from the East. I bring news of the Lord of Crequy, who has endured a captivity of ten years."

The lady, at these words, dismounted, so great was her emotion. But on recovering the first shock, she looked earnestly at the pilgrim, and said:

"Your report, alas! is I fear incorrect. My lord fell with his brothers and their squires leading on their banner with honour. All who accompanied him perished, with the exception of seven who escaped by flight."

"Raoul de Crequy did not perish, noble lady; behold him! he stands before you."

A general murmur and excitement was expressed by the attendants at these words.

"Look at me," continued the count. "Despite so much misery and the many hardships I have suffered, can you not recognise your faithful husband, once so dear to you?"

"I can scarce believe you," exclaimed the lady, interrupting her sobs, "unless you give me some proof. If you are my husband, tell me what you did on the day of your departure for the Holy Land?"

"I broke in two your wedding-ring: I left you one half, and took the other with me, and I have kept it in pledge of my love. Here it is."

The knight removed, from round his neck, a little reliquary, from which he took the half ring, and presented it to the lady. On seeing it, she fell on his neck embracing him, and exclaimed:

"You are, indeed, my beloved husband! You are my dear lord!"

She then gave full vent to her raptures on recovering him, which excited the greatest sympathy in the bystanders.

The Lord of Renty, relative and friend of the Count of Crequy, was still incredulous of a fact which deprived him of a charming wife. A struggle arose in his heart between friendship and love.

"He certainly possesses the form and size of Raoul," thought he, "but I cannot recognise his features."

The countess's father, however, said:

"I now see the features of my lost son-in-law, although suffering has somewhat altered them. When we see him dressed, I think you will all recognise in him your long-lost lord."

The child, who was now ten years old, had also timidly approached. He felt new sensations come over him on hearing that his father lived; and when his mother took his hand and said, "Behold, my dear son, your father! show him how you love him," the child threw his arms round his father's neck, rejoicing at his recovery. The count covered the boy's face with tears of joy, and pressed him to his heart. The boy seemed not to have any childish fears at the uncouth appearance of his father, but said:

"It was for you that my dear mamma wept so often,

continually repeating, 'We have lost everything, my son, in losing your father, my beloved husband.'"

The ladies and knights who had been invited to the wedding pressed round to see and speak to the count. The abbot of the monastery was apprised that the wedding would not take place, and was summoned to attend at the castle. The count having been shaved, and dressed according to his rank, and wearing a wig, which quite changed his former wild and eastern appearance, led his lady to the banquet which had been prepared for the marriage feast. The whole of the company were also invited to seat themselves; and having recounted to them his sufferings, and miraculous deliverance, and sudden transportation to the forest, the hall resounded with toasts to the health and long *vivas* to Raoul, Lord of Crequy.

He even invited his brother Baudoin; and having pardoned him his treachery towards his wife and child, made him sit by his side. The *fêtes* were continued for some days; and the people, who came from far and near to see the long-lost Count de Crequy, were well received and entertained.

The chains with which he had been loaded in his dungeon were found in the forest near the spot where he awoke; and the count, in thanksgiving, built a monastery in the wood, and richly endowed it. He also made presents to all the neighbouring chapels of our Blessed Lady.*

* This story has some affinity with that of the Three Knights of St. John. A still more extraordinary story is familiar to the people of Brittany. The Lord of Garo was taken prisoner, with his esquire, in Palestine, by the Saracens, near Bethlehem. They were placed in a large strong box, and told by the infidels to ask their God to get them out of it if He could. They then closed it, and were about to bury it in the earth. The esquire began to lament, but the Count Garo commended himself to God, and most particularly to our dear Lady of Bethlehem—vowing to erect a chapel in her honour, if he should escape his dreadful entombment alive. They then felt that they were moving; and the esquire, after some time, said, "Why, surely it is the cock of Garo I hear crow!" The count at these words blessed heaven and our Lady, who he felt confident had saved

them and transported them to their native land. Shortly some peasants passed, and seeing this large trunk on the wayside, opened it, and set free the Lord of Garo and his esquire, whom they recognised with astonishment. He instantly fulfilled his vow, and erected a charming Gothic chapel in honour of our Lady of Bethlehem, which is to be seen at the present day, with its old stained glass recording pictorially the wonderful deliverance of Count Garo out of the hands of the Saracens, and his miraculous transmission to his own estate in Brittany.

THE MIRACLE OF TYPASUS

Evening was setting in over the ancient city of Carthage, and bringing to its close a day of great and solemn rejoicing; bells had been ringing the whole day long, solemn processions had passed up and down the city, and on men's faces there was the impress of a joy too deep for utterance,— such joy as is known only to those who have endured the extremity of suffering. For the church of Carthage had received as her bishop this day the saintly Eugenius, after four-and-twenty years of widowhood and desolation; and all those earnest faces which crowd that ancient Basilica have known what it was to have been left orphans, without a head, to face alone the fury of a persecution almost unrivalled even in those ages of blood. Enter into the church, and you will feel that the mere surface of humanity has been swept away; the men and women and children even who surround you have tested the realities of life; and the future has nothing terrible for those who have borne themselves so manfully through the past. There is a calmness and grandeur about some amongst them which at once attracts your attention,—they seem, by common consent, honoured above the rest; if you look more attentively, you will see the insignia of their rank. Some maimed limb, some terrific gash or scar, bears witness that they have resisted unto blood for the faith of Christ; and thus the rage of the persecutor, while it has disfigured their earthly bodies, has placed upon their brows an aureole of glory even in this lower life. Listen: the heart of that mighty multitude goes up as the voice of one man in thanksgiving to God. That solemn ancient chant, it bowed the heart of the great Augustine, and made him weep, when but a few years before he heard it in that very church: what would he have felt had he heard it as it burst from the lips of those noble confessors and future martyrs of Christ! They thought not of themselves or their own sufferings; not one thought of self-gratulation marred the perfection of their self-abandonment; they thought but of the wrongs of Jesus; their hearts were bursting at the remembrance of the insults which for more than fifty years had been heaped upon Him before their very eyes; they were making an act of reparation, they were making atonement, they were thanking God for those mysteries of faith, that Christ was God, that God had died in human form for man. Far away over the blue Mediterranean the fisherman caught the sound, and stood up in his little boat, which looked all golden in the setting sun, and joined his heart to theirs. Far away the soft breeze bore it to the villages scattered amidst the Mauritanian mountains, sleeping in such a flood of light and spiritual beauty as is only to be seen beneath the sunsets of the south. And far, far above them all, and beyond them all, the watching angels caught the sound, and bore it before the throne of God. In its eager impetuosity of love it tried to make amends to the Sacred Heart of Jesus for more than half a century of blasphemy. Oh, who can doubt that it attained its end!

And now the newly-consecrated bishop stood upon the high-altar steps, his priests and attendants ranged in semi-circles on either side. He was a man of tall stature and commanding countenance; but that peculiar expression which rendered it so different from others cannot be described, and is best understood when we remember that even in life he was reckoned among the number of the saints. As he stood there, addressing for the first time the flock which had been committed to his care, the first impression his calm clear voice made on the hearts of all was one of recollection, humility, and peace. The dove, wherein reposed the adorable body of the Lord, brooded above his head, and his words seemed rather the echo of the breathings of the dove than any thought or speech of earth. Few would have recognised in the calm subdued tones of that voice the expression of the ardent passionate spirit, who, like another St. Paul, would have wished himself anathema, rather than behold one of his children fall away from the faith; whose daily prayer was that he might die for Christ; whose nightly dream was that the crown of martyrdom was within his grasp. And while the saintly bishop goes back into the past, with his whole soul filled with thoughts of those among whom he had to labour, we too must look back and explain in brief words the circumstances which were the forerunners of the facts we are about to record.

The Roman provinces in Africa brought under the empire of the faith were at the very height of peace and prosperity. The voice of the great Augustine, that column of the Church, against which the fretful waves of false doctrine broke themselves in vain, was scarcely hushed in death; the Church of Carthage seemed to sit enthroned like a queen, by the shores of that sweet southern sea whose waters brought to her feet the learning, wealth, and respectful salutations of the rest of Christendom; on a sudden, men were roused from this deep sleep of security by a storm which overwhelmed them ere they were well aware of its approach. In the year 428, Genseric, the king of the Vandals and Alans, burst upon these fertile provinces with his huge barbarian armies, and in an incredibly short space of time the whole country was laid waste. These Vandals were, for the greater part, Arians, and joined the sacrilegious malice so peculiar to heretics to their native barbarity. We have neither power nor heart to describe what the Christians of those times were forced to look upon: the adorable body and blood of the Lord spilt and scattered on the pavements; the altar-linen made into shirts and under-garments by the blasphemers; bishops burnt alive; the virgins of Christ scourged, tortured, insulted; and the Catholics of noblest descent disqualified from holding any office, and condemned to keep cattle. Genserie died, and was succeeded by his son, Huneric, under whom the persecution went on more hotly than before. At last, at the earnest intercession of the Emperor Zeno, Huneric permitted the Church of Carthage to elect a bishop, after the see had been vacant twenty-one years. There had been small time for ceremony or preparation; the shepherdless flock, eager to enjoy the comfort of a pastor, with common consent pitched upon Eugenius, who had grown up amongst them from childhood in the odour of sanctity; and he, well knowing what he was doing, accepted the solemn call, knowing that the spousal ring with which he espoused the Church of Carthage was one of certain suffering, and almost certain death; knowing that the present lull in the storm would be of short duration, and that as soon as Huneric's policy would allow him to follow his fierce inclinations, he would be the first victim of his rage. Perhaps even his unshrinking heart would have quailed, if he could have seen in that moment the real life that lay before him; the long lingering martyrdom, harder far than death; the agony of betrayal and apostasy amongst some he trusted most. But we will not anticipate; but listen as he stands now, with the full glow of the setting sun upon his brow, and his piercing eye searching the very hearts of those whom he addressed. "Therefore, well-beloved children and brethren in Christ, bear ye the trial patiently, and wait for the end. Go on in the way of loftiness with the foot of lowliness, fearing only sin, which will easily make an apostate of a confessor. For how shall they be strong to confess the faith of the divinity of Christ, who dare to defile the members which are His? or how can they follow the meek Lamb in lowliness, whom any thought of pride uplifteth? Chastity, therefore, being the splendour of charity, and martyrdom the particular crown of both, humility is their safest guardian. Where these gifts abound, I have no fear that the weakest amongst you will fall away beneath any temptation: yea, even the tender and delicate woman shall be strong, and offer up her child to death, gazing on the Mother of God beneath the Cross."

The sun sank into the sea, and sudden twilight fell upon that mighty crowd; the mystic dove glittered in the lamps which burnt around the relics of the martyrs. Something in the solemnity of that moment thrilled upon the chord so closely buried in the heart of Eugenius. He burst forth: "O angels of my God, intercede for us! O glorious patriarchs and prophets, plead for us! O blessed Peter, keep not silence now! O great and most beloved Father Augustine, more great and beloved now than when on earth, from the secure haven unto which thou hast attained, look down on us, thy desolate flock, tossed and driven on these stormy seas!

"And you, O children of saints! O brethren of martyrs! remember ye belong to Christ, who suffers in your torments, and prepares for you an immortal crown. Soon shall the Red Sea of martyrdom be passed; soon shall the maimed and tortured body rest in peace; soon shall the everlasting nuptials of the Lamb be celebrated, and He will lead the choice ones of His flock into those heavenly pastures, whereof, methinks, the very grass are joys. Therefore go on with steadfast foot, praying for yourselves and for our unworthiness that we may attain this crown." Then raising his hand, he blessed them in the name of the thrice Holy Trinity; and men left the "house and the dove" in peace.

We will conduct our readers over some space of time, in which the pledge Eugenius gave that day was well redeemed, and leaving Carthage, travel westward to the ancient city of Typasus. The little Arab village of Ifessed now occupies its site; and the ruins which attract the admiration of the traveller of the present day sufficiently prove its grandeur in the days of its Roman occupation. But at the time of which we are speaking, the graceful columns which surround the forum had escaped unscathed from the hand of the barbarian; and the arches which spanned the broad "Via Scipiano," which led to it from the city gates, still told the tale of earthly triumphs which had been celebrated there. That way was soon to become a "Via Crucis," and the power before which the mistress of the world had sunk into the dust was to be laughed to scorn upon that spot. But now through the deserted streets of that old city two men are passing quickly: one a venerable old man in the dress of an ecclesiastic; the other clearly showing by his fair complexion, keen blue eyes, and short, firm-set stature, that he was one of the warlike children of the north. As they passed by house after house, whose open portal and unkindled hearth showed that it was forsaken, a party of men brushed rudely past them, the foremost of whom was speaking in a loud voice of the measures soon to be taken with that "dog of an intruder, Eugenius." The hot blood of the northman mounted to his cheek in a moment, and, clenching his teeth, he drew the short sword which depended from his belt, muttering, "The wretch! the blasphemer! never shall he take that venerable name within his lips again while I—" "My son," said the old priest, laying his trembling hand upon his lips, "well may it be seen that you are but a catechumen in the school of Christ, when words like these spring to your lips so readily. For the sake of your saintly Master, hold your peace until we reach the open shore; there shall we be in safety from the unfriendly ears which now may overhear our speech." Theobald bit his lips till the blood came; but his hand traced, the sign of the cross, and the fury which his Scandinavian ancestors deemed perfectly uncontrollable yielded to its might. They passed on in silence along the broad-way, across the forum, until they gained the sea-shore. Calm and wonderfully beautiful was the scene they gazed upon: the long level sands, where the waves rippled up to the very line they had worn when the ships of old Rome bore Scipio to the conquest of this new world. To the east lay the mausoleum of the royal family of Massinissa, now vulgarly called "the tomb of the Christian." Above the resting-place of the dead, one fair solitary palm-tree stood out against the deep blue sky, bringing remembrance of her of whom the Church sings, that amidst the desert and the tombs of earth she was exalted as a palm-tree in Cades. The quiet of the time and place seemed to still the stormy spirit of the northman; but when the priest turned to him, as though to ask his thoughts, he burst forth, "Men live amid these scenes of blood till they learn indifference. Your people are driven into exile, and you walk calmly through their desolate homes; you near those savage threats against Eugenius the holy, the wise, the good, and it scarcely stirs your blood." The old man gazed out upon the waste of waters, as though other scenes than those he looked on were before his mind's eye. He paused long before he spoke, and then seemed rather thinking aloud than answering his companion: "Four little months ago yon sea was alive with boats, bearing their living cargoes to the ships which lay in the offing. All along this line of sand there were groups of people in tears; there were partings between those who shall meet no more on earth. Son was torn from mother, friend from friend, priest from people. As each little boat bore the exiles from the shore, they stood up and stretched out their arms towards Typasus, and mournfully waved their adieus to those they had left to die within its walls. One old man was amongst them, whose spirit was worn out by the long harassing struggle with the Arian intruders. His flesh quivered and shrank with inexpressible horror at the thought of torture and insult and violent death. He looked to the distant shores of Spain as a land at least of rest and a quiet grave. He was one of the last to embark, and as he looked back sorrowfully to the land he was leaving, a form seemed to float upon the edge of the blue waters, and that face of unspeakable sorrow gazed reproachfully upon him, and a voice breathed into his inmost soul, 'Can it be that thou fearest to stay and feed those few sheep in the desert?' He hesitated not a moment: he leaped from the boat into the water, he rejoined the forsaken band of those who, from infirmity or poverty, could not embark,—the little knot of noble confessors, who, from their longing for martyrdom, would not embark. Love rekindled the failing torch of faith. He went with joy and singing in his heart to console his children,—to suffer and to die with them. My son, call not the old man *indifferent* because his God has given him the gift of patience." Theobald fell on his knees and pressed the old man's hand to his lips, he would have poured out his repentance for his unjust and hasty words, but the priest checked him, saying, "Enough, my son; I know all you would say. Now may you deliver to me in all safety the bidding of our holy bishop; but first will it please you to declare, in brief words, all that has passed at Carthage since the last burst of this fierce storm. Small communication hath there been between the churches since it broke forth, and the last messenger Eugenius despatched to us was taken and slaughtered on his way."

"My Father," replied Theobald, "it is but little I can tell of the first outbreak, for I was not in Carthage; I only joined Huneric with the last troops which came from Spain; but I found Eugenius' name on the lips of all, as one whose sanctity and wonderful gifts made him master of all hearts, and excited against him Huneric's especial rage. I heard the first order Huneric sent him was to shut the church against the Vandals, who were beginning to embrace the faith in numbers. Eugenius' reply was, 'Tell Huneric that the door which the King of kings hath opened, none may dare to shut.' Huneric burst out with a torrent of curses, and the next day witnessed a scene that it passeth my poor wit to describe. Guards were placed at the doors of the churches; and when any one passed in clothed in the habit of a Vandal, they struck them on the head with a short, rough, jagged staff, and twisting it into the hair, violently dragged off both hair and skin together. The agony was so intense that many died, and many lost their eye-sight; but not one would give up their faith." Theobald covered his eyes, as though to shut out the horror of the remembrance. The priest asked him in a calm voice, "And the women,—did they stand firm?" "Most steadfast," answered Theobald; "it was the sight of the strength made perfect in their weakness that first drew me, a wandering sheep, into the fold. I saw one, Dionysia, a matron of noble birth and most delicate nurture, scourged till she sank fainting in her own blood. During the torment, I saw her gaze fastened on her young son, Majoricus, who stood weeping beside her, with a devoted tenderness such as in our colder lands I never witnessed. All the mother's heart was in that gaze. When they had wreaked their will on her, they turned to the son. His cheeks grew pale at the horrid preparations, and at the first touch of the torturer's hand he uttered a shriek of horror. That shriek roused the mother from her death-like swoon; she started to her feet, and in a voice which thrilled through the whole place, she said, 'Remember, O my son, we were baptised in the name of the Holy Trinity, and the bosom of our Mother the Church.' Then, with most lofty words, she went on encouraging him, as he endured the torment with heroic courage and when he could no longer stand, his burning head was laid upon her lap; and while the flesh to which she gave birth was quivering in agony before her, she perpetually traced upon it the healing sign of the cross, until she received the last sigh of the victorious martyr. That scene, that martyrdom, that mother, purchased for me the gift of faith; and not for me only,—four of us, ere that night closed in, knelt at the feet of Eugenius to ask for admittance to the Catholic Church." "O noble confessor of Christ!" exclaimed the priest softly, "thou like Abraham hast sacrificed thy only son, and thou hast become the spiritual mother of many children in Christ. And the end, my son?" "She so longed to possess the precious remains of her child, that several of us went in the night to the place of execution, and succeeded in bringing them to her. She buried them in her own house, that, as she said, she might day by day offer to the Holy Trinity her prayers over his grave, in the lively hope of a glorious resurrection with him. And there the childless solitary mother offers the daily sacrifice of her life." "And the clergy?" asked the priest— "are any spared?" "Scarce any are left in Carthage," replied Theobald. "Eugenius does everything, and is everywhere; he moves like an angel of consolation through the miseries of the times; and the love of his children for him is strong as death. The moon is not new since nearly 5000 bishops and priests, and noble Catholic laymen of Carthage, were banished by the tyrant's order to the deserts. There they were to be left the prey of scorpions and venomous serpents, to be fed with barley, like beasts. Numbers of the people followed their bishops and priests to the very borders of the desert, as though in triumphal procession, with tapers in their hands. Eugenius stood forth, an envoy between the living and the dead, and said they must now return, for their time was not yet come. Then the air was rent, not with the cries of those who were descending into this living grave, but of those who were returning to life. Mothers cast their babes at the feet of the confessors, and exclaimed, 'O confessors of Christ, ye pass on swiftly to your crowns, but to whom do you leave your desolate flock? Who will baptise our children? Who will bury us with solemn supplication after death? By whom shall the Divine Sacrifice be offered up amongst us?' Then Eugenius raised his voice, and stilled that mighty cry. He told them a beacon should be kindled that day amid the dreary sands of the desert, which should lighten the Christian world; that if their voices were hushed in death, God would raise the dead, or make the dumb to speak, rather than allow His truth to be without a witness. Then prostrating at the feet of the principal bishop amongst them, he kissed them, and asked his benediction, and all the people prostrating to receive it. Eugenius led them back to Carthage, with solemn hymns of thanksgiving for those who were counted worthy to suffer for the name of Christ. Tidings have since been brought us, that not one of those terrible serpents have dared to approach the confessors."

"Yea, the desert shall blossom as a rose," said the priest, fervently. "How sweet is the perfume it is now sending up in the sight of the company of heaven! But, my son, the hour is waxing late, and I may not tarry longer from my post at this moment; I would fain hear the message of the blessed Father Eugenius ere we part for the night."

"They are evil tidings," said Theobald, after a pause. "I would I had not been their bearer. Father Eugenius bids me say that secret intelligence has reached him that the fury of Huneric is especially directed against Typasus at this moment. The Arian bishop has informed him of your steadfast opposition to his intrusion—of your courageous celebration of the Tremendous Mysteries—of the unshaken constancy of your band of confessors. Huneric is mad with fury at the fruitlessness of his efforts; and Eugenius says that even now his fierce bands are preparing to do their worst. What that worst may be no one knows; but the bishop sends you health and benediction in the Lord; and not doubting of your crown, he bids you remember him when you shall have entered into rest."

A slight paleness overspread the countenance of the old priest as these words reached his ear; but it passed in a moment, and raising his eyes he exclaimed, "O my dear and well-beloved Master, for fourscore years and more Thou hast done good things unto me, and now thou dost suffer me to give Thee all that remains of this miserable life. Blessed be Thy Holy Name." Then turning to the youth he said, "Blessed be thou of the Lord, my son, for the good tidings thou hast brought me this day. Return to Eugenius by the way of the sea, that thou mayest escape the hands of the barbarians; and tell him, by the grace of God, we will redeem his word, that the beacon which has been kindled in the desert waste shall be caught and answered on the towers of Typasus; and men shall know and own that He is God who giveth victory to the weak and contemptible things of this world. And now depart quickly, my son," he said, laying both hands on the head of the youth, who knelt in speechless emotion to receive his parting blessing. "It seemeth to me that the sun will soon rise, which shall not set until thou hast given thy best heart's blood for thy Lord. But the time is not yet; therefore depart in peace, and do my bidding with the holy bishop. Farewell."

Day dawned over the fair city of Typasus, but found it not as the sun had set upon it. In the dead of the night the furious tramp of the wild undisciplined troops of Vandal barbarians announced to the devoted band that the hour of their trial had arrived. It found them prepared and watching. It had been agreed that three strokes of the bell should assemble them all in the house where they were wont to celebrate the Divine Mysteries; and the old priest and the subdeacon Reparatus kept watch. The solemn signal sounded about the hour of midnight, and they had scarcely collected all that remained of the inhabitants of Typasus ere the armed barbarians poured in at the city gates, and in a moment seemed to fill the streets and the air with their cries and blasphemous imprecations; hundreds came, and thousands followed, to sieze this helpless band of Christian heroes. It seemed as though Huneric hoped by the mere multiplication of animal strength to subdue that spiritual energy and force which had so often proved too much for him. They soon discovered the little assembly of Catholics, and drove them mercilessly before them to the forum outside the gates. "Even so He passed beyond the gate of

Jerusalem," said the solemn voice of the priest, as urged by the pitiless goading of the swords, their ears stunned with the blasphemies and insults shouted around them, some of the weaker sort stumbled and fell. As soon as they reached the forum they were fastened all together in the midst with thick ropes; a strong band of horsemen was left to guard the place till morning dawned, and the rest of the Vandals dispersed throughout the city to spend what remained of the night in revelry and feasting. Meantime the confessors received the last words of reconciliation and blessing from their pastors; they strengthened one another for the fiery trial which awaited them; they gave each other the kiss of peace, and sang their "Nunc dimittis" with joy. As the sun rose gloriously out of the sea, they saluted it with a hymn of triumph, as the dawning of that happy day which should see them suffer for Christ. About the hour of Prime the forum was surrounded with their eager persecutors; and it was with great difficulty that the chief of the band secured silence for a moment with a flourish of the wild unmusical horns they were accustomed to use in battle. Then riding slowly into the arena, he shouted, "Citizens, the children of the north deal not in many words. One change, and one only, of life and liberty and honour lies before you. Submit to the bishop whom Huneric by rightful authority has placed over you; deliver up the fellow who has dared to act as your priest; consent only to be baptised amongst us, and you shall be received like brothers, and Huneric will show he knows how to treat his friends. This, of his mercy and great clemency, he offers once; he *never* offers mercy twice." There was not a moment's pause—clear and strong went up the voice of that united band, "We were baptised in the faith of the Catholic Church, and in her bosom we will die. For Christ is very God, and the virgin Mother of God stood beneath the cross of her Son." There rose a sound from the surrounding soldiery like the growl of a wild beast; scarcely could their commanders hold them back from darting on their prey, and tearing them to pieces. "Dogs!" shouted the chief through the tumult, "hear, then, the too-merciful decree of Huneric. Your blasphemous tongues shall be torn out by the roots, and your right hands cut off, and dogs shall devour them before your eyes." More he would have said, but the roar of the angry multitude drowned his words. Every semblance of order vanished.

A troop of ruffians appointed for the purpose rushed into the place. They seized them as they stood, and, without any preparation, began the work of butchery. The old priest was the first victim. He was violently seized by the hair and hurled to the ground; and as he meekly stretched out his right hand to the gleaming axe of the barbarian, he murmured, "Holy Father, grant me only in that day to say, Of those whom Thou hast given me I have lost not one." The Vandal then knelt upon his breast, and spitting in his face, pulled the tongue out by the roots with such terrific force, that it is marvellous life remained. And so it went on. The subdeacon Reparatus was the next, uttering his confession of faith while the torturer's hand was in his mouth, till all those noble confessors lay prostrate in a Red Sea of blood; their mutilated members lying all around them, sometimes cast to the dogs by their savage foes. And now even *they* seemed satiated. Human nature seemed laid as low as human hands could thrust it. Speechless, bleeding, mutilated, what more could those well-nigh lifeless bodies do? what more could be feared from them?—so at least their persecutors thought; and preparing to leave them to their fate, the foremost, giving a contemptuous kick to the prostrate form of Reparatus the subdeacon, exclaimed, "Ha, blasphemer! thou art silenced once and for ever now: why stand ye not up and preach as of old, of a God dying on a cross, and a woman, the mother of a God? Choice witnesses are ye truly, lying there speechless, of the divinity of your Christ!" Reparatus knelt up: soft, low, and clear arose the words from his lips, "I believe;" and then a chorus of voices joined in from that prostrate band, finishing the sentence, "The Christ is very God of very God; and Mary the Mother of God stood beneath the cross of her Son." Then as the mighty marvel flashed upon their minds, a cry, strong, thrilling, but most musical, burst from their lips, "Alleluia, alleluia to the Lamb who sitteth on the throne; He hath done all things well; He maketh both the deaf to hear and the dumb to speak." Earth and heaven and hell stood attentive as that wondrous song went up. Huneric's fierce barbarians fled in wonder and amaze; and hour after hour the confessors knelt on the spot of their torture, giving God thanks for the miraculous gift He had vouchsafed that day. Their sound went forth into all lands. Constantinople, and the Isles of the Sea, and the fair fields of France, were blessed by the presence of these wondrous witnesses of the truth; and ever as the "Credo" came from their lips, it carried conviction to the hearts of all who heard them, of the might of God's power, and the strength of His Church.

Years passed on: the career of Eugenius was still bright with saintly deeds and unfailing perseverance. In long exile, in imprisonment, under every kind of contumely, with his head laid upon the block and the axe gleaming over him, he was still the same,—the unshrinking confessor of that precious faith, dearer to him than life. Still it seemed as though the yearning longing of his soul might not be gratified; he was to live and suffer, not to die. A winter night had set in drearily; the holy bishop sat alone in a rough, rude hut, which scarcely offered any resistance to the piercing blast which swept through it from the mountains. The wide desert country of Tripolis lay round him. He was a prisoner in the hands of Anthony, an Arian bishop, who made his exile one unvarying round of sufferings, to which his eager love of the Cross continually added more. He was writing by the dim lamp, when suddenly a mysterious awe and terror fell upon him, for which he could not account "The Evil One is busy," he muttered to himself; and leaving his writing, he betook himself to prayer. It was no wonder that the pastor should suffer and fear exceedingly, for that night two stars had fallen from heaven. The next night the door of the hut was softly opened, and Reparatus the subdeacon knelt before him. He spoke no word, and the strong man's face was wet with tears. "Speak, my son," said the bishop; "is Eugenius so little used to suffer, that thou fearest to toll thy tidings?" Reparatus lifted up his face, and spoke in the low tone of one whose heart is torn by every word he utters: "The lamps of the sanctuary are defiled, and their light is gone out in utter darkness. The two confessors whom you wot of at Tripolis have fallen into deadly sin, and they are speechless. In their misery they have fled away into the desert, and we have come to ask counsel of your holiness." The bishop clasped both his hands over his face, and bowed it on the table before him; and when he raised it, the trace of agony left upon it was deeper than that left by years of exile and suffering. He rose and gathered his mantle round him, as though he would have started instantly to seek the lost sheep; and then the remembrance of his imprisonment came upon him, and he sat down again and wept. At last, recovering his calmness, he said, "Let prayer be made for them throughout all the Churches, that the mercy of God may bring them to repentance: and do you, my son, bid those of our brethren who remain steadfast take heed lest they fall. Let them count that forgiven them from which they have been preserved through grace; and for that in which they have not been tried, let them walk heedfully, and be instant in prayer."

Eugenius died at last in exile, full of good works, and in a monastery which he himself had founded. Perhaps, as he looked back upon all the varied sufferings of his long and agitated life, the agony of that night was the only one which seemed worth remembering. But the tears which the saints of God weep for the sins of others shall all be wiped away in the morning of the resurrection.[*]

* The truth of the miracle recorded above is as well ascertained as any fact in history. It has recently been critically examined, and the proofs thrown together, by Victor de Buch, of the Society of Jesus. The facts of the Vandal persecution in Africa are too well known to require any authentication here.

THE
DEMON-PREACHER

There was in a town of Italy in the early part of the 14th century a convent of Franciscan monks, who followed the rule of their holy founder in its utmost strictness. The spirit of Francis seemed to be alive again among his children, so rigidly did they adhere to the constitutions he had left them, and specially to the religious poverty which he had loved and chosen as his bride. Never had they departed from that law which sent them daily from house to house, begging the alms of the faithful as their only support. You might meet them every day, treading barefoot through the dirty streets in their poor rough habits, carrying a coarse bag on their backs to receive the scraps of food which some would give, who were too poor to offer more; or driving the convent ass before them, laden with the wood-chips they had gathered together. Pictures they were of that meek, patient, suffering spirit which is the heritage of their order; and yet, for all their lowliness and poverty, they carried about with them a certain air of spirituality that made you feel disposed to uncover as they passed, for they bore back your imagination to Judea and the streets of Jerusalem, and filled you with the thoughts of One who was the first to stamp the mark of holiness upon the abjection they imitated so well. Now, at the time of which we speak, the inhabitants had lost something of that fervent charity and devotion that had made them at first so ready with their alms when the friar's little box was offered at their door. They were growing rich, and their hearts were narrowing; and often the poor Franciscans were driven away with curses and abuse, and many a hard word was levelled against the "idle mendicant." Still they lived, hardly enough, yet contentedly; contempt and ill-treatment were like a sweet savour to their scanty food; and they never thought of complaining at what seemed as much a part of their state as the habit that they wore.

Now this resignation and lowliness of spirit were very displeasing to the great enemy of souls, who eyed these poor despised friars of Lucca as the greatest adversaries he possessed in the town. He determined, therefore, on making a powerful effort to shake their constancy and endurance; and in order to effect this, to shut the hearts of the citizens yet more against them, by temptation of avarice and selfishness, which he knew well enough were the likeliest to prevail, and could scarcely fail of success. His designs answered as he expected: the people of the town became gradually more and more hardened against the friars; and the very appearance of one of them in the street was a signal for every door to be closed. At length the alms, which were their only resource, entirely failed, and the distress of the brethren became excessive. There was one of the citizens named Louis, the richest man in the town, who had lately married a young and virtuous wife, and to his door the Father-Guardian directed the last appeal for assistance to be made for Octavia (such was the name of the merchant's wife,) was known to entertain friendly and charitable feelings for the order, and had never yet allowed the friars to go away without giving them some trifle for the love of God.

It was late in the day when the poor brother whose charge it was to beg for alms knocked at the door of Louis's house. He had been on foot for many hours, and his bag was still empty; and he felt weary and discouraged. It was a timid knock that he gave; and perhaps the faintness of its echo told the master of the house what kind of visitor was standing at his gate; for when the door opened, and the good friar raised his eyes from the ground, half in hopes to meet the kind looks of Octavia, he saw that the merchant Louis himself stood before him, and in no gentle mood, to judge from his knit brow, and the quick rough movement of his hand.

"What brings you here, friar?" he said, with a contemptuous sneer; "back to your convent and pray, as is your trade; or if that suits not your holinesses, why, work like honest men; we will have no vagrants here."

"May it please you, good sir," replied the trembling friar, "I thought to see the Lady Octavia. It has pleased our Lord to try us during this last week as seems good to Him, and none of us have broken fast this day; but you will scarce refuse to help us for His love;" and he held out his little box with a hesitating and pitiful glance.

"The Lady Octavia forsooth!" returned the other; "let her look well to it ere she have aught to say to you. Begone, I say; for I make not my money in order to throw it after all the beggars that may choose to hang about my gate. Begone, and fast if you will; you are ever ready to tell us it is profitable to our souls." He turned, and would have shut the door; but the friar made another attempt to speak.

"Good sir," he said, "I beseech you to be patient; we have verily toiled all the day, and have taken nothing; send me not away empty, and God will reward you for your charity, even as though you did it to Himself. The Lady Octavia hath ofttimes bidden us ask freely when we were in need;" but his words were interrupted by the heavy blow of a stick.

"Say that name again, and I will send you home with broken bones to fill your bag," was the angry reply. "Here, good neighbours, help me to drive this fellow to his hole again;"

and at his words the bystanders, who had gathered together at the sound of the altercation, pressed closer round the
person of the friar, and began to hoot and clamour after him
as he moved away, whilst some, bolder than the rest, threw
mud and stones upon him, bidding him carry them back
to the convent to fill his bag. And as he passed along, the
crowd grew every moment more numerous and angry, till,
when they came to the convent-gates, it was a hard matter
for the poor friar to effect his entrance, without receiving
serious injury from some of those who pressed about him.

That evening the friars went indeed to their refectory, but
it was not to eat. They sat, with heavy hearts and downcast
eyes, whilst one of them read aloud, as was their custom;
and the tables were covered as usual, but there was not a
morsel of bread. And the next day things were worse, for
the riot of the previous evening had roused the attention
of the governor of the town; and he came to the convent,
and tried, partly with threats and partly with persuasions,
to induce the brethren to abandon a place where they had
become the object of popular dislike, and where their presence only disturbed the public quiet. The courage of many
of the friars was fast failing them; they made a fair show to
the governor, but as soon as his back was turned, the general
feeling of discontent and despondency began to manifest
itself.

"We had done better to have accepted lands like other
of our communities," said one. "Our Father Francis meant
not that his children should perish for their keeping of the
dead letter."

"It were well to sell the silver vessels," said another; "perchance this trouble comes on us for over-richness in our
church furniture: if we be sons of poverty, wooden vessels
will serve our turn, and befit us best." The Father-Guardian
heard it all, and knew not how to answer.

"Know you not, my children," he said at length, "that we
may neither retain lands, nor sell any goods for our own

maintenance, without breaking those twenty-five precepts which our Father left on us, and which bind us under mortal sin? Fear not for the future; for God Himself has surely promised His help to them that keep the same; and His promises are not void." But though he spoke thus, the brothers could hear in the tremour of his voice that his heart was not wholly with his words; his confidence was faltering with the rest; and the triumph of the devil seemed as though it were soon to be complete.

And he knew it. He was there in the midst of those fearful failing hearts, terrifying them and tempting them,—filling them with a strange unaccountable dread, by the unseen influence of his presence. And as they yielded to the cowardly suggestions he was whispering in their ear, he was every moment gaining more and more power over their hearts. He was then watching them with an infernal joy; but the joy was very short: it was broken by a light that glanced across his vision; and a voice sounded in his ears, whose echoes were well known to him, and filled him with the old anguish, and reminded him of his conquest and defeat. It was the voice of Michael. "Fallen Star of the Morning," said those angelic tones, "wherefore art thou here? I come to drive thee hence, and once more to humble thy pride."

"Thou mayest do thy will," returned the malignant spirit; "but I, too, have had mine: there is not one of all these friars but has done me good service this day, for they have doubted God's word and mistrusted His promise. I am well content to go, and leave them thus.

"But not thus shalt thou leave them, O perverse and evil serpent," returned the archangel: "if thou hast done thy work, thou shalt also undo it; thine own lips shall recall these poor children who have erred through weakness, and shall bring Louis also to a better mind, and shall restore charity to the hearts of the citizens; yea, so that of their own will they shall build another convent within these city walls, where God shall be served and praised, and the rule of Francis, which thou so hatest, shall be strictly kept. This is the decree of the Most High, who changeth not."

The demon gnashed his teeth. "I am no preacher," he cried; "and I fight not against mine own house,— least of all will I do work for that Francis of whom you speak, for he was ever my deadliest enemy."

"Therefore is it given thee as a punishment for thy malice to do even as he would do were he again on earth," replied Michael; "and thou must obey. Thou shalt take the form of one of his friars, and shalt enter the house; and good words shall flow from thy lips against thy will; and thou shalt recall the friars to trust and confidence, and shalt reproach them for the shameful yielding of their hearts; and shalt strengthen them with holy speech and words of comfort. Moreover, thou shalt thyself procure them the means which they lack, so that their sufferings shall cease, and they shall have wherewith to feed the poor at their gates as of yore; and so shalt thou learn well what it is to fight against God and His saints."

There was a knock at the convent-gate, and the porter opened it timidly, for he scarcely knew what to expect. A monk, dressed in the rough habit of the order, stood without; but it was not one of the community, and the good friar did not recollect ever to have seen him before. A singular majesty of bearing might be discerned even through that poor despised garb of poverty,—something too much of the air of command, as some might have thought; but yet the grandeur and nobleness of his aspect, and the bright flash of his eye, gleaming beneath the thick hood covering his face, seemed to compel respect. "I would speak with the Father-Guardian, he said; and the tone of his voice was signally musical. The porter bowed in silent wonder, and led him to the presence of the assembled religious, who were in the act of making their final preparations for removal.

"Deo gratias, my brethren," was his salutation; and the sound of his voice startled them strangely.

"Mother of God!" exclaimed the astonished guardian, "who are you, brother, and whence do you come?"

"I come from very far, and I was led here by the hand of God," replied the stranger; "so very far away was I when it was laid on me to come hither, that doubtless were I to name it, you would not know it; for it is a country little spoken of, and the sun itself shines not on it as on yours."

"And your name, good brother; you are of our order?"

"I am called Obedientus Obligatus; and I wear your habit, as you see. In old days, before I put it on, they called me Cherubino."

"Well, good brother," replied the guardian, "you are surely welcome. I would we had aught to offer you; but the times go hard with us, and you have chosen an untoward moment for your visit. The men of this city have risen up against us, and will do nothing for our support; and we are even now preparing to go forth and seek new shelter; for we fear lest if we tarry here, we perish for very want."

The tall form of the strange friar assumed an air of yet greater majesty as he heard these words; he pushed back the cowl, and displayed a countenance which struck awe into all who beheld it. The shaven crown was encircled by a single ring of coal-black hair; the brow was lofty; and the eyes, deep-sunk in their recesses, sent forth a gleam of fire, as he gazed on the guardian with a look that seemed to penetrate into his heart. His face, too, was pale, and had that look of suffering which might be worn by one who ever bore about him some secret pain; and as he spoke, his lips assumed for a moment a curl almost of contempt.

"O faithless and perverse generation!" he said at length, "are these the soldiers of their Lord, the sons of him who wore the wounds of the crucified, the children of the saints, and the followers of martyrs? Two days of want have come upon you, and where is your confidence? You trusted and prayed when God gave you abundance, and were ready with pious speeches and brave words when the alms-boxes came home full; and now, after two days of trial, your faith and courage have all fled away, and you are ready to believe that God's word, which He promised to your fathers, is about to fail! Therefore do you err grievously, inasmuch as you do wrong to the truth and fidelity of the Most High."

And as he spoke, an expression of new pain shot across his face.

"Saw you that?" whispered one of the younger brothers to his nearest neighbour; "he is surely a saintly soul, whom it grieveth even to speak of sin; but he is about to speak again. I wot well the secrets of our souls are manifest to him."

"Yea, they are manifest," said brother Obligatus, turning the lustre of his sparkling eyes full on the last speaker. "And thou who so lately didst give thy vows to God, standest now before Him half resolved to break thy faith, and dally with the gifts and lands of worldlings, lest perchance thou shouldst suffer too hard an abstinence for thy delicate frame. O fools and slow of heart, did ye not know that sooner than one word of His should fail, the angels themselves would bring you food? nay, the very demons would be forced to serve you, and minister to your needs."

"My Father," said the guardian, with a low reverence, "you are all unknown to us, yet we see well that you speak by the Spirit of God. We cannot resist or gainsay your words, for they have a strange power with them; and, for my part, I feel that, come what may, I will now die a thousand deaths ere I abandon this house, or infringe one letter of the rule of Francis."

"Nor I, nor I!" burst from the lips of the brothers. "You have conquered, Father, and are to us even as an angel of God; do with us as you will, for we know verity that He speaks by your mouth."

What a moment for the tempter! for it was even he; he saw how the momentary weakness of the poor friars had but been the occasion of their gaining a new title to the favour of heaven, by their quick penitence at the first word of exhortation. Gladly would he have retired from a scene that only tortured him; but brother Obligatus had no will of his own; there was a stronger power than his compelling him to say words which were not his, and which were an agony for him to utter. So covering his face for a moment with his hand (the brethren thought it was to hide the emotion which their words produced), he continued:

"My brethren, God has been angry; but He will be appeased by your prayers and humiliation. As to me, the task is mine now to provide in His name for all your wants."

"Good Father," said the guardian, "if you purpose seeking alms, know that there is none to give them in this town."

"Fear nothing," replied Father Obligatus; "but get you to the choir, and cause the gates to be opened, for I will not return empty-handed."

And now the unwilling preacher found himself compelled to go through street after street, stilling up the cold hearts of all he met by his wonderful eloquence. Men gathered after him, and hung upon his words; they felt that nothing could resist the force and magic of his appeals for charity, and all for the love of God. The love of God! words which came forth with so sad and sweet a music from his lips, while his very heart was torn with their utterance. And oh, as he felt forced on to speak to them of the vanity of riches, and the danger of that covetousness which takes the heart from God, and binds it like a galley-slave to Satan,— and of the pride and self-love that likens them to devils, and defaces in them the image of the Most High, what a bitter humbling thing it was! and how he writhed and struggled against the hand that forced him on, whilst men thought it all but the energy of one who laboured for fit words in which to utter his idea, and the zeal for the salvation of souls which so kindled the words of the impassioned speaker! The alms poured in from all sides, and he was forced to take it, and to carry the heavy bag on his own shoulders, into which every hand was now eager to put something, and so bring his load back to the monastery.

This went on day after day; the fame of the wonderful preacher extended even beyond the walls of the city, and stranger's crowded to see him from all parts; and when they had once heard him, they felt a new spirit revive in their hearts; it was a wonderful change. And what was worst of all was to have to wear that meek, lowly look of the poor Capuchin, and to rattle his little box, and cry, "Charity, my master, charity, for the dear love of God!" and as they dropped their coins into it, to bow low, and promise prayers for his good benefactors, and to ask God to bless them and reward their liberality. At a week's end the alms had increased to so enormous an amount that it was judged fitting the surplus should be appropriated in some way, and the universal cry of the citizens was for a new monastery; it seemed as though they could never now be weary of Capuchin friars; and brother Obligatus was forced to go about seeking for labourers and masons, urging them on, so that they worked with extraordinary rapidity, they hardly knew how; for the walls seemed to grow under their hands with supernatural speed whenever the brown frock of that wonderful friar was seen standing near the spot. Meanwhile, the friars themselves were not a little perplexed to guess who their strange helper could really be. Some said it was Francis come back to earth to help his children; but those even who most admired Br. Obligatus looked doubtfully on this suggestion; for with all his holy, pious words, they felt as though there was a different air and carriage about him, from that of the meek and lowly founder of the Friars Minor. The Father-Guardian kept a prudent silence; men said he had received a divine revelation as to the truth; and so indeed he had, but he did not allow any word of it to escape his lips. Now, on a certain day it chanced that, as he walked to and fro within the convent-garden, he met Obligatus coming from the new building; and though usually he did not seek his company, yet this time he could scarce avoid addressing him. He was the first to speak: "Brother," he said, "how goes on the convent? is it well advanced?" "It is finished," said Obligatus, concealing his face as he spoke; for he had become uneasy in the guardian's presence, and did not much relish the glance of his clear grey eye. "How? finished! why, it was begun but five months since!" "And they have been five years to me," said the demon, bitterly; "nevertheless, had I been so permitted, I could have done it in five days." "God does not work miracles without necessity," answered the guardian coldly, for he thought it well not to seem to know more than others. But Obligatus saw that he was discovered; and not caring to dissemble any longer, he turned fiercely towards his companion, saying, with an impatient gesture, "God! always God; *I* could have done it, I say. I am powerful enough for that." "I know you," said the guardian, "and I know that God permits your presence here; I know, too, that with all your boasted power, you are less strong than our Father Francis." "*He* powerful!" said Obligatus; "yes, when he prays; a poor sort of power: mine at least is mine own." "And yet you have failed; the friars have returned to their first faith; the citizens are more devout and liberal than before; there remains but one task laid on you by heaven to be accomplished, and all your malice will be baffled. Go, then, and convert the merchant Louis from his gold; for it seems to me that there yet lies in store for you a great humiliation."

In fact, the conversion of Louis was the hardest of all the tasks imposed on Obligatus. He laboured at it night and day, but always without success. The merchant could not refuse to see him, for the friar Obligatus was a great man in the town, the popular favorite, and the confident of the governor and the city council. Moreover, there was that in his manner which no one dared openly to affront; so Louis endured his presence and his exhortations; but he listened to them unmoved, and his heart grew every day harder and harder. At length he fell sick; the physicians declared him in danger of death; his wife hung over his bed, and implored him now at length to think of his soul; but still he babbled of his money and his trade, and would not hear of priest or prayer, and turned away his head when they showed him the crucifix: it was a hopeless case. "Oh, would to God," said the weeping Octavia, "that the holy friar Obligatus were but here! Run for him, good Beppo," she added, turning to an attendant, "and tell him that Master Louis is growing worse; and pray him not to delay, for there is sore need of his presence." "I am here, my daughter," said the deep voice of the friar in her ear; "Master Louis is indeed in need of prayer and holy words, for his hour is come at last." Then turning to the sick man, his whole form seemed to dilate, as he burst forth in one of those strains of thrilling eloquence which had so often fascinated the ears of the people during the last five months. He spoke of the soul and of its loss; its death that never dies, and the anguish of that remorse that comes too late, and never goes away. He spoke of the unquenchable fire, and the hair of the hearers bristled on their heads. "That man must surely have seen the things whereof he speaks," they whispered; "speak he of heaven or of hell, it is all one; it is as though he gazed on them with his very eyes." Yes; and he spoke of heaven— not enjoyed, not possessed—but of the eternal regret of one that had been created to enjoy it and to possess it, and had once half tasted of its happiness, and then had lost it, and lost it through his own fault. Oh, the wild weeping, and mourning, and gnashing of teeth, and the cry of long despair of that loss! How, as he spoke, the doleful sounds of the eternal prison seemed to rise round the bed of the dying man! it was the loss of God whereof he spoke, of God the supreme beauty, the supreme truth; of God the end of all desires and all love (and the plaintive echoes of his voice seemed full of an unspeakable regret), all lost—lost—lost!

"My master is a bold man," muttered Beppo to another attendant; "I would not for all his money-chests that such words as those should be spoken over my dying bed." But scarcely had Louis heard them, even as Obligatus had uttered the last syllables, the death-rattle was in his throat; and as that last word "lost" came forth from the lips of the speaker, he gave one convulsive motion of the hands, and fell back upon his pillow. Obligatus bent eagerly over him; he was quite dead. "Mine!" cried the demon with a tone of triumph, "mine own at length. Michael, thou art baffled now!"

"Alas! the good friar is beside himself," said the bystanders. "Holy Father, you have indeed done your utmost with the unhappy man; we pray you take some rest; your much speaking has overwrought your strength." But as they spoke they perceived that the friar was wrestling as with some strong power, which forced him against his will. Broken sentences burst from his lips: "I cannot—nay, I will not—he is mine, I say." Then turning to those who filled the room, "Follow me to the Great Piazza," he said; "I cannot resist that voice." And so saying he rushed from the room, and into the street; with hurried step traversed the piazza, till he came to the spot where he had been wont to address the multitudes who flocked to hear him. The news of what had happened soon spread through the place. "The merchant Louis has died impenitent, and demons have carried off his soul," said they one to another; "doubtless, Father Obligatus hath witnessed the same, and hath much on his mind to speak to us; it will be a rare discourse." And so curiosity, the hope of hearing, the well-known eloquence of the friar on so terrible and stirring a subject, soon gathered a vast crowd that filled the piazza from end to end.

Obligatus stood up before them. What kind of words they were he spoke we dare not attempt to chronicle; but his audience at least had never heard the like. How many a sinner was roused from his dream of luxury and ease by those words, that seemed as though they opened hell beneath his feet; how many a cold, indifferent heart now felt for the first moment what it was to have, and to lose, a soul. Yes, Louis had indeed become the victim of his own avarice and impiety; but the loss of that one soul was the conversion of thousands. And many a man had afterwards reason to thank God for having witnessed the tragedy of that day, which first brought him to penitence, and saved him from a like fate.

The last sermon of the demon-friar was ended. He knew the souls it had lost him; and his moment of triumph was over. Tearing off his friar's habit, and casting it from him, he cried, "Francis! the truce between us is at an end. I have done thy work, and thou hast conquered." Then turning to the astonished multitude, "Go to the Father-Guardian of the Capuchins," he said, "and tomorrow he will declare to you what these things mean; but never more will ye behold the Friar Obligatus." As he spoke, he disappeared, men scarcely knew how; nor was he ever seen again. The strangeness of his last words, and the casting away of the holy habit, perplexed them sorely, till the truth was declared, and then a yet more solemn awe fell upon their souls; nor has the tradition of this event ever been lost; but far and wide, through many a city of Italy, and in other lands, may still be found, in broken fragments, the story of the demon-preacher.

THE
MARTYR OF ROEUX

At the time when the children of Clovis reigned in Gaul," says an old chronicle, "there was in Ireland a king by name Finnloga, who had a brother, the pious Bishop Brendan. Adfin, one of the kings of Scotland, had a daughter named Gelgès, who had embraced the religion of Christ. King Finnloga's son was smitten with her beauty, and married her, but privately, because it was necessary to conceal it from King Adfin, who was an implacable enemy of the faith. He soon discovered it, however, and had his daughter seized and condemned to be burnt. In vain his relations and other persons of influence represented to him that man ought not to separate what God had joined; he ordered the stake to be prepared. But no sooner had Gelgès placed her foot upon the burning wood than it was extinguished. Her father was not convinced by this prodigy, but he consented to spare the life of his daughter, and he condemned her to perpetual exile. She retired with her husband to good Bishop Brendan, her uncle, and there gave birth to three sons—Fursy, Foïllan, and Ultan. On the death of their grandfather, Finnloga, their father was raised to the throne; but instead of returning to the court, they resolved, by Brendan's instructions, to devote themselves to the service of God, and they embarked as missionaries for Gaul." So far the chronicler.

Fursy, after many labours and hardships, attained the crown of martyrdom. Foïllan, the second brother, was preparing on the 31st October, 655, the day on which our narrative commences, to leave Nivelles, where he had been resting for a short space. Gertrude was at this time the abbess of the convent of Nivelles, and had given to Foïllan, in 633, the domain of Fosses, where he had built a church and monastery, the tower of which, in fact, exists to this day. His brother Ultan was now at the monastery of Fosses, and Foïllan was about to join him; but before doing so he wished to celebrate the festival of All Saints with his friend the blessed Vincent Maldegher. He took his journey therefore through an opening in the forest by the route of Soignies, where he was to receive hospitality for the night in the monastery of Vincent.

After traversing many intricate paths in solitude and silence, without meeting any living being; and having moreover, as he thought, lost his way, he began to look about for some human habitation where he might obtain shelter and direction. At last he perceived some rude straw-built huts, and thither he accordingly directed his steps. This was the hamlet of Sonetto.

Foïllan seeing that it was now late, and that he had not completed half his journey, was glad to enter a hut and ask for a guide. The frightful appearance and fierce looks of the inmates of the cabin would have frightened anyone but the holy missionary. But, like the glass which we read of in the Arabian tale, that did not reflect any deformed object, the heart of the saint suspected no evil, and he at once desired two of the men to accompany him as guides.

Foïllan conversed with the men from time to time as they proceeded along the rough and unequal path; but they said little in reply. Finding they were still pagans, he spoke to them of God, His goodness and mercy, of the redemption of man by the blood of the Crucified, and of the paradise prepared for those who believe and do His will. All his words, however, fell unheeded on their ears, and he could only be silent and pray for them. At last the saint arrived with his guides at a part of the forest where an idol was worshipped; and there, whether it was that these pagans wished to force him to sacrifice like them to their god, or whether they thought only of robbing him, the four men threw themselves upon him and dispatched him with their clubs, heedless alike of his entreaties, or of the prayers which with his last voice he offered up for his murderers.

Night now set in cold and dismal. A violent wind began to howl among the trees; and next morning a thick snow, which lay for several months, covered the face of the country.

Meantime, the companions of Foïllan became alarmed at his prolonged absence, and at not having seen him at the feast of Christmas, which he was accustomed to celebrate at Fosses. The most dreadful fears began to be entertained, which were confirmed by several visions. His brother Ultan, as he was at prayers, saw pass before his eyes a dove white as snow, but with wings reddened with blood; a similar prodigy was seen by the abbess Gertrude; and on the 5th January, 656, information was given her in her cell at Nivelles, that in a certain spot of the forest of Soignies the snow was red. Next day she repaired thither, guided by a bloody vapour which hovered in the sky, and discovered the dead body of Foïllan. It was at first carried with pomp to Nivelles, but Ultan desired it might be buried at Fosses, as the martyr himself had requested. In order to arrive at this monastery it was necessary to cross the Sambre, then swollen by the melted snow and ice. Not knowing where to cross, it is related that Gertrude ordering them to leave the horses free, the latter passed, followed by the crowd, through the place which has ever since been called the "Ford of St. Gertrude."

The body of the martyr was afterwards enclosed in a

beautiful chapel; and on the same spot, at a later period, was raised a magnificent church, to which was added, in 1123, an abbey of Premonstratensians. The colour of the snow, which had revealed the place of the crime, gave to this place the name of Rood (red), which was afterwards known by the name of Le Rœux, an important barony in the middle ages, and at this day a thriving little village. Soneffe, whence the murderers of the holy Foïllan came, continued, and still continues, to bear the marks of the divine malediction; for while all the other hamlets around became flourishing towns, this alone has remained as in the times of paganism, a collection of miserable huts.

THE
STORY OF ST. CAEDMON

It is a common thing amongst us to speak of the gifts of genius; and the phrase is never more frequently used than in allusion to those poetic powers which, when found in any very high degree, convey to the rudest understanding the notion of coming from a higher source, and of being far out of the reach of those on whom they are not originally bestowed: yet few who use the term, and still more of those on whom those gifts have rested, ever think of the Giver. By another phrase as common as the first, they are wont to term the different manifestations of genius the gifts of nature; and in the annals of the saints there are not wanting an abundance of examples which seem as if given with the direct intention of teaching our forgetfulness and presumption that these gifts of nature are only the gifts of God. The very remarkable instance of Albert the Great is one example; another, equally striking, is to be found in our own early history: it is that of the great Saxon saint and poet, Caedmon.

Attached to the great abbey of Whitby, which was founded in the seventh century by the Abbess St. Hilda, there was a certain poor rustic employed by the steward of the monastery in the work of the farm, and whose ordinary occupation was the care of the horses and cattle. He was neither young nor of natural abilities, and had passed all his life in the drudgery of his servile calling, which, however, was seasoned and made sweet to his soul by a holy and simple life, and the habit of prayer.

He was accustomed at times to join in the merrymakings and entertainments of his neighbours, at which meetings, according to the favourite Saxon custom, music and singing, of the rude and unpolished style of the day, were often introduced. But poor as were these performances, they were far above the capacity of Cædmon, who was wont to sit a rapt and marvelling listener to what doubtless seemed to him a display of incomprehensible talent.

One evening, as he sat with his comrades round a blazing winter hearth, one of the company proposed that all present should sing in turn to the music of a small lute, which being handed from one to another, should indicate the person who was next called on to amuse the assembled guests. The proposal was agreed to, and the singing began. We should probably think but little either of the music or words, were they produced in our own day; the rude war-songs of our Saxon forefathers were given in barbarous phrase, to a rough and unharmonious chant; there was little skill in the execution, and still less in the composition; yet Cædmon watched the approach of the lute to the corner where he sat with a sensation of nervous terror. It was not the first time when he knew he should be obliged to make the humiliating avowal that he could not sing; and good and holy as he was, it gave him pain. Cædmon was an English saint, and he had an English temperament,—a certain shyness and aptitude to blush, and the inability to carry off a failure well, and the painful consciousness of being awkward and stupid amid his gay companions. So, as the little lute came nearer and nearer, he grew more abashed, and shuffled about, and heartily wished himself safe in bed, or in the stable with his horses. Two more turns, good Cædmon, and the lute will be in your hands, and you will have, as usual, to pass it on and say, "I cannot sing;" and to-night, moreover, there are strangers present; for there has been a meeting of bishops and clergy who have come to hold council at the monastery, and a crowd of attendants in their train; and mingling with the master's guests you may see the equerry of his lordship of York, a huge Northumbrian, with a voice that would fill the abbey nave; and, worse still, there is the house-steward of Archbishop Theodore, whose keen Italian eye has more than once rested on you as you sat a little awkwardly in your corner, with a glance that said, as plain as glance could say, that he considered you as little better than a barbarian. What was to be done? To bear the ridicule of the whole company, and of that foreign fellow with his look of conceited superiority, was not to be endured; before the instrument left the hands of the next but one to himself, Cædmon had determined on flight, and rising from his chair as softly as he could, he stole to the door, and before his absence was noticed, found himself in the quiet refuge of his stable. He sat down on the heap of straw that lay against the wall in somewhat disconsolate mood. Why was he so different from others, he thought, that he should not be able to do what seemed so easy and so natural to them? "I marvel," he muttered, "that I can go among them, I that am so dull and heavy, and can find not a word to say, while other tongues are so glib and busy with the sea-kings and the like trumpery. Though, truly, could these great fingers of mine find their way among the strings of yonder lute, and knew I but the fashion of speech which they call singing, it should not be on the heathen Vikyngs that I would waste my breath; no, nor on the praise of strong ale, which nevertheless was the chief burden of the Northumbrian's song." And then good Cædmon's heart smote him a little to think how vexed and shamefaced he had been because he could not do what, after all, was scarcely worth the doing; and how far better it was to sing God's praises in his heart,

and remain the dull rustic hind that he was, than to abuse
God's gifts by an unworthy use of them; and lastly came a
doubt whether the sweetest song he could have offered his
Lord that night would not have been to have sat quiet in
his chimney-corner, and borne the jests and ridicule of his
companions with a patient will. And with these thoughts
in his head, and the echoes of the last chorus yet ringing
in his ears, Cædmon leant his head on the straw-heap and
fell asleep.

In his sleep he had a singular dream; it seemed to him
that he was still lying on his bed of straw, close by the horses' stall, when the door of the stable opened, and a stranger
entered and stood before him. "Cædmon," he said, bending
over his sleeping form, "I pray you rise, and sing me a song
to-night." And the voice in which he spoke had a sweetness
in it more exquisite than the finest music of the abbey choir.
"I cannot sing," replied Cædmon, sorrowfully; "it was even
for that reason I left the house and came here; for they were
merry and cheerful, and I was dull, and so I came hither to
hide myself, because I could not sing." "Nevertheless, thou
shalt sing," said the other. "And what am I to sing about?"
asked Cædmon; "I am fit to speak of nothing save the beasts
and oxen that I tend, and the fields I till." "The beasts and
the fields are God's creatures, and show forth His praise,"
replied his companion; "fear not, therefore, but sing as
you find words, and it shall be of the beginning of created
things."

Then Cædmon felt a marvellous change in his soul:
thoughts and shapes came flocking on his mind, and they
were not so much new things as old things with a new light
shining on them and making them glorious. The images
traced on his memory through the long years he had spent
in the broad forests and healthy uplands of his native land,
seemed to start up fresh and beautiful within him. He heard
the larks carolling sweetly in the morning air, as they were
wont to do when he went early into the plough-field; and

the mystic glory of many a sunset swam in golden floods before his eye, which he had been used to watch as he plodded home from his daily labour, scarcely knowing how much of their beauty was sinking into his soul. Nor was this all; for, mingling with the images of nature and the excellence of created things, there came thoughts of the Lord who had made them, notions about God, and aspirations after Him, which had filled his simple heart as he had toiled at work, and which in old time had seemed plain and homely like himself, but now were all bathed in a new beauty, as though the sunshine had suddenly been let into his heart. And soon he thought there followed words, not slowly and heavily, as Cædmon had been wont to speak, but flowing forth with a fulness and impetuosity like the waves of a broad and noble river; he felt that something mightier than himself was struggling within him for utterance; and when at last those prisoned words found vent, and shaped themselves into song, the sound of his own voice startled him, for it was rich and musical, even like the voice of him who had first addressed him and commanded him to sing.

Now if this were all, and the story of Cædmon were nothing but the story of a dream, there would be little to make it worth our notice beyond other dreams. Most men can remember times when the mystery of sleep has bestowed on them a fancied power, which fled from them when the grey daylight brought them back to commonplace and common sense; but with Cædmon it was not so. He went on making verses and singing them in his sleep; and when he woke he still found himself making verses, and could remember all he had made and sung during the whole of that night. Moreover, though when the cock began to crow outside, he started up from his straw, and yawned and rubbed his eyes, and found he was still the herdsman Cædmon, and knew that his first business was to lead the horses out to drink, and sweep their stalls, yet for all that, he knew he was at the same time another man. That wonderful gift was within him which makes all things new; that gift, whose joys, too rare and excellent for earth, are ever mingled with a pain, yet whose pains are worth all the common joys of rude souls; that gift so like the prophet's inspiration, which kindles us with a fire that surely first came down from heaven, and was meant to keep alive the altar-fire, though they on whom it falls too often forget from whence it came, and profane it to unhallowed purposes, so that it loses the pure light of its celestial glory, and burns with the dulled and faded lustre of an earthly flame.

Not so, however, did Cædmon treat the power which had been given him from God: reflecting within himself that the change which could have transformed a rustic herds-man into a poet, in the short space of a winter's night, was nothing short of miraculous, his next conviction was, that he was bound to impart the news of this strange transfor-mation to his master the steward; and having come to this conclusion, he presented himself before him, and informed him, with his usual simplicity, that he had come to sing. "To sing!" exclaimed the steward; "now thou art surely beside thyself, or the strong ale thou drankest overnight hath got the mastery of thy brain. Never hast thou sung since I have known thee; and I would fain know, if thou be such a schol-ar in thy music, why thou ever sittest silent in thy comer like one of thine own beasts, when it is time for merrymaking; and now, when thou shouldest be abroad with the cattle, dost come to me to prate of singing: thou wast not given to such vagaries."

"So please you," replied Cædmon, "it is neither the ale nor mine own folly that speaketh; but a strange vision was given me last night as I lay in the stable; and none other than an angel of God, as I deem him, hath taught me how to sing: wherefore I pray you to listen to the verses that I have made, for truly I would have other man's judgment than my own what these things may mean."

When the steward saw by his words and the unusual

earnestness with which he spoke, that some marvel had befallen him, he gave him leave to sing; and Cædmon begun
his poem on "The Beginning of Created Things." Scarcely
did the steward know what to think; for the words were
so lofty, and the strain so musical, and the mysteries on
which he discoursed were so profound and excellent, that
it seemed to him as if he had never heard poetry or music
until then.

"Good Cædmon," he said, when the song was finished,
"thy case is past my counsel to decide; and whether thy music come from heaven or hell, it must be for the Lady Hilda
to resolve: for to her shalt thou surely go, and sing even as
thou hast sung to me; and see well that thou tell her truly all
things that have befallen thee, and all the words which were
spoken to thee in the stable;" and so saying, he carried the
inspired ploughman to the abbey-gate, and sent a message
to the Abbess, that he craved to speak with her on a matter
that would admit of no delay. They were admitted into her
presence, and not a little did the purport of their coming
perplex her.

"Thou desirest me to hear this man sing," she said, addressing the steward in a tone of some severity; "it is a
strange, and methinks scarcely a fitting request. Of what
does he sing, that thou shouldest call me from choir and
prayer to listen to his idle carols?"

"Reverend mistress," said the steward, "I pray you to have
patience with me; for even as I stand here, there is a mystery in this matter which spiritual hands alone can unravel.
A spirit hath surely spoken to the man, but whether good
or bad it is for your reverence to declare; only this much I
know, that words like those that Cædmon spoke this morning have I never heard before."

Then Hilda commanded that he should begin his song
again; and when she had heard the Beginning of Created
Things," she marvelled as greatly as the steward had done.
The words of the heaven-taught poet found a quicker and

readier response in her soul than they had done in that of his less spiritually-minded master. He began by an address to God, and devoted himself to the praise of the Maker of all things, and of the power of the Creator and His counsel, and the deeds of the Father of glory. The Eternal God was, he said, the author of all miracles; and when He made the world, He stretched out the heavens to be the roof of that house which His Majesty had erected for the sons of men, and the earth was to be the place of their abode. All things were of Him, and all things should end in Him; therefore in creatures men should worship God, and praise the Creator who had made them. This was the burden of his poem.

When Hilda had listened for some time in profound silence and attention, she rose and addressed the poet:

"Cædmon," she said, "if thy tale be true, and these words thine own, the matter is too high for my poor wit to judge of; but the Lord Theodora of Canterbury and the Abbot Adrian are even now in the house, and thou shalt speak to them: it may be their learning may see farther in this matter than doth my simplicity."

Perhaps no young poet in the first flush of newly developed powers has ever been put to a harder ordeal than was poor Cædmon on that eventful morning; thrice within an hour's space to repeat his verse, and each time before a noble presence. It was no small trial for him to stand before the Abbess Hilda, whom he had been used to consider as the greatest person in the whole world; but to be brought before the Archbishop of Canterbury, the most learned man of Christendom, as men were wont to call St. Theodora, and the not less learned or less holy Abbot Adrian, who, between them, as we are told, made men talk Greek and Latin as though they were their native tongues.* However, there was no help for it; once more he had to tell his dream and repeat his verses, that all might determine what the dream

* Bede, b. iv. c. 2.

was, and whence the verse proceeded. And when they had heard him speak (says V. Bede), they all concluded that heavenly grace had been conferred on him by our Lord.

"Yet since we know not surely whether these verses are his own," said the abbot, "were it not well, my lord archbishop, that some farther trial should be put upon him?"

"You say rightly," answered Theodore; "therefore will we choose out a passage of Holy Writ, and if he can put the same into like verses with those he has even now recited, we may no longer doubt that the hand of God is on him for some high purpose; if not, let him look well to it that he be not treated as knaves deserve."

The passage was selected, and Cædmon went away. When he returned the next morning, he gave them the whole composed in most excellent verse; and moreover the grace of God was so evident in the luminousness and holiness of his thoughts, far more than even in the marvels of his versification, that his hearers began to feel that they had not only found a poet, but a saint in the poor herdsman Cædmon.

"Whereupon," says V. Bede, "the abbess embracing the grace of God in the man, instructed him to quit the secular habit and take upon him the monastic life; which being accordingly done, she associated him to the rest of the brethren* in her monastery, and ordered that he should be taught the whole series of sacred history. Thus Cædmon, keeping in mind all he heard, and as it were chewing the cud, converted the same into most harmonious verse, and sweetly repeating the same made his masters in their turn his hearers. He sang the creation of the world, the origin of man, and all the history of Genesis, with many other histories from Holy Writ; and of the incarnation, passion, and resurrection of our Lord, and His ascension into heaven...

* In the monastery of Whitby, or Streaveshalch, as it was then called, there were two separate and distinct communities, one of men and the other of women, both governed by the same head.

besides many other things about the divine benefits and judgments, by which he endeavoured to turn men away from the love of vice, and to excite them to good actions." "And by his verses," adds the same historian, "the minds of many were often excited to despise the world, and to aspire to heaven. Others after him in the English nation attempted to compose religious poems, but none did ever compare with him, for he did not learn the art of poetry from men, but from God; for which reason he never could compose any vain or trivial poem, but only those which relate to religion suited his religious tongue."

We have given the story of Cædmon as furnishing a fitting illustration of the true vocation of a poet, who receiving his powers directly from the hand of God, is bound by his calling to dedicate them to those objects which are here so beautifully pointed out, namely, the praise of God, and the exciting of men's hearts to aspire to heaven. The first to write in his native tongue, Cædmon may be considered as the father of English poetry. He lived many years in the monastery, where his life was as sweet and holy as were his words; "for he was a very religious man," continues the same author, "humbly submissive to regular discipline, for which reason he also ended his life happily." We will give the account of his death in the words of his biographer. After telling us that he was taken with a moderate infirmity, and desired to be carried to the house prepared for the sick, he continues: "The person to whom he made this request wondered why he should desire it, because there were no signs of his dying soon; nevertheless, he did as he had ordered. He accordingly went there, and conversing pleasantly and in a joyful manner with the rest that were in the house, when it was past midnight, he asked them whether they had the Holy Eucharist there? They answered, 'What need of the Eucharist? for you are not likely to die, since you talk as merrily with us as though you were in perfect health.' 'Nevertheless,' he said, 'bring me the Eucharist. And having received the same into his hands, he asked whether they were all in charity with him, and without any enmity or rancour. They answered that they were all in perfect charity and free from anger, and in their turn asked him whether he was in the same mind towards them. He answered, 'I am in charity, my children, with all the servants of God.' Then strengthening himself with the heavenly viaticum, he prepared the entrance into another life, and asked how near the time was when the brothers were to be awakened to sing the nocturnal praises of the Lord? They replied, 'It is not far off.' Then he said, 'Well, let us wait that hour, and signing himself with the sign of the cross, he laid his head on the pillow, and falling into a slumber, ended his life so in silence. Thus it came to pass, that as he had served God with a simple and pure mind and undisturbed devotion, so he now departed to His presence, leaving the world by a quiet death; and that tongue which had composed so many holy words in praise of the Creator, uttered its last words whilst he was in the act of signing himself with the cross, and recommending himself into His hands."

Miracles followed on his death; and in the days of the Conqueror his body was granted an honourable translation. He is commemorated in the English martyrology on the twelfth day of February.*

---

* The resemblance between portions of Cædmon's poem on the *Fall of Man* and passages on the same subject in the *Paradise Lost* have been judged by several writers so remarkable as to justify the opinion that Milton was familiar with the English version of the Anglo-Saxon poem. Conybeare, comparing the passage referred to, says, "the resemblance of language is so striking, that much of this portion of Cædmon's ode may be literally translated by a hundred lines of our great poet."

THE SHEPHERDESS
OF NANTERRE

It was the summer of the year 429, and the little village of Nanterre, near Paris, presented a scene of unusual bustle and festivity. The fronts of the houses were gaily decorated with boughs and many-coloured banners, and the very streets, strewn with rushes, seemed to indicate the presence of some illustrious guest. People of all ranks and ages were crowding to the open door of the church, not, indeed, as might be supposed, to join in the celebration of any festival solemnised there on that day, but rather that they might catch a glimpse of two great men who were to lodge that night in their humble village; these were the two Bishops Germanus and Lupus.

They were on their journey towards the island of Britain, which at that period was gaining its first melancholy celebrity as the seat of heresy; and it was to oppose the rapid and alarming progress of Pelagianism, that a council of Gallican prelates had selected them as champions of the faith, and despatched them to Britain, where Germanus was to bear the office and authority of papal legate.

Nanterre was a poor and insignificant place, and the population which filled the church was chiefly composed of rude shepherds and village artisans. The chance which had given them two such distinguished visitors as the Bishops of Auxerre and Troyes was a great event in their simple history; and when it was known that the legate was about to address the people in a discourse, and would afterwards assist publicly at the singing of the divine office in the parish church, the satisfaction of the villagers was at its height.

Germanus was in all respects a remarkable man; his call to the priesthood and episcopate presents us with one of those instances of sudden conversion which were so common in the early days of faith, and so hard of comprehension in our own. A successful courtier and imperial favourite, he had incurred the displeasure of his Bishop Amator by a passionate love of field-sports, which had led him into practices which the jealous watchfulness of that prelate denounced as savouring of heathenism. For Germanus was wont to adorn the city with the heads of the beasts he had slain, and to hang them solemnly on an old tree which stood in the middle of the city, in accordance with certain superstitions of pagan times; and when the Bishop summarily stopped these proceedings by ordering the tree to be levelled to the ground, the young noble vowed never to rest till he had taken vengeance on the meddling prelate who had spoiled his sport. His anger obliged Amator to fly from the city; but it was at this very moment that, by a divine revelation, the venerable prelate became aware that his persecutor was the very man chosen to be his successor. As the moment of his death drew near, he ordered his ecclesiastics to seize Germanus by force, and give him the tonsure, assuring him at the same time that such was the will of God: the command was obeyed, and he who but a while before had seemed so firm and untameable a spirit, offered no opposition to their proceedings, but gave himself blindly and unresistingly to the course marked out for him by Amator. When the unanimous voice of the clergy and people chose him to succeed that prelate in the government of the Church, Auxerre marvelled at the spectacle of the wild and half heathen noble transformed into another man; his life was one of penance and extraordinary sanctity, nor was it long before the universal reputation which he enjoyed raised him to the highest station among the councils of the Gallican Bishops.

Such was the man who, standing on the altar-steps of the church of Nanterre, was now addressing his simple audience in a few brief and appropriate words of exhortation. One of the most learned and accomplished men of the day, he was perfect in the art of adapting his thought and language to almost any company; and with the facility of a truly great speaker, he gracefully fitted himself and his eloquence to the intellectual littleness of his audience. Never had the good people of Nanterre heard such preaching before; and perhaps its power over their hearts was not a little enhanced by the affable and winning courtesy which Germanus showed to the rude peasantry who crowded about him. He spoke to each in turn with a fatherly sweetness; and many a mother's heart was made prouder and happier till her dying day by the thought that the lord legate had even noticed her ragged urchins of children, and, it may be, given them a kind word as they knelt to receive his blessing. Among those who were thus presented before him, was a little child scarcely seven years of age, whose singular beauty was apparent in spite of the extreme poverty of her dress. The parents of Geneviève were indeed of the humblest class; the wretched shepherd's hut, in which her father Severus lived, was the poorest in Nanterre: and, young as she was, her life had already begun in hard labour, as she toiled about the hills after the sheep, whom it was her daily care to watch and drive home in the evening. And so when we speak of the beauty of Geneviève, it was a beauty which certainly had little of worldly accompaniments to set it off, and to many it might perhaps have seemed a perversion of terms to call her beautiful at all. The charm lay rather in the innocence which was expressed in every look and gesture, and the earnest gravity of her countenance; and such as it was, it seemed in an extraordinary manner to rivet the attention of Germanus; for when she came to him in her turn, and knelt with her little companions before the spot where the Bishop stood, a very singular expression of interest passed over his countenance. "Who is this child, and who are her parents?" he inquired of the priest of Nanterre, who stood beside him, and who noticed his manner with no small surprise. "It is the little shepherdess Geneviève," he replied, "the child of one of our oldest villagers. Severus and his wife Gerontia are among the poorest dwellers in Nanterre; but they serve God faithfully, and Geneviève knows how to say her prayers better than many who are twice her age."

"Are her parents here?" said Germanus; "if so, call them, that I may speak to them;" and in obedience to his summons, the astonished couple found themselves called from the crowd, and brought, to their no small embarrassment, to the presence of the prelate. Taking the child by her hand, Germanus addressed them with the air of one who was yielding to a Divine inspiration: "Severus," he said, "guard this child as the most precious gift of the Divine goodness; her nativity was celebrated in heaven by the hymns of angels, and the day is not far distant when she will recal sinners from the error of their ways, and perfectly accomplish the resolution even now formed within her heart. And you, my daughter," he continued, turning to Geneviève, "will you not consecrate yourself wholly to Him who has chosen you from all eternity to be His spouse?" The singular address of the prelate, and the curiosity and attention of all the spectators, did not seem to disturb or confuse the tranquillity of the little Geneviève. She scarcely seemed aware that she was an object of interest, and that the eyes of all present were bent on her with a gaze of wonder and admiration, for her own were never raised from the ground, and to the inquiry of the bishop she replied simply, and without hesitation, "It is what, by God's grace, I have always resolved."

"Then be of good courage," replied Germanus, "and prove by your actions, that your heart firmly assents to what your lips profess. Neither be afraid of the opposition of man nor devil; for the Lord will support you, and strengthen you with grace."

When this extraordinary dialogue was concluded Germanus desired that the singing of vespers might be begun; but the wonder with which the people had witnessed what had passed, was not diminished when they observed that he kept the child near him during the whole of the office, and that his hand rested on her head. When he retired from the church, he again called Severus and Gerontia, and charged them to bring their daughter to him on the following morning before his departure for Paris.

The impression which these incidents made on the little world of Nanterre may be easily supposed; when the people left the church, every tongue was busy with the strange prophecy of Germanus; for the miraculous gifts which he was known to possess gave a character to his words which would not have attached to those of an ordinary man; and when, very early on the following morning, Severus and his daughter were again brought into the Bishop's presence, not a few of those who had witnessed the scene on the previous day contrived to join themselves to their company, eager to see the end. Germanus was sitting with some of the ecclesiastics of his suite as they entered, and calling the child to come close to his knee, he looked earnestly in her face. "Listen, Geneviève, my daughter," he said; "do you remember the promise you gave me yesterday, that you would consecrate your soul and body wholly and entirely to God?" "Yes, Father," she replied, as simply and readily as before; "I do remember it." Germanus was about to speak again, when something lying at his feet caught his eye, and he paused to pick it up. It was a piece of bronze, probably some coin of the country, which chanced to be marked with the rude figure of a cross. He took it in his hand, and gave it

to Geneviève, saying, "Always carry this round your neck
in memory of me, and of the words you have spoken to
me this day. Suffer no richer ornament ever to touch your
neck, and resolve, were the world to offer you all the jewels
and pearls of the empire, to trample them under your feet."
Then giving her his blessing, he rose to depart; and in a
few hours the little village was again left to the quiet and
tranquillity which the excitement caused by his visit had
for a moment interrupted. For a time, indeed, the singularity of his conduct towards Geneviève formed the subject
of many long speculations; but gradually the interest died
away, as they every day saw the little shepherdess leading
her ordinary life among them, with no change either in her
manner or occupation which could indicate that the prophecy of Germanus had roused within her any consciousness
of her own importance, or impatience for any other kind of
life. It is true, neither her neighbours nor even her parents
saw much of what passed in Geneviève's heart; for her time
was spent for the most part on the lonely hills where she
watched her sheep, and so the habits of prayer and aspira-
tion which day by day deepened in her soul, filling it with
the perpetual memory of Him to whom she had been so
solemnly consecrated, grew in secret, and unobserved by any
human eye, leaving no trace by which they could be guessed,
save in a certain spirituality in her look, which those who
surrounded her were scarcely quick-sighted enough to discern or understand. Her mother Gerontia, though good and
kind-hearted in her own way, was in no degree superior to
the common faults of her class; of a quick and hasty temper,
she was little in the habit of restraining her tongue; and
whilst she was far from comprehending the quiet gravity of
Geneviève's manner, so different from that of ordinary children, it often provoked her into angry speeches and somewhat rough treatment.

Now it happened that not very long after the visit of the
Bishop of Auxerre, Gerontia was preparing one morning to

set out for the village from which their little cottage was situated at some little distance. It was a fête-day, and she had
dressed herself in her holiday attire to appear in church as
gay as her neighbours; but as to Geneviève, she desired her
to remain at home, and mind the house in her absence. For
once, however, she was surprised to meet with something
like opposition from the child, who rather pertinaciously
pleaded that she too might be suffered to go to church and
keep the fête, by hearing Mass. Gerontia was very angry:
"Thou shalt stay at home and bridle thy tongue," she said,
"which is over-forward for thine age; a fine thing, indeed,
if all the children and babies of the village are to be crying
thus to keep their fête like grown women. You will be wanting earrings, and a silken kerchief next." "I want no earrings,
mother," replied Geneviève, "for the Bishop told me I was
never to wear them or any ornament save my little bronze
cross; but he told me likewise to serve God, and always to
hear Mass on feast-days; wherefore, I pray you, suffer me to
go with you today, for I promised him I would faithfully do
whatsoever he bade me."

"The Bishop hath turned thy head, I think," exclaimed
Gerontia, who felt a secret consciousness that the pleasure of exhibiting her own gay holiday dress had no small
share in the delight of a village fête-day. "May I never see
the church-town of Nanterre again, if I do not rid thee of
thy whims;" and as she spoke, she struck her daughter a
heavy box on her ear. Scarcely had she done so, than she
seemed seized with a sudden fear. "Geneviève, child, where
art thou,— what hast thou done?" she cried, extending her
arms, as one who feels in the dark, "it is surely a jest of thine;
thou hast closed the door, hast thou not? for I cannot see."
"O mother!" answered Geneviève, who was terribly frightened, "the door and window are wide open, and it is quite
light;" and as her mother still looked wild and confused,
and felt about her to find the door, Geneviève began to cry,
and throwing herself into Gerontia's arms, continued to sob

with childish vehemence, "See, dear mother, won't you; you can surely see now." But Gerontia could not see; the penalty she had called down on her own head had fallen on her hasty words, and she was quite blind. Nearly two years passed away, and though she tried many remedies, nothing availed to restore the smallest gleam of sight to her eyes. The terrible privation, however, was not without its effect; and whilst Geneviève served and tended her with devoted care, Gerontia's temper grew more patient, and her tongue was learning a gentleness or civility to which it had before been a stranger.

Now it happened one day that Geneviève had gone to the spring which was at a little distance from the house to draw the water. Tired with the hard work which now fell to her exclusive share—for her mother's blindness prevented her from taking any active part in the affairs of the household—she sat on the brink of the well to rest; and as she sat and thought of her mother, and the affliction which had come upon her, she began to weep. "Oh, that our Lord would give sight to my mother!" she sighed; "if He were here, He could do it in a moment: and He is here, for He is everywhere. And Germanus called Him my spouse; if He is my spouse, He will surely do what I ask Him; and when I go back I will ask Him to cure my mother." And with these thoughts revolving in her mind, she filled her buckets with the clear sparkling water, and tottered back to the cottage. "Is that you, child?" said Gerontia, as she heard the footstep on the threshold. "Come here; for our Lord has put a thought into my heart, and bring with you some of the water which you have drawn; for I verily believe that this day He will give me back my sight." "O mother!" exclaimed Geneviève joyfully, "it is what I have been praying for; but what will you do with the water?" Gerontia did not immediately answer: with a movement of great reverence she took the water in her hands, and raised them and her sightless eyeballs to heaven; she prayed for a few moments in silence, then holding out the vessel to her daughter, she desired her to make over it the sign of the cross. Geneviève having obeyed, Gerontia bathed her eyes several times in the water, whilst her daughter stood watching her with feelings of extraordinary tenderness and anxiety. And as she so stood, her mother looked up, and she saw that her glance was no longer wandering and expressionless. Gerontia's sight was restored; and as she herself hesitated not to acknowledge, through the merits of her child. Her time of suffering had produced its effect, and the gratitude and reverence with which she had now learnt to regard Geneviève showed itself in the care which she now displayed in cherishing and forwarding the holy design to which the child had so resolutely consecrated herself. It was not long before an opportunity presented itself for this consecration to be made in a formal and solemn manner, according to the custom of the times, on the occasion of the Bishop of Chartres visiting Nanterre. Geneviève was presented to him, with two others older than herself, to receive the religious veil from his hands. When they all three stood before him, Geneviève, as being the youngest, was placed the last in the rank; but a secret inspiration revealed to the Bishop that a more than ordinary degree of sanctity was concealed under her simple and modest exterior. Regarding her earnestly for some minutes, he delayed commencing the ceremony; and then turning suddenly to some of the attendant priests, he said, "Bring that youngest child to the front, for God has already sanctified her."

"It is Geneviève," said one of those standing by; "and the holy Father Germanus did indeed in some sort consecrate her when he came here eight years since, and prophesied that great designs of God should be accomplished in her."

And so for a second time the attention of the people was directed to the little shepherdess, who was now once more pointed out to them as the chosen favourite of Heaven. In those times the holy virgins consecrated to God remained in their own homes, and followed a life of devotion and mortification, without wholly withdrawing from the society of their families. But very shortly after the reception of the sacred veil, the death of both her parents obliged Geneviève to seek a new home with her godmother, who resided at Paris; and with her change of residence a new life opened before her. The celebrity attaching to her name accompanied her to the capital, and was increased by the innumerable miracles which followed her prayers, and the visits of charity in which her time was spent. These visits extended far beyond the boundaries of Paris,—all the chief cities of France became familiar with the presence of one whom they regarded as a kind of messenger from heaven. The secrets of consciences were laid open to her; and her arbitration and judgment were accepted in many a feud which might else have found its settlement in a sea of blood. It is to be regretted that so much of the history of this period of her life is sunk in the obscurity of the times; yet if we may judge from the imperfect notices preserved, it seems to have borne a striking resemblance to that of St. Catherine of Sienna. For whilst constantly engaged in long journeys and troublesome affairs, living before the public eye and accompanied by a number of those who were living like herself in a state consecrated to religion, whilst yet not wholly separated from the world, and who considered themselves her spiritual children, neither the distractions nor the fatigue which she suffered had the effect of disturbing for one moment the interior calm of a soul which united the contemplation of a solitary to the labours of an apostle.

Like St. Catherine, she had her enemies; and for a time the world banded against her, and denounced her as a hypocrite and a visionary. Like her, too, the mysterious and supernatural life of ecstasy and miracle mingled with the thread of her ordinary existence; and whilst the marvels of such a life made some venerate her as a saint, many others were equally ready to persecute her as an impostor. She was

scarcely more than twenty when St. Germanus returned
from England after an absence of thirteen years; and we
give the events that followed in the language of an old account of the fourteenth century. "Then having returned to
France, he came to Paris; and all the people went out to
meet him with great joy. But before all things the blessed
Germanus asked how fared the virgin Geneviève; and the
people, who are ever more ready to speak evil than well of
good people, replied that there were no good tidings of her.
But as they tried to blame her, their words did themselves
praise her; wherefore he took no count of their evil speech,
but as soon as he had entered the city, he went straight to
the dwelling of the virgin, whom he saluted after so humble a sort, that the people who beheld the same marvelled
greatly; and then he showed to those who despised her the
ground watered by her tears, and related to them the beginning of her life, and how it had been made known to him at
Nanterre that she was chosen of God, and therefore he had
recommended her to the people."

The steadfast friendship and protection of Germanus
turned for a while the current of popular feeling, and silenced the busy tongues that sought her ruin; but his fresh
absence in Italy in the year 449 was the signal for a renewal
of the persecution of her with greater violence than before.
They even determined to take her life, and were preparing
to drown her as a witch and impostor, when once more the
intervention of Germanus was the means of restoring her
to the popular esteem. At the very moment that they were
dragging their unresisting victim to death, the archdeacon
of Auxerre arrived on a mission from the Bishop, and im-
peratively demanded to be permitted to speak with her. The
character and authority of Germanus commanded respect
for his messenger, and the brutal mob were awed into gentleness when they beheld the archdeacon present her with
the usual ceremonial, a portion of the blessed bread, which
Germanus, after a custom of the time, had sent her as a

special token of esteem, and as a token of communion. This had the effect of changing the rage of the fickle populace into a veneration for her person, which they continued to retain during the remainder of her life. But events were at hand which were destined to exhibit Geneviève to the world in a new character, and to give her a claim on the gratitude of the country, of which she was now to become the defender. News came to Paris that Attila, the felon-king of the Huns, was ravaging every part of France, and had sworn to subdue it to his rule; wherefore the citizens of Paris, by reason of the great fear that they had, sent their property into other cities that were more secure. In this general alarm Geneviève undertook to reanimate the drooping courage of the people, and to encourage them to a manly defence. "She admonished the women," continues the ancient writer before quoted, "that they should watch in prayer and fasting, whereby they should powerfully resist and overcome the tyranny of the enemies, even as the two holy women Esther and Judith did in old time. And they obeyed her, watching many days together in the church in fasts and prayer." But she was not content with this; leaving her companions in the church, she herself appeared in the streets and public places, calling on the men to arm themselves and remain at their posts, and promising them the protection of Heaven. Each day the danger appeared more imminent; for tidings were continually reaching the terrified inhabitants of the nearer approach of the barbarian hordes, whose way was marked by a track of devastation; and still each day was Geneviève to be seen going about among the fearful and faint-hearted people, and assuring them that the day of deliverance was at hand. Some, indeed, disregarded her prophecies, and treated her as an impostor; but the greater part so far yielded to the extraordinary power which she had over them, that they remained in the city, and consented to prepare for its defence. And at length the intelligence arrived, that when within a day's march of the capital Attila and his savage army had suddenly changed their course, and abandoning their designs on Paris, had returned in the direction of Orleans. The reason of this unexpected change in the plan of the barbarians was not explained; but the people of Paris were not slow in attributing it to the particular grace of God, who had guarded the city by the prayers and merits of Geneviève.

It was this circumstance that subsequently caused St. Geneviève to be considered as the patron saint of Paris; and yet, perhaps, the city did not owe her less for the influence she exerted in sanctifying and christianising it, than for its deliverance through her means from the scourge of the Huns.

Every Saturday night there might be seen a long procession of women winding through the rough and dirty roads that lay between Paris and the mountain of Mont Martre, which had been the scene of the martyrdom of St. Denys. Geneviève was at their head; her piety was constantly united to a patriotism as fervent, and, if we might so say, as romantic, as that which in a subsequent age animated the breast of Joan of Arc; and this devotion to the great apostle of France had been instituted by her to implore his protection on the country, which was then sharing in the terrible sufferings that attended the final dissolution of the western empire.

One night, as they were on their way, the rain descended in torrents, and they could scarce keep their footing in the dirty roads; yet still they kept on, brave and undaunted, singing psalms and litanies, and battling with the wind, which arose with tempestuous violence, and rendered their progress slow and difficult. At length the lamp which was carried in front of their little company was blown out, and they were left in total darkness. Many of them were frightened and disheartened, and began to weep; but Geneviève reassured them. "Give me the lamp," she said; and the sound of her sweet and gentle voice restored courage in the hearts of her children, even though they could not discern her form; "I will light you to the church." And taking it in her hand, she had scarcely touched it, when it instantly relighted of itself; and bearing it in front of them, so that its clear ray fell over the whole company, she thus led them on to the church-door, and so accomplished the night's pilgrimage.

We have instituted a comparison between the characters of Geneviève and St. Catherine of Sienna,—a comparison which is forcibly suggested in the public and patriotic passages of their lives; in their interior sufferings, and the martyrdom of love which each endured, they were not less alike. "The precious virgin Geneviève," says her historian, "did most hardly torment her body all her life for the preventing of sin; her only delights were fasting, prayers, and penances." At length the Bishops laid her under obedience to moderate her penances, and to take a more nourishing kind of food. She obeyed; and yet, "whenever she did eat," continues her biographer, "she did use to look to heaven and weep; and it was thought that she did then verily see our Lord in open vision, according to the gospel promise which saith, that it is well with the pure in heart, because they see God." We shall not pause to enumerate the many miracles which she performed; but hasten to another scene in her life, when she was called from her prayers and pilgrimages to the service and defence of her country. A new enemy was fast establishing itself in Gaul, and after having taken possession of the western and southern portions of the country, was now preparing to advance against Paris. These were the French under their King Childeric, who, appealing before the city walls, commenced a siege which they afterwards turned into a blockade that lasted ten years, during which time the sufferings of the half-starved inhabitants reached a terrible height. A vast number perished of hunger, and the cries of the famishing populace fell on the ear of Geneviève with a power she could not resist. Yet what could she do? her own scanty portion was every day divided among the most distressed; but the sufferers were to be numbered by thousands; and as she passed through the streets, her heart, which felt like a mother's heart for the people whom she loved so dearly, was torn to see them lying in her way in the agonies of despair and destitution. That heart was, however, one of too truly heroic a nature to be content with giving pity and compassion where there was room for action. With her usual resolution and composure, she proposed to some of the boatmen of the river to endeavour to make their way up the Seine to some of the distant villages, whence they could procure a supply of corn and other provisions for the distressed city. The proposal seemed nothing short of madness, for the banks of the river were crowded by the hosts of the enemy, and every avenue from Paris was strictly watched and guarded. Geneviève's plan therefore met with a sturdy and abrupt repulse. "Boats," they said, "there are in plenty; but we will not man them: as well die in Paris for want of bread as on the swords of the barbarians." "Moreover," said another, "all the world knows that the Seine is now scarce navigable; *for* higher up, near Troyes, a great tree has fallen over the river, and many boats that have attempted the passage have been wrecked, and their crews have perished. Neither is it possible to reach the higher stream till the hindrance be removed." "Well then," replied Geneviève, without the smallest appearance of disturbance, "since you have none of you the heart to go, I must needs go myself and so saying, she loosened one of the smaller boats from its moorings, and pushed it from the shore. "We are shamed for ever, if our mother perish alone," said one of the men; "I for one will surely go with her; one can die but once." His words revived the courage of another; and so she set out on her perilous journey with her two companions, whose dangerous course she herself directed, exhorting them not to fear, but to put their whole trust in God.

The citizens had gathered in great numbers on the banks at the news of the departure of their protectress; and followed her with their eyes, as they watched her little vessel, until the windings of the stream hid her from their gaze. Days passed on, and still no news of her return reached their ears; and the possible loss of one they counted as their mother was for the time a sorer trouble than the perils of the city or their own sufferings in the famine. At length, on the third day, the men who were set to watch on the towers which commanded the river gave notice that a boat was to be seen coming down the stream, which bore every resemblance to that in which the three adventurers had embarked. The tidings brought all the populace to the shore; and in a short space Geneviève landed safe amid her fellow-citizens, having succeeded in bringing them a welcome supply of provisions, which she had collected at the peril of her life from the surrounding villages on the Seine. Even the noble exertions of Geneviève, however, could only defer the fate of the city, which fell into the hands of Childeric after the blockade had lasted ten years. Geneviève, however, had still a part to perform, even in the hour of defeat and surrender. She presented herself to the pagan conqueror, with a noble daring, to solicit the lives of the prisoners, and to exhort him to clemency and humanity in the hour of victory. What power there must have been in the eloquence of that appeal, we may judge from the fact, that the barbarous chief, who had made other cities of Gaul run with the blood of his victims, is known to have signalised himself, on the taking of Paris, by a clemency which formed no part of his usual character. Nay, even though Geneviève's name was well known to him, as having been the foremost among those who rallied the citizens to their long and obstinate defence, and though her exploit on the Seine had reached his ears, and he might naturally have conceived some enmity against one who had proved herself so steadfast an opponent, yet he could not resist the extraordinary influence which she exerted over all who approached her, and whose most powerful element was probably to be found in that union of heroic strength with childish simplicity, which was the most striking feature of her character.

Childeric continued to treat her with respect and veneration during the remainder of his life; and his successor, Clovis, who embraced the Christian faith in 496, was often wont to take her counsel on matters of consequence, and frequently at her suggestion released prisoners, and performed other acts of generosity and mercy.

She lived to the age of eighty-nine years, all her life being illustrated by miracles of every kind. They continued to be worked at her tomb, and to those who sought her intercession, in what might be called a profusion; so that the shrine of "Madame Saincte Geneviève," as she is called in the old story, became the place of pilgrimage for all France. The lame walked, the blind saw, and the lepers were cleansed. But this was not all. "All this was worked in the bodies of the sick by the holy virgin," says her biographer, "who did even yet more accomplish spiritually, by her merits, in the souls of men." For indeed the conversions which she made, both during her life and after death, were far more numerous and more glorious to her name than all the other offerings which long adorned her sepulchre, and bore testimony to the relief which her invocation had brought to the sick and maimed.

Such was the career of the humble shepherdess of Nanterre, the holy Geneviève; and we may safely venture to say, that rich as the subsequent history of her country has been in both characters, France will scarcely find any to equal her as a heroine, or to surpass her as a saint.

THE MONK'S LAST WORD

"O yes, certainly, the last word of a man who dies as in the presence of God, is carried on high all entire."—F. Englegrave.

"God, who sees all, will see this too."—*Song of the Blind*

THE Ash Wednesday of the year 1649 was darkening the city of Rome with its aspect, so melancholy and yet so cherished among the Catholic nations; and yet at noon, that same day, in a vast room which served as studio to a painter, and which looked upon the Tiber, five joyous strangers were just going to seat themselves before a festive table.

It was clear that the Roman carnival, so bustling, so lively (a childish joy which the northern nations obscure with scandals and orgies), had not been enough for the five guests; for they were going to prolong it on that day of penance when the Catholic Church prays, asking the forgiveness of excesses, and reminding the faithful, by putting the ashes on their foreheads, that man is dust, and that the mortal part of his being must return to dust; *Memento, homo, quia pulvis es, et in pulverem reverteris.*

The room into which we are introducing the reader was raised one story above the Tiber, which washed the foot of the house. Three large windows opened on the river, which was swollen by the winter rains; and the artist who inhabited this dwelling might enjoy, without leaving his house, the calm pleasure of angling; as he sometimes did.

He had copiously decked his abode with sketches and objects of art. But it was seen, from the character of these objects, that their master was not one of those believing painters of whom Rome is always the country. Nothing of that sublime magnificence which faith inspires warmed the cold representations of material nature displayed upon those walls. The sketches were of feasts, hunting-parties, attacks of robbers, rural diversions, and grotesque scenes.

In the middle of these compositions, varied, however, and often full of life, strutted a fiddler with his bow. The artist was also a musician, and was wont to put himself into spirits by playing an air before seizing his pencil. Ill-shaped, a little hunchbacked, like an ape in the length of his arms and legs, proud of his rough moustaches drawn up like hooks on the two sides of his nose, and which threatened the sky, this painter, nice and correct in design, vigorous and transparent in his coloring, redeemed the disgrace of his outward form by a jovial spirit, a noisy good humor, and appreciated talents. He was named Peter van Laar. The Italians had surnamed him *Puppet* either on account of the singularity of his mind and form, or of certain of his pictures still described as *Puppet-paintings*.

Puppet was thirty-six, and had lived for sixteen years in Rome. Poussin, Claude Lorraine, and Sandrart were his friends. But it was not with them that he practised his irregularities. His guests on that day were Roelant van Laar, his elder brother; Claes van Laar, his younger, born, like him, near Naarden, in Holland; Andrew Both, born at Utrecht, and John, Andrew's brother; two artists of renown, who were about Peter's age. The five young painters were thus all Dutchmen. Let us add, that all the five were of the sect of Calvin.

A little more good sense would have made them feel, however, that, although they had no faith, yet, at a time when their country did not tolerate the children of the Roman Church, they ought at least to have respected in Rome, while enjoying its hospitality, the laws of its sovereign; and these laws make Ash-Wednesday a fast-day there. But accustomed to the mildness of the Roman clergy, they went without fear in their own ways; and their table was served with many dishes reserved from the preceding day, and among the rest shone an enormous ham from the Tyrol.

"Before we begin," said Andrew Both, inspecting the table, "Peter is going to play upon his violin a little and rather lively air, to put life into us."

"True," added Claes, "we shall be more in cue."

The others supported the proposition so well, that Puppet, who had not the fault of wanting to be pressed, began to play, with contortions and gambols, a burlesque dance, which had complete success. At half-past twelve, the five artists at table began their dinner, to the noise of bursts of laughter, which presaged a tumult at the end, and some broken glasses at the dessert.

"We are wrong to excite ourselves so strongly," said Puppet, however. "Let us have a little more respect for the usages of the country in which we dwell. See how quiet all our neighborhood is."

"Bah! bah!" replied Roelant; "it is known we don't give in to the Roman superstition. Artists are free. Send round the wine."

And the noise went on increasing.

At four, the five friends were more than half intoxicated: some sang detestable songs, others disputed or whistled; and the hall resounded with the hoarse tumult of their confused voices.

At the same hour, a poor Franciscan monk, passing in front of the house, was struck with this mixture of savage cries. Not suspecting that Christians could be feasting on such a day, he fancied there was a quarrel there, and made haste to enter, with the hope of recommending peace.

Directed by the noise, he arrived at the door, opened it, and recoiled with horror at the sight of such orgies.

"Enter, Father," said John Both with effrontery, and stammering with drunkenness; "you supply me with a good model; come and drink a round."

And as the monk did not come forward, John Both rose briskly, ran to him, took him by the arm, and led him in front of the table.

"Sirs," said the religious, gravely, "I thought I was coming among Christians. But I see I was mistaken."

He made a movement toward the door.

"We are Christians as well as you, Father," replied Roelant, retaining him; "but we don't think we offend God in eating a slice of ham."

"What enters the body can't be a defilement," said John Both, in a doctoral tone.

Claes van Laar added with a careless air, "Was it not said to the Apostles, 'Eat what you find?'"

"You seem to me hardly in a condition to reason, my brethren," answered the monk. "Forgive me for telling it you so freely. But, even were you cool, I should confine myself to telling you, that when the Church commands it is for her children to obey, and not to dispute. One augurs ill of a family where the children dispute, of a house where the servants reason, and of an army in which the soldiers deliberate. As for the rest, it is well known that it is not any kind of food that defiles, but disobedience to lawful authority."

"It seems to me," said Andrew Both, in a voice all at once become gloomy, "that the Capuchin Father is insulting us."

"No, my brethren, I pity you," replied the monk; "and on such a day I beseech you to abstain from giving scandal. If instead of me one of the Fathers of the Holy Office saw you, you would probably be subjected to fifteen days' penance in one of their convents."

"He is right," curtly replied Puppet: "let the Father go, and let us leave the table."

"Not at all," cried Roelant; "but what thou sayest frightens me; and if he is right, as thou pretendest, this monk is going to denounce us. John, shut the door. Claes, lay hold of the Father. It is not fifteen days' imprisonment we should have to undergo; we should be shut up till Easter; I know the usages."

"And who knows," pursued Andrew Both, "whether we shouldn't be banished from Rome? We are Calvinists."

At this word the monk's face was contracted with grief. Claes, however, held him forcibly by the arm, though he made no resistance.

"We must be sure," said he, "that he won't sell us. And this can only be by making him do as we do. Roelant, fill the glasses; John, give the Father a slice of ham."

These words were received with applauses. But at the same instant the visage of the monk, so mild and simple, seemed impressed with a marvelous dignity. He repelled, with the hand which remained free to him, the dish which was offered him; and, after the drunken artists had emptied their glasses in drinking his health with a mocking voice, he said to them,

"If it is true that you have deserted our common mother, the holy Roman Church, if you are no longer in her bosom, I ought only to pray and weep for you. But you cannot be ignorant that children who have remained faithful obey."

"That shan't prevent," said Roelant, striking the table with his fist, "his eating the slice of ham."

"He shall eat it," continued Claes; and, taking up on the dish the morsel that was cut, he brought it near the lips of the monk, who recoiled with horror.

A frightful scene developed itself at that moment, and such as one cannot well describe. The night came on; the sky was streaked with gloomy clouds; a stormy wind arose, and had just violently opened a window. The table, loaded with fragments, presented a scene of frightful disorder. The five heated artists bore, in their dull eyes, husky voices, glances, movements by turns tottering and violent, all the hideous marks of drunkenness. To these were added the fear of being denounced, proud malice, and hateful anger. The good religious, in their hands, was the object of an obstinate vengeance. Now up, now held down on a seat, stretched on the ground, driven against the table, he no longer heard anything but threatening words, or saw anything but ill-omened gestures.

Andrew Both pressed to his lips a glass of wine; Roelant brought the slice of ham close to his teeth; Peter van Laar, more gentle, tried to persuade him; and Claes sought to open his mouth with violence to make him eat it by force. The monk silently resisted; and, when an instant of relaxation was granted him, was content with repeating these words, "My God, forgive them, and save me!"

After this frightful struggle had lasted half an hour, Puppet, who alone preserved a lingering ray of reason, sought to put an end to these excesses. "We are going too far," said he; "let us leave the Father at liberty, or else we shall repent it. Let us be satisfied with his promise not to betray us."

"No, no," cried Claes: "after what we have just done we are too much compromised. Besides the violation of the laws of his church, he will accuse us of outrage on his person. He must sin along with us, or become acquainted with the points of our daggers."

He drew his own while thus speaking. Roelant, John, and Andrew Both imitated him.

"A murder!" cried Peter van Laar in Dutch, "you would meditate a murder! you would be assassins! But you are destroying yourselves, my friends."

The daggers were arrested in their progress at this short speech.

"Sirs," then said the Franciscan, "though you may have deserted the Holy Church, you still, perhaps, know the gospel. Well, God is here: He sees you, and it is He who has said, 'Whoever shall use the sword shall perish by the sword.'"

"The Father is right," replied Peter, troubled: "down with the daggers! you shall not stain this dwelling with blood, you shall not be infamous murderers."

"Ah!" pursued Claes, whose excitement was not lessening, "the Tiber!"

And pointing to the window, below which rolled the river swollen by the hurricane, he was dragging the poor monk in that direction.

"Ah, the monk will sell us!" said Andrew Both, springing up.

"Ah, he will deliver us up to the Inquisition!" added John and Roelant.

And, all the three uniting their efforts to those of Claes, they pushed the religious to the edge of the window.

"My God!" cried the monk, divining their project.

What he said more was carried off by the wind of the storm: the Franciscan had fallen into the Tiber, into which the four artists had thrown him.

Peter, struck with horror, took no active part in the crime; but he did not prevent it.

And when his four friends had withdrawn from the window, smitten with a sudden terror, which chilled them and recalled their senses, he went as if to see whether the river were not giving back its victim, who might yet demand vengeance.

But he saw nothing but the gloomy night. He remained some minutes bending over the flood. Reassured at last by seeing nothing float, and hoping the crime had no witnesses, he returned toward his companions, all fixed on their seats in a melancholy silence.

A quarter of an hour passed without any one opening his mouth. At last Puppet regained the power of speech.

"What have you done?" said he.

No one answered except Claes, who said, "It is

unfortunate; but at least we are delivered from fear."

"Provided," resumed Peter, "the crime be not discovered."

"The crime!" repeated the others, looking at him with stupor, and fell back anew into their motionless attitude.

Thus a frightful murder had been committed, at the end of a debauch, by five eminent artists.

Peter van Laar had an extended reputation: his works were in request, and high prices given for them. All the amateurs wished to have from him a rural feast, or an encounter with brigands, or an anglers' scene, or a hunting party. His compositions, full of life, the truth of lush skies and landscapes, the delicacy and spirit of his figures, the charm of his coloring, were all admired. The museum of the Louvre, at Paris, is still proud of possessing two of his pictures.

His brothers, Claes and Roelant, painted in his style. Less perfect than he, they also had a nattering celebrity.

John and Andrew Both, pupils of Bloemart, and emulous of Claude Lorraine, who saw them rival his successes, have left works which will always be praised for fine execution, striking effects of light, lively and brilliant coloring, and figures full of spirit and delicacy. United by nature, friendship, and talent, these two brothers worked always together, and formed, so to speak, but one artist, John painting the landscape, and Andrew the figures. The connoisseurs have never ceased to look upon *a view of Italy at sunset*, painted by these two masters, as a capital picture and a masterpiece.

And these were the men who, at the end of a drinking-bout, were the assassins of an inoffensive monk.

They separated, on the evening of the murder, in a condition of mind which could not be without disquietude and terror. It was not till two days after that the lifeless body of the Franciscan was found, a little lower down. The certainty of not being even suspected did not bring back serenity to the brow of the culprits. Without doubt they were the subjects of remorse: but what is remorse without expiation and penance?

Sad and grave, the five artists, formerly so joyous, spoke no more of festivities nor of rejoicings. Instead of seeking each other, as before, they fled from each other; and Puppet soon announced that, long wanted in his own country, he was going to return to it. The others, to whom a residence in Rome had become painful, declared that they would leave also; and they began to set their affairs in order.

"It is at least fortunate," said Peter sadly, "that you did not imbrue your hands in his blood. For he said, 'He who uses the sword shall perish by the sword;' and the last words of a dying person are terrible."

"Ah, bah!" answered Claes, "superstition! According to thy doctrine, because we drowned him we shall perish by drowning also." He began to laugh aloud. But his gaiety had no echo. A gloomy cloud passed over the brow of the others, who said as they rose, "Let us speak no more of that, and let us go hence: the sooner the better."

If we were inventing a story, what follows would seem very odd. We might be accused of leisurely constructing a chronicle of violence, to support the imposing opinion of Joseph de Maistre on the temporal government of Providence. But we are here only simple narrators of historical facts, real, known, authentic, avowed, incontestable, and which can be verified by all the world. We shall relate them unembellished by any ornament.

The day after this last conversation the five friends dispersed. Claes van Laar went to find, in his villa near Rome, an old lord, who was to pay him the price of a picture. He was mounted on an ass. In passing over a little wooden bridge, which joined two rocks, the ass stumbled, and precipitated himself with Claes into a torrent just formed by a storm-flood. The body of his drowned brother was brought to Puppet as he was packing up. After he had had him interred, he hastened to Holland with John Both.

Roelant van Laar and Andrew Both, under particular engagements, had set out, one for Genoa, the other for Venice.

They had payments to get in these two towns. Neither was destined to see his country again. Six months after, Puppet was settled at Haarlem, when he received the news that his brother had just been drowned at Genoa. In the spring of the following year (1650), John Both, who was opening a studio at Utrecht, found, in a packet brought from Italy, the statement of his brother Andrew's death, who was drowned at Venice.

Struck with terror and giddiness at reading this, John Both, out of his senses, fled from his house, flew like a mad-man across the country, and precipitated himself into the Rhine, where he perished.

There remained only Peter van Laar.

Devoured by a black melancholy, and become, say the historians, insupportable to himself and others,—he, who had been known so easy and so gay,—Peter lived, because God, perhaps, was leaving him a little time for repentance. But, on the Ash-Wednesday of the year 1673, his cookmaid having served him up a ham at dinner, he rose, uttering a cry, and went and threw himself into a well, whence he was taken out drowned.

KEEP HOLY THE SABBATH

THE following legend is an old, historical tradition, of which all modern nations have got hold. It is told in the South as well as in the North; it is particularly popular in Lorrain, in Champagne, and on the borders of the Rhine; but it is no less so in the Iberian peninsula. Schiller heard it at Manheim, and made of it a little poem, which has become national among the Germans.

He was wrong, however, in attributing the deed to the count of Saverne, an imaginary personage, while he might have preserved the truth by respecting the real names of this beautiful story, which are,—Denys, the king of Portugal, a violent prince, whose reign began in 1279, and his wife, Elizabeth of Arragon, who was enrolled by the Holy See in the catalogue of the saints.

We have thought it right, while following as far as possible the touching and lively narrative of Schiller, to re-establish throughout the historic truth.

Fridolin was a worthy servant, brought up in the fear of God by his mistress, the pious Queen Elizabeth, wife of King Denys, who reigned over Portugal. She was so mild, so good. But, had she had the caprices of pride, Fridolin would have forced himself to satisfy them joyfully, for the love of God.

So, in presence of all her household, the good queen praised him; an inexhaustible commendation flowed from her mouth. She did not look on him as a servant; her heart granted him the rights of a son, and her serene looks were fixed with pleasure on the youthful page.

These favors kindled envenomed hatred, and made envy boil in the bosom of Robert, the king's favorite huntsman.

One day, as the prince was returning from the chase, he approached him.

"How happy you are, Sire!" said he, perfidiously: "the sharp tooth of doubt does not snatch sweet slumber from you. It is true that you possess a noble and chaste spouse, and that Satan himself would not succeed in the attempt to tarnish such a virtue."

The king, who was rude and savage, knitted his gloomy brows. "What dost thou mean? Should I reckon on a virtue variable as the waves, and which can so easily be seduced by the voice of the flatterer?"

For Denys believed little in virtue.

The other replied, "You are right, Sire; but the madman who, born a vassal, raises his eyes to his queen, deserves nothing but contempt."

"Speakest thou of any one of my court?" interrupted the king, trembling.

"Yes, certainly; does what is in all mouths escape my lord? But if it is concealed from him with so much care, I ought perhaps to be silent about it."

"Speak, wretch," cried Denys, in a terrible voice; "who dares lift his eyes to Elizabeth?"

"Sire, the young page Fridolin. He does not want attractions. Have you not observed how he follows the queen's looks with his eyes? It is even said that he makes verses to her, full of tenderness. The noble princess, without doubt, conceals it from you through compassion. But I repent of what has escaped me. I cause you uneasiness, Sire, when, in fact, you need fear nothing."

The king, bounding with fury, dived into the neighboring wood, where burning furnaces were always lighted for his service; there his armor was fabricated, there the fire was kept in night and day by the active hand of forgemen; the sparks leaped forth, the blows rang, the heavy hammers fell in cadence, and, under these powerful efforts, the iron was softened.

The king, gloomy and determined in his cruel resolution, perceives two black forgemen, makes a sign to them, and says,—"The first person I shall send hither, and who will bring you these words, 'Have you executed the masters order?'— throw him into that fire. Let him be reduced to ashes; and let no one ever see him again."

The coarse pair reply to this order by a satanic smile. The heart which beats in their bosom has become harder than the iron they shape.

Next morning, which was Sunday, at the dawn of day, Robert, with a hypocritical and deceitful air, says to the young page, "Quick, comrade, don't loiter. The king wants you instantly."

"Repair directly to the forge," said the king to Fridolin, and ask the workmen there, 'Have you executed the master's order?'"

Fridolin answered, "It shall be done, Sire."

It was Sunday, then. Before departing, he presents himself before the queen. "I am sent to the forge," said he; "what are your orders, noble queen? Can I go directly? For, after God, my service belongs only to you."

The good queen answered, with sweetness,—"My son there is ill. As you assist at the holy Mass, pray for him and for me."

Happy at such a message, Fridolin departs directly. He had not gone far into the country, when the bell sent forth those joyous sounds which called the vigilant faithful to Mass.

"Never leave the good God if He places himself in thy way;" and "Put not off to another moment, what thou oughtest to do for the Lord's service"—Fridolin recollected these two proverbs. He could not miss the Mass on a Sunday; and did he know whether he should be back soon enough to attend at the court chapel? He entered, then, the little church; it was, as yet, empty; seeing no one ready to serve the priest, he drew near, and piously fulfilled those holy functions for which God blesses the youthful age.

After hearing Mass with recollection, he resumed his journey, bearing with him the quiet of a good conscience. He took the way toward the forge, sanctifying the holy day by sweet prayers, and humble meditations on the greatness of God.

Half an hour after the page had left the court, Robert, sent in his turn by the king, and impatient to know if his revenge was satisfied, had also taken the path to the forest. He arrived in sight of the burning furnaces as Fridolin was saying his last *Ave Maria*, before leaving the little church. Not suspecting the pious station he had made,—for Robert thought as little about Sunday as his master, he approached, without foreseeing aught, and asked the fierce workmen whether they had done what the king had said? These men of horrid look, taking Robert for him whom they had been ordered to dispatch, answered only by seizing him, without understanding his protests, and, in spite of his frightful cries, threw him in, and buried him with their iron pokers in the furnace, where nothing but the ends of his feet were seen when Fridolin arrived.

"Have you done," said he to the workmen, "what the king commanded?"

They, twisting their mouth with a triumphant air, showed him the burning gulf, and said, "It is done, and well done: the king will be satisfied with his servants."

Fridolin carried this reply diligently to his master, who would find it an enigma. Denys, seeing him come from far, could not believe his eyes.

"Wretch!" said he, "whence comest thou?"

"From the forge, Sire."

"Impossible, unless thou didst stop by the way."

"Only, Sire, long enough to assist at the holy Mass, where I prayed for the queen, for your sick son, and for yourself."

The king fell into a profound astonishment, and said, as if struck with terror,—"What answer did they give thee at the forge?—speak."

"Sire, the men's words are obscure: they showed me the furnace, and said smiling, 'It is done, and well done; and the king will be satisfied with his servants.'"

"And Robert?" still asked Denys, while a cold shivering ran through his limbs, "Did he not meet thee? I had sent him, too, into the forest."

"My Lord, neither in the woods nor in the fields, did I see the least trace of him."

"Well!" said the king, in great consternation, "God himself in heaven has judged."

Then, with a goodness quite new to him, he took the page's hand, and led him with emotion to his spouse, who understood nothing of the matter.

"This child," said he, "is pure as the angels. He deserves all our good graces; for God keeps him, and His saints accompany him."

THE STORY OF TANCHELM THE HERETIC

"Dans une voie aussi large
Tout est profit pour Satan." -Moncriff.

"In that broad, flowery, but deceitful way,
At every step the Devil meets his prey."

IN a beautiful evening of spring, a youthful citizen of
Antwerp, on his return from fishing, held in his hand a
small nosegay, which he appeared to dread tarnishing, so
carefully did he carry it. It was a tuft of those pretty plants
which grow on the banks of rivulets, and which bear above
their elegant stem small sheaves of flowers of a sky-blue colour; their rounded lobes resemble a festoon of azure around
an aureola of gold. In Brabant and Flanders, this ear of
flowerets is generally designated as the eyes of the Blessed
Virgin; the Dutch and the Germans call it Forget-me-not.
Our Antweipian, whose name was Peter Vanderheyden, was
hastening to the street Des Crabes. There stood the house
of Jean Meleyn, a rich merchant rope-maker, whose daughter, Pharailde, had been promised to him and betrothed. He
knocked at the door, which he was surprised to find shut, as
on a great holiday. There was left in the house only an aged

domestic, who came to let him in.

"Are you then alone, Lambert?" said the young fisher-man. "Where are Master Meleyn and Pharailde?"

"Alas! Peter," answered the old man, with a sigh, "need you ask where they are? The town is being lost a second time. What would St. Amand say, or the good Eligius, or St. Hillibrond, if God permitted them to return amongst us? May the good St. Dympna, and the generous St. Walburga deign to protect us!"

"But, withal, where are they, my good Lambert?"

"Do you not understand me, Peter? They are gone to the preaching-house of the heretic."

"Tanchelm, then, has returned to Antwerp?"

"Unfortunately for us."

"And he is still permitted to corrupt the people?"

"They are flocking to him in crowds. Undoubtedly, God is abandoning us."

"Does he preach in the Champ des Flamands?"

"No; he has established himself at the wharf, among the seamen. His meeting is there, opposite the very church of St. Walburga."

"I must away to it," said Vanderheyden.

But the old man, in a manner horror-struck, held him back, "Would you also go to blaspheme?" said he.

"I do not go there for the sake of the impostor," replied the youth, calmly; "but I hope to bring home Pharailde."

"In that case, may God be with you!"

And the aged Lambert, having made the sign of the cross, shut himself up, in solitary sadness, in his master's house, whilst the young man ran to the bank of the river.

All the ancient wood-yard, which projected like a tongue of land into the Scheldt, and which today, although it be confined within a very narrow compass, is nevertheless still called the werf (wood-yard), all the large sloping quays, all the space which surrounded the church of St. Walburga, the first Christian temple erected at Antwerp, and which no longer exists, as well as all the neighboring streets, were encumbered with a crowd so dense that it was almost impossible to get through it. The river was covered with hundreds of barques, full of sailors and fishermen, who were arriving from every quarter, and advancing as near as possible to an immense husting, which stood at the extreme end of the wharf, built partly on the bank and partly on the waters of the Scheldt. It was painted white, and ornamented with streamers. In the midst of this platform was a personage, magnificently arrayed, who was speaking with vehemence, and enforcing his arguments with a profusion of ridiculous gestures, as the heretic Tanchelm, whose name, mutilated in certain chronicles, is sometimes written Tanchelinus, instead of Tanchelmus, so that he has often been called Tanchelin. The deepest silence prevailed around him.

It was only after prolonged exertions that Peter Vanderheyden reached the Place St. Walburga, where he observed Jean Meleyn and his daughter seated in front of the church, and listening to the discourse of Tanchelm. Although Peter was only twenty-seven years of age, and although already, in the course of nineteen years, the heresy of Tanchelm had made immense progress at Antwerp, where the clergy were not sufficiently numerous to oppose it, Peter had been so fortunate as to remain untainted. He was a young man of a mild and quiet disposition, who followed, in the simplicity of his heart, the religion of his mother, and who, after God and our Lady, had no other love in the world than Pharailde. Having become sufficiently rich to pretend to her hand, he had no idea of happiness except in his union with her; and if in the evenings he saw the object of his affections, his day was not spent in vain.

A band of armed men, whom he could not separate, kept him apart from Pharailde. He saluted her from a distance, deeply grieved by the kind of attention she appeared to give to the harangue of the corrupter. He would have thrown to her his nosegay, but one of the guards took it from his hands; and, threatening him with his naked sword, to make him be silent, whispered in his ear, "There is no worship here, except that of the master." At the same time, he threw the little bunch of flowers on the platform where Tanchelm was gesticulating, surrounded with nosegays and crowns.

This Tanchelm, now environed with the splendor of power, was a simple layman. He was born at Antwerp. His character was a compound of boldness and evil inclinations. His poverty not permitting him to satisfy his desires, he had resolved to profit by the ignorance of the people; and, whilst the religious and brave men who were capable of throwing obstacles in his way, were absent in the Holy Land, he had made himself the chief of a sect. He immediately found companions who became his supporters. He was gifted with fluency of speech, and a certain rude and animated eloquence, which made impression on the multitude.

In 1105, he commenced his preaching against what he called the abuses of the Christian religion. His easy doctrines speedily brought him numerous partisans in Flanders and the islands of Zealand, in Holland, and Brabant. Like all innovators, he asked at first only slight reforms. It was not long, till he treated religious beliefs as stupid errors, meritorious actions as deceptions, the crusades as follies, the sacraments as abominations. He taught, that priests, bishops, and the Pope, were not different from plain burgesses. He condemned the payment of tithes and attendance in the churches. In addition to this, he declared himself a prophet, whom God had sent to enlighten the world.

He acquired so much credit, that he was as much respected as a sovereign. His magnificence was equal to his pretensions. He arrayed himself in purple, and carried a sceptre. He wore a radiated crown, and environed himself with all the pomp of royalty. In vain had Godfrey the Bearded, count of Flanders and marquis of Antwerp, endeavored to stay his progress. When Tanchelm was in the states of this prince, he never went abroad without an escort of three thousand armed men; and when he went to preach to the people, his officers bore before him his standard unfurled. His guards attended him with drawn swords.

He delighted in feasting and debauchery. He availed himself of his power to give himself up to these enjoyments with impunity. He was held in such high veneration, that the stupid people purchased, as holy objects, the parings of his nails, hairs of his head, his beard, the water of his baths, &c. He could likewise, on occasion, imagine other resources for defraying his royal expenses.

From 1105 to 1123, Tanchelm had thus lived, defying his enemies and priding himself on his crimes. Morality was at an end; religion was in its death-agony at Antwerp. The men of God were persecuted, and wept in secret, whilst Christian women dared not leave their retirement. Matters were in this state, when Tanchelm, having seen one day the daughter of the tribune of Antwerp, became enamoured of her, and boldly asked her of her father. The town, so early as the period in question, was beginning to be governed by a municipal body. This body consisted of aldermen, whose chief, afterwards called the ecoutete, and now known by the title of burgomaster, was at that time styled the tribune. The indignation of the aged magistrate was at length aroused. He called together his council, and awakened those honorable feelings which had become dormant in the minds of men. He made an appeal to all good citizens, who came forward at his call in greater numbers than could have been hoped, and Tanchelm was obliged to flee. He escaped to Italy, disguised as a monk. But, at the commencement of the year 1124, he reappeared in the Low Countries, and preached at Antwerp, as powerful and as audacious as ever.

Nevertheless, being without money to maintain his numerous guard, he had recourse to a stratagem, which he put into operation the very evening on which we have seen him on his platform, a few moments after our friend Vanderheyden's nosegay was snatched from his hand. The heretic had just concluded an harangue quite to the humor of the multitude, who preferred his accommodating morality to the austere precepts of the priests of Jesus Christ. His officers then dragged up to the scaffolding beside him a painted statue of the Blessed Virgin, whilst his guards placed on the right and left-hand sides of the platform six large boxes within reach of the people, who stood on the ground, as well as of the auditors who were in the barques. Tanchelm, rising, spoke as follows:—

"Listen, all of you, and bear witness. And you, Virgin Mary," continued he, turning towards the statue, "I take you today for my beloved wife."

At these words, he kissed the statue on the forehead, placed upon her head a crown as magnificent as his own, and then resumed, addressing anew the eager crowd:—

"I have just received as my loving spouse the Virgin Mary. It now belongs to you to provide for the expenses of our chaste espousals. Let the men put their offerings into the boxes that are on the right hand, and the women into those on the left. My spouse and I will thus know which of the two sexes has the greater love for myself and her."

If you are scandalized by these details, bear in mind that they are strictly historical.

Tanchelm had scarcely done speaking, when all eagerly brought their money to the boxes. There was the greatest emulation in this work of blind enthusiasm. The women, in order to give more than the men, divested themselves of their necklaces and ear-rings; and Peter Vanderheyden saw with joy that his dear Pharailde, who was hurried along by her father, who emptied his own purse, put nothing into the box before which she passed, although Jean Meleyn would fain have forced her to throw into it the ring which had been given her by the youth who aspired to her hand.

Meanwhile, Tanchelm, to whom fathers, as formerly, offered their daughters, and husbands their wives, although he was more than fifty years of age, had no sooner cast his impure eyes on Pharailde, than the fresh and gentle appearance of the young girl, her beautiful chestnut hair, her large blue eyes, her rose-like lips, her elegant person, completely captivated him.

"Brother," said he, addressing Jean Meleyn.

At this word of the personage who was called the prophet, the rope-merchant fell on his knees.

"Brother," resumed the heretic, "in an hour hence, Spierinck and Oudaghen [two of his satellites] will be here, in this very place; you will give your daughter in charge to them;—she will come to obtain my blessing."

Jean Meleyn, beside himself with joy, called out that he would be punctual. Taking his daughter's arm, he conducted her home, in order that she might appear in her richest dress, without leaving her time to say anything else to Peter than the words, "Save me!" which she uttered in a trembling voice.

The armed bands once more separated Pharailde from her betrothed. Tanchelm withdrew, in the midst of his guards, preceded by his banner; and poor Vanderheyden, after having remained for a moment utterly stupified, not knowing what support to find among men, knelt down, and addressed a prayer to St. Walburga, the patroness of Antwerp, and to St. Amand, one of its first apostles; after which he regained, his heart wrung with grief, the street *des Crakes*. He counted on softening Jean Meleyn, who had promised him his daughter in marriage. But he found not opportunity of speaking to any other than the aged Lambert, who, knowing what was in preparation, wept till his eyes were red, and tore out his grey hair, in the excess of sorrow.

"You shall not suffer it," said he to Peter, as soon as he saw him; "you will presently call your friends to arms…"

"I have so very few friends," said the youth, in a desponding tone.

"Well, I will second you. Time is passing rapidly; do not

lose sight of your betrothed; and may God restore to me, for a moment, the strength of my youth!"

No sooner had the old man spoken these words, than he ran towards the rampart, to the cloister St. Michael, where the pious Norbert, Bishop of Magdeburgh, had just arrived, accompanied by some other holy personages.

Whilst he was going to claim their support, Jean Meleyn came out of his house, with his daughter sumptuously dressed. Peter knelt in the way, in order to prevent him from advancing. But the burgher, in great anger, raised his stick to strike him; whereupon, Pharailde sprang between them. She was pale and confused; but contrived to make Peter observe a poniard she had concealed in her dress.

"Follow us," said she, with animation, "and if you cannot rescue me, I shall die, rather than offend God and the Blessed Virgin."

Encouraged by these words, Peter arose, and followed the young girl and her father to the Place St. Walburga, hoping somewhat from the devotedness of the aged Lambert, and appealing to all the fishermen whom he met. Spierinck and Oudaghen were waiting, each with a drawn sword in his hand. As soon as Jean Meleyn had given Pharailde into their charge, they commanded him, as well as the crowd, to withdraw. They all obeyed. The aged rope-maker departed, singing hymns for joy. Peter alone ventured to follow, at some distance, accompanied by two sailors, his comrades, who were armed with their boathooks.

The two satellites of Tanchelm went by the streets *de la Prison* and *au Fromage*, and then directed their steps through some deserted lanes to the den of their master. Peter began to feel alarmed, when he found that there was no appearance of succour. He was in the middle of the long lane *de la Mouche*, a few steps behind Pharailde. Quite near to him were the dwellings of the principal disciples of Tanchelm, in the street *des Livres*, and in the street *des Prédicateurs*; and just beside him was the little palace of the chief, at the spot called, even to this day, *Le Coin Joyeux* (the merry nook), in remembrance of the orgies of which it was the scene. It was not long, however, till he beheld coming to meet the two armed men a venerable man, whose hair was white with age. He wore a surplice, and held in his hands a small shrine or reliquary; two youths, clad in white, walked at either side, each having a lighted wax-taper in his hand. Lambert walked behind, bareheaded; he carried a canopy, shaped like a parasol, and gave notice of their approach by ringing a hand-bell. The old man was the servant of God, whom our fathers have since paid reverence to under the name of St. Norbert. He bore a relic of St. Amand.

"Kneel down!" cried Lambert, as soon as he was only a few paces from the two bullies.

"Down with the priest!" was their only reply.

They sprang upon the old man, to kill him, when the two sailors, moved by the presence of the holy relic, rushed upon Spierinck and Oudaghen, struck them with their hooks, and left them dead upon the street.

Night having come down, Peter and Lambert, who were now following the prelate, conducted Pharailde into the house of some Christian women, where she could, in all freedom, return thanks to God.

Tanchelm, meanwhile, finding that the young lady had not arrived, sent in search of her. The dead bodies of his two guardsmen were brought to him, as the only result of his inquiry. He suppressed his anger till next morning. He then called an assembly of the people, who met at the *Coin Joyeux*, on a large open space, now called the *Esplanade*. There was soon an immense crowd; they amounted, it is said, to twelve thousand persons. The Bishop Norbert, the canons, the tribune, and the aldermen of Antwerp, all the honest citizens, all the Christians who had remained faithful, warned of what was in preparation, and resolved at last to show their power, had also come. A terrible hurricane, mingled with hail, lightning, and thunder, arose, almost suddenly. Tanchelm appeared. He availed himself of the tempest, and spoke of it as a sign of the anger of God.

"Yesterday," said he, "I was robbed of the girl I had selected for myself; my two dearest disciples were slain; avenge me, or tremble for yourselves."

A portion of the people, and all the followers of Tanchelm, gave vent to their fury in loud cries. But a powerful voice, the voice of Norbert, was heard above the tumult.

"If God has sent you, prove your mission, and we shall believe in you."

"Who has spoken?" called out one of the satellites, brandishing his heavy sword.

At the same moment, all the guards displayed their arms.

But those who had come to call the corrupter to account at last, showed that they also were armed. The clamour of the multitude was immediately succeeded by a grave and gloomy silence. A firm voice was again heard:

"WE DEMAND A MIRACLE."

A deeper silence now prevailed throughout the compact mass of people.

"A miracle!" said Tanchelm, impudently. "Have I not done enough of miracles?"

"They are right," was the prompt reply of a man who appeared to be a stranger. "If you possess the power attributed to you, I offer you, in my own person, an opportunity of giving proofs of it."

This man, as he spoke, went to a spot where the ground rose a little, and showed himself to the people. His back was disfigured by an enormous hump, which would have graced the back of a camel. Some laughed, when they saw him; others opened wide their eyes, in the hope of what was about to be done."

"What you ask, I grant," said Tanchelm; and, addressing one of his disciples, he added:

"Touch the back of this man, and let him become straight."

The comrade of the worker of miracles, stretching forth his hand, struck the back of the deformed man.

The excrescence immediately disappeared; and the hump-back stood erect and handsome. Clamours of enthusiasm burst forth. The stranger came down from the little mound, anxious to lose himself in the gaping crowd; but he found himself surrounded with burgesses, who required that he should undress, in order to let the miracle which had just been worked upon him be more thoroughly appreciated. It was necessary to remove his doublet, and the result of the search was that the hump Tanchelm had done away with was a bladder filled with air.

The fickle multitude appeared to be enlightened all of a sudden. The heretic grew pale, as if he had foreseen his downfall.

"If you are the friend of God," called out the people in every direction, "put an end to this tempest, which threatens us with destruction."

The storm at this moment raged over the city. The waters of the Scheldt rose in high roaring waves, as if they would have swallowed up Antwerp; the fragile shipping in the river seemed at every moment as if it would have been dashed to pieces against the banks; the crowd dragged the impostor to the wharf, and, as he harangued no more, but supplicated, and, trembling, acknowledged all his hideous actions, the indignant people were on the point of precipitating him into the water, when a man came to extricate him from this danger. It was no other than the Bishop Norbert.

"Leave him time for repentance," said he.

God now resolved to show that he had compassion on Antwerp. The holy prelate, victorious over the fury of men, commanded the winds and the waves also to be still. He threw his episcopal ring into the Scheldt, and the tempest was immediately appeased. The people all knelt down in thankfulness. Religion now returned to heal the wounds the heretic had inflicted. Tanchelm, hardened in crime, departed for Germany, where he was slain in 1125. Jean Meleyn lamented his error. The marriage of Peter Vanderheyden and of Pharailde was celebrated in a small chapel dedicated to our Lady,* which occupied the site where today is admired the magnificent cathedral of Antwerp.

---

* This chapel of our Lady had no doubt been built by Godfrey of Bouillon, he being understood to be its founder.

A "FLAPPER"*

W E were talking, the group around the Bishop, about the way that one person can affect the course of history. A man falls away from the faith for instance, and two generations later all his descendants have forgotten that any of their family ever were Catholics. One woman decides not to give up her religion; her children... and grandchildren...

"I was a very young priest," said the Bishop, "when I ran right into a case just like that. The housekeeper rang my bell, and I hurried down to the parlor. Bells might mean anything, from a tramp looking for an easy touch, to a child waiting breathlessly to tell me that grandma was dying. Life is exciting for a young priest in his first parish.

"Only this time I blinked. The parlor was filled to overflowing with two people. The man was large, husky, aggressive, well-dressed, and prosperous, the kind of fellow who takes over a room and makes you the guest in your own parlor. But it was the girl who made my eyes pop.

"The word *flapper* had only recently been invented. One look at the girl, and I knew it had been invented to apply exclusively to her. Her hair was a drugstore blonde, and even an amateur like myself knew it. Her clothes had all the refined reticence of a jazz band's rendition of boogie-

* Narrated by a priest in Fr. Daniel A. Lord's book *These Tales Are True.*—*The Publisher*, 2021.

woogie. And even as I entered the room, she was repairing her face with tools from a painter's kit large enough to need a redcap.

"'Hi'ya, Fawther,' she said. And from that point on I give up all attempt to reproduce her accent. 'Meet the man I'm going to marry.' She waved a manicured hand in his direction, every nail tipped with a red flag of danger.

"The man did not offer to shake hands; so with an inward sigh I sat down and motioned them to chairs. For a few seconds there was silence broken only by the rhythmic champing of the girl's gum.

"'Sir,' said the man, deliberately discarding the 'Father,' I'm going to marry this girl. But Honey says something about promises a fellow's got to make when he's marrying a Catholic. I don't go into anything blind, not even when I'm in love. So can I have a quick look at the papers I sign?'

"I got him a set. He read them through with a frown that crescendoed as he read. When he finished, he took a swift look at the girl, who wordlessly kept on chewing and gazing off into space while one bright slipper served as a metronome for the rhythm of her chewing. He seemed to be wondering whether she was worth the promises.

"Suddenly he rose, tossed the promises on the table, grabbed the girl by the wrist, and cried, 'Come on, Honey. I'm a free American citizen. And if you think for a minute I'm going to sign away my rights and the rights of my children to a future they can choose for themselves, you've got another guess coming. Sorry to have bothered you'—this was directed to me—'but from this point we're going out to find a justice of the peace or some minister. A Catholic marriage is out.'

"I had been watching the girl out of the corner of my eye. She sat impassive through the tirade. She didn't move even when he caught her wrist. There was nothing I could do about it. Just a weak sister, I decided, who'd go out of the Church, taking with her her children and generations still unborn.

"The girl rose to her feet with affected grace. She shook off his hold and struggled back into her short, snappy coat. Then she looked at him, still without a sign of expression on her enameled face, and spoke her first words since the introduction. I need say only that her voice was tuned to her general appearance.

"'If you think I'd marry you anywhere but in the Catholic Church,' she said, 'it's you that's got about ten more guesses coming. It's a priest or nobody. Thanks, Father.'

"'Honey!' cried the man, in amazement.

"'Don't waste time honeying me. You heard me. A priest and the promises—or no marriage.'

"She was out of the rectory like a rainbow in transit and before the man had recovered. I stood in the doorway as she swung into a taxi and he, stranded at the church, watched her go.

"Two nights later the housekeeper rang my bell again. Again my duo were in the parlor, she again chewing gum, he still dour and determined. Her raiment this time took even larger chunks out of the rainbow and the rules of good taste. As before she spoke not a word.

"'Listen Father,' he said, and I noticed that he had progressed to the 'Father' stage, 'we're back.' Master of the obvious, I thought. 'I'm making the promises. Honey won't have me any other way. Now listen, both of you. I don't want to sign those promises. It's all against my principles. But if I sign'em, I'll keep'em. That's the kind of a guy I am. Give a promise, keep a promise; that's me. Let me read 'em again, and then I'll give my word.' He read the promises thoughtfully again, took his own pen out of his pocket, and signed on the dotted line.

"A week later, after the instructions—which he accepted stolidly and with no sign of interest—I married them.

"And that was that. How long would the marriage last, I wondered. For if ever there was a girl obviously unsuited to homemaking and child rearing, it was this flapper with the mechanical jaws and the taste in clothes that was like the scream of a tortured artist.

Then one day he came to the rectory again.

"'Remember me?' he demanded, and this time he shook hands with me on his own impulse. 'Honey's going to have a baby pretty soon now. Grand, ain't it? She's getting a little embarrassed about going to church; and what's more, she's not feeling any too well. But she thinks somebody in the family should go. I'm not a Catholic or anything like that, but we want to know will it be all right if I go as substitute for her until the baby comes and she can go herself.'

"It was a new point in theology for me, but I assured him he would be most welcome. So on three successive Sundays I saw him sitting sheepishly in a pew in the farthest side aisle, looking around in embarrassment, plainly the strange dog in the strange back yard.

"Then he stopped coming. And presently they, both arrived for the baptism of their first child—a baby boy.

"Not very long after that he came again (I saw nothing of him in the interval, though she was regularly at the parish Mass), and he again made his offer to substitute for her. In fact this happened for four successive babies.

"Before the fifth baby came, he was in to see me again.

"'Congratulations!' I said, anticipating him. 'Another on the way?'

"'Listen Father,' he mumbled. 'Seems sorta stupid, traipsing into church when I don't know what it's all about. It's all right substituting like this; but maybe it would be better if I wasn't just a substitute Catholic but the real thing. Honey and I talked it over, and I told her that I'd take instructions again. And if you persuade me...'

"Three weeks later he was a real Catholic going to Mass because it was part of his faith. For as it turned out, the next baptism in that family wasn't a baby's but the father's. The fifth baby was the sixth to be baptized in that family.

"Well he was one of the trustees in the parish when I

was moved along to my next appointment. Honey was still wearing clothes that were designed for a flapper of eighteen, and all the seven children were brought up to chew gum and hold on to their faith with jaws nobody could shake loose. And all this because one girl refused to give up her religion and made the man respect her for her loyalty.

"So when some girl who looks like a saint out of a stained-glass window or some boy with a complete Catholic education behind him gives up the faith and drags generations still unborn out of the Mystical Body, I think of Honey and pray for a few more like her. A little courage at the turning points of life, and no one would ever be lost... need ever be lost to the faith."

Out of our own experience we knew how right the Bishop was.

BORNE ON THE WAVES*

THE freighter, lights all sealed or extinguished, crept along the Virginia coast, the chaplain told us.

It was during that fearful period of World War II when the German submarines had nosed right up to our Atlantic coastline and the shore was strewn with wreckage and the rumors of wreckage—almost as much of one as of the other.

Its engines throttled down to kill all possible noise, the freighter eased through the sea, black and oily and thick in the moonless darkness. No one on the ship seemed to be breathing. And the ship itself seemed to be afraid to nuzzle into the track along which so many of her sisters had smacked a torpedo and called it a night and a day.

The captain was just descending from the bridge when it happened.

There was no mistaking what had hit them, for the ship shivered and reared slightly. Every hand of the waking crew instinctively touched the life preservers—which the crew constantly wore—as the explosion ripped open the blackness of the night, the side of the ship, and whatever hopes there had been of the ship's reaching harbor.

No one ever saw the sub. It was a smart sub; it hit and ran. Why, the commander figured, waste ammunition on

* Narrated by a priest in Fr. Lord's book *These Tales Are True.*—*The Publisher*, 2021.

merchant seamen when one could knock the ships right out from under their feet? And ships were what mattered, ships that could be sent with their precious warbound cargoes deep down into the bed of the sea.

The crew had been trained in pessimistic anticipation of this minute, and every man was at his post. The few who had been asleep were on deck almost before the sound of the explosion had died away. The lifeboats swung free; and though the ship started to list, the men had already moved toward safety.

Then someone noticed what shouldn't have been missed even for so short a time—that the captain was not at his post in his lifeboat.

His Filipino mess boy dashed across the slanting deck and toward the ladder that led to the bridge. At the foot of the bridge he found the captain. He was lying completely unconscious, pinned to the deck by the heavy freight derrick that had crashed when the explosion ripped the ship.

Half a dozen willing men from his lifeboat tugged at the heavy length of wood and steel that fastened him helplessly. They tugged furiously and feverishly, for the ship was sinking fast and the lifeboats had all been swung into the sea—all but the captain's and theirs. But the derrick defied even their united strength.

Then the eyes of the captain opened slowly. Swift intelligence came back into their depths. He swept a glance down at his pinioned leg and then gave an amazing order.

"Unstrap my leg," he cried.

They looked at him in the sad certainty that he was raving.

"It's an artificial leg," he exclaimed, impatiently. "The straps are up here at my hip."

Even as they were unstrapping the wooden leg, some of them marveled that in all the time they had shipped under this captain they had never guessed that his light limp was, not a mere limp, but the result of a missing leg.

The leg was soon unstrapped, and with his arms around two brawny shoulders he was on his way to the lifeboat and safety.

The chaplain who had been telling the story paused and then smiled.

"That is the point at which I enter," he said. "He was badly chilled from exposure and more bruised and smashed from the falling steel and timber than he himself had known. They took him straight from the lifeboat to the shore hospital, where I called on him often and came to know him well.

"He was a seaman of what we like to call the old school. He lay there, chafing at the necessity that made him lie in bed when he wanted to be back on the deck of a ship that was carrying the stuff that would win our war.

"'But even after the doctors let me get up, it will be weeks before I can get another leg to replace the lost one.' He looked out the hospital window, a view that took in the stretch of sea which now rolled in unconcern over his lost ship.

"In disgust and resentment he eyed the crutch which the doctor had placed against the wall.

"'A captain on a crutch!' he sniffed, angrily. 'I want my leg. Chaplain, if you have any pull with the powers that be, say a prayer that there are no priorities on game legs. I want my leg fast. I want my ship again. I want to get back and help finish this business.'

"Well the long arm of coincidence this time turned out to be a leg. A story writer wouldn't dare use this for a yarn. It's fishy, too fishy for fiction. But it's not too fishy for fact. And this is fact.

"We looked around as the door opened. In the doorway, grinning, was his Filipino mess boy. The face of the bright little lad was wreathed in smiles. In his unreproducible dialect he addressed his captain.

"'Me got old friend to see captain,' he said, 'old friend captain love very much.'

"'Bring him in,' shouted the captain, in his best storm-and-stress manner. 'Bring him in.'

"The Filipino vanished, then reappeared, bearing, as if it were a precious baby, the lost leg—yes the very same identical lost leg. It had floated to the beach and lain there, gently rocking, in anticipation of its return to a good master and his ship.

"I don't know where my captain is now. But I'm sure he's pacing a deck, gloating that the submarine menace has been licked, that the war is over, and beating out a triumphant rhythm with a limp and a leg that wanted to go back to sea with its master."

LA MÈRE DE DIEU

Don't worry if I'm late getting back," he said to the brother porter. "I'm off for a long hike in this glorious sunshine." *Monsieur le Curé* Demers went down the walk from the old Spanish mission and headed up the rolling road among the hills to the sea. The priest was enjoying an ordered rest from the worries, smoke, and ennui of his small parish of *Saint Henri* in the Province of Quebec. The bright California weather was doing wonders for him, and he could feel new power in his limbs as he strode along the hard road. When he entered the path that led down to the beach, the wind whipping up the valley from the Pacific bent the front dip of his shovel hat and swirled about his cassock. Occupied with gripping his hat and adjusting his cassock, he didn't notice the oncoming band of masked horsemen until they were right upon him.

They swung from their horses and gathered him up. A gag was snapped in his mouth, a blind placed over his eyes; and without saying a word, they galloped off with their captive. The silent cavalcade rode on at a brisk pace for a long time. Then the going became rougher, the animals laboring up steep hills and straining down precipitous embankments. The priest had plenty of time to think after the first shock of his capture wore off; but try as he might, he could not resolve the terrible situation that encompassed him. He heard the sound of running water and the singing and calling of birds; he noticed the change as the heat of the day gave way to the cooling dampness of the early evening mists. The fatigue of the long ride began to lay wearily upon him, and his imagination began to trouble him with frightening pictures of possible tortures and a violent death. Why had he told the brother at the mission not to expect him early? It would be late at night before the *padres* would be sufficiently worried about him to organize a searching party.

At last the party stopped, and he could hear the men dismounting. The priest was lifted down from his horse, and the blindfold and the gag were removed. They had stopped at the opening of a cave. The men paid no attention to the priest. They unsaddled their horses and led them to water.

One of the bandits took the priest gently by the arm and led him into the hide-out. It was a hollow place in the solid rock. Twenty or more tough-looking men were sitting around, playing cards, smoking, drinking, and swearing. When they saw the frail cassocked man enter, their amazement was so great that they were stunned into silence. His guide led him past the long table of surprised men and down the cavern to a blanket-covered entrance to another room.

"I owe you an explanation, Father," he said, as they paused at the doorway. "My wife is in this room. She is dying, and she asked me to bring her a priest."

"I see," *le curé* answered.

"Don't worry about these fellows here. They will do you no harm. I give you my word. But help her." Pulling the blanket aside, he motioned to the priest to enter.

The place was surprisingly well furnished. An Indian woman ushered him to the bedside of a wide-eyed feverish woman. When she realized that a priest was standing at her side, she relaxed and breathed deeply. "*Dieu soit beni,*" she murmured.

Father Demers was astonished at the sound of his native

tongue so many miles away from the French of Quebec, in this California wilderness. Automatically he reached into the deep pocket of his cassock. He brought out his stole and drew it over his shoulders.

Simply, contritely she confessed her sins and received absolution. There would be no viaticum for her, no extreme unction; but she rested quietly, a happiness in her eyes, for she had made her peace with God, and she knew now that He would welcome her to paradise. The Indian woman re-entered and walked to a makeshift cradle at the other side of the four-poster bed.

The mother smiled and pointed to the crib. "My baby," she said.

The weary priest sat on the edge of her bed. The day had been like a nightmare for him. The shock of being freed so suddenly was almost as great as the shock of being captured. After the long hours on the hot, dusty trail, his mind a riot of weird speculation as to his fate, he was asked to hear a dying woman's confession. He lowered his head into his hands and tried to adjust himself. This had been the most unusual evidence of God's providence that he had ever known. When he lifted his head again, the woman began to speak.

"My father was a *coureur-des-bois*," she said, slowly, deliberately. "My mother was French too. Both pioneered in the country bordering the Great Lakes, and during their restless, roving life all my brothers and sisters were born. One day—I was seventeen at the time—as I was out alone picking blueberries, three men came upon me suddenly and forced me to go away with them. They made me do the cooking. I tried to keep track of the directions in which they went so that I might find my way home again. But soon we were so far away that I knew that escape was impossible. I would have been lost in the great woods.

"The leader was kind and always protected me. In his own way he showed me his affection and after a while made me his wife, according to the customs of these lawless men. That baby is our first child. I knew I was dying. I went through the horror of pain and sleepless nights, praying *la Mère de Dieu* to send a priest to me before death came. I am so happy, so grateful to her and to you, *Monsieur le Curé*. The Blessed Mother has answered my prayers."

When dawn broke over the hills and on the placid waters of the Pacific, a handful of hard-riding masked men halted their horses down the road a piece from the mission and left a bewildered, weary priest standing in the dust as they turned and rode off.

ABOUT THE AUTHOR

Augusta Theodosia Drane, in religion Mother Francis Raphael, OSD, was born near London in 1823. Her parents were both Protestants, her father being managing partner in an East India mercantile house. Her remarkable natural gifts were developed by wide reading at a very early age. In 1837 she moved with her family to Devonshire, where she read much of the early literature of the Oxford Movement. Burnet's "History of the Reformation", she declared, was the real cause of her conversion. It was not, however, till 1847 that she grew uneasy as to her religious beliefs, whereupon she consulted Keble and Pusey, but without satisfaction. The influence of Maskell, then Vicar of St. Mary Church, helped her more and she confided to him a scheme called "Ideal of a Religious Order". He told her that such an order existed in the Catholic Church, naming the Third Order of St. Dominic. This made a profound impression on her mind and gradually she was drawn to the Catholic Church. She was received in 1850, and in 1852 entered the Third Order of St. Dominic at Clifton. She professed vows at the new convent in Staffordshire, and was there employed in teaching and in writing various books, meanwhile making great spiritual progress. In 1860 she was appointed mistress of novices, but in 1863 became mistress of studies instead, thus obtaining more leisure for writing. In 1872 she became prioress under her friend, Mother Imelda Poole, and on the death of the latter in 1881 succeeded her as provincial. Her character was well summed up by Bishop Ullathorne, when he described her as "one of those many-sided characters who can write a book, draw a picture, rule an Order, guide other souls, superintend a building, lay out grounds, or give wise and practical advice with equal facility and success." She continued to grow in remarkable sanctity till her death, which took place a fortnight after she had ceased to be provincial, April 19, 1894.

Her works include: *The Morality of Tractarianism* (1850), published anonymously; *Catholic Legends and Stories* (1855); *Life of St. Dominic* (1857); *Knights of St. John* (1858); *Three Chancellors, Wykeham, Waynflete and More* (1859); *Historical Tales* (1862); *Tales and Traditions* (1862); *History of England for Family Use* (1864); *Christian Schools and Scholars* (1867); *Biographical Sketch of Hon. H. Dormer* (1868); *Songs in the Night* (1876); *New Utopia* (1876); *History of St. Catherine of Siena* (1880); *History of St. Dominic* (1891); *The Spirit of the Dominican Order* (1896), and some smaller pieces. She translated the *Inner Life of Père Lacordaire* (1868), edited a *Life of Mother Margaret Mary Hallahan* (1869), Archbishop Ullathorne's *Autobiography* (1891), and *Letters of Archbishop Ullathorne* (1892).

Made in United States
North Haven, CT
22 February 2022

16381383R00157